Withymead

Anthony Stevens

WITHYMEAD

A Jungian community for
the healing arts

COVENTURE

London

Photoset and produced by
R James Hall Typesetting and Book Production Services
Harpenden, Herts.
Printed and bound by
Redwood Burn Ltd., Trowbridge, Wilts

CONTENTS

Illustrations: facing pages 24, 25 and 56, 57.

ACKNOWLEDGMENTS

Of all those who knew Withymead and who have given me unstintingly of their time, their memories, and their reflections, I owe a particular debt of gratitude to each of the following: Ben Belton, Juliet Berry, Theo Brown, Margaret Button, Evelyn Clark, Rupert Cracknell, Douglas Crosse, Carol Diss (née Paul-Jones), Doris Eyles, Richard Fritzsche, Barbara Hannah, Robin Johnson, Molly Kemp, Jill and Martin Lambourne, Frances Lane-Claypon, Peter Lyle, David MacLoughlin, Kenneth and Vera Petrie-Ritchie, Mary Pye, Veronica Sherbourne, David Sime, Pat Somerset, Guida Swann, Euanie Tippett, Audrey Wethered, Sylvia Wiess, Elizabeth Wills, Kathleen Wright and Lena Zamish.

I received helpful comments, suggestions and criticisms on earlier drafts of this book from Anne Acland, Edward Adamson, Maurice Ash, Michael Austin, Christopher Booker, Salley Brown, Margaret Button, Douglas Crosse, Michael Edwards, Betsy Garrett, Molly Kemp, Jane Mayers, Spencer Millham, Mary Pye, Henry Rollin, Peter Scott, John Timlin, Ingaret van der Post, Sylvia Wiess, Elizabeth Wills and Michael Young.

I was also given much help by the following, who are now, alas, deceased: Leonard Elmhirst, Kenneth Folkes, Hardy Gaussen, Doris Layard, Eve Lewis, Joan Macworth, Freda Platts, Jo Sawyer, and Florida Scott-Maxwell.

In addition to allowing me to tape many hours of interviews, Irene Champernowne made available to me all her papers, both private and professional, relating to the whole Withymead experience, and gave me *carte blanche* to make of them what I would. If my account is inaccurate or deficient in any way then the fault is entirely mine.

Finally, I must express my gratitude to the trustees of the Elmgrant Trust, the Francis Scott Trust, to Peter Scott, and to the Trustees of the Frances Wickes Foundation for grants which made it possible for me to research, write and publish this book.

Chapter I

Withymead and the Champernownes

Irene Champernowne was not a beautiful woman, and photographs do her less than justice. She had a large, rather homely face, frizzy hair, enormous, penetrating eyes, and she was undeniably plump. But her presence was compellingly attractive: her voice warm and endearing, her smile had great charm, and her generosity of spirit was so evident that few people met her without being captivated. I was no exception. From our first encounter, one bright morning during the spring vacation of 1956, I experienced feelings of affection for her which, in the months and years that followed, ripened into love.

Our meeting marked my first visit to Withymead. I was 23 at the time, a first year medical student at Oxford University, and I was looking for an analyst. Before Oxford, I had completed a degree course in psychology at Reading University, a dispiriting experience which had taught me a lot about rats but next to nothing about human beings. I looked to analysis to make good this deficiency, and when medically qualified I was determined to specialize in psychiatry.

There were also personal reasons which led me to Withymead. An only child, brought up by loving, solicitous parents, I was finding it hard to cope with the emotional realities of adult life. My desire to find an analyst had been growing for years, and a recent unhappy love affair heightened this desire into an imperative.

My good fortune in discovering Mrs Champernowne and Withymead was due to the kindness of friends living 20 miles away at Dartington Hall, once the seat of the Champernowne family, but by then, thanks to Leonard and Dorothy Elmhirst, an internationally famous centre for education and the arts. Close links existed between Dartington and Withymead, and when approached on my behalf, Mrs Champernowne readily agreed to see me.

She received me in her large consulting room, a converted bedroom on the first floor of Withymead overlooking the garden. It was full of plants, books and sunlight. We sat in comfortable arm chairs beside a log fire. She gave me coffee and oak-meal biscuits and within minutes I was pouring out my story. I was aware of her concentrated attention and scrutiny but I found this strangely undisconcerting: indeed, I had seldom met anyone to whom it was possible to speak freely. I knew that she was *on my side*. She said little during that first hour, I remember, but at the end of it I felt accepted, understood, and very concerned that she should take me on as her patient. She must have sensed my state of mind, for she reached across the hearth and took my hand. 'When would you like to begin?' she said.

We agreed that my analysis should start at the end of the summer term and that, subject to the agreement of the rest of the Withymead staff, I should spend the whole long vacation of four months at Withymead.

At the end of our session I was invited to stay on for the rest of the day in order to meet the staff and 'residents' as the patients were called, and then handed over to Hilary Bates, the Centre's psychiatric social worker. Hilary, busy with files, suggested that since there was still half an hour before lunch and it was a sunny day I might like to have a stroll round to get my bearings.

I wandered out into the garden and looked back at the house. Built towards the end of the eighteenth century, it was a stone building of good proportions, capable of providing ample accommodation for a large family and its servants. Situated at the south east corner of Exeter near Countess Wear, one approached it down a leafy Devon lane whose hedges were a mass of wild flowers. The house itself was surrounded by well stocked gardens and orchards. A mill stream ran beneath an ancient stone bridge into a duck pond and on through spacious meadows of the River Exe. Behind the house a group of stone stable buildings, converted into pottery and painting studios, clustered round a busy courtyard and through open windows I heard the sounds of talk and laughter mingled with a young woman singing Mozart to a piano accompaniment. The courtyard led out to the lane on the other side of which lay other properties and gardens which had evidently been acquired by the Withymead community: a handsome seventeenth century farmhouse called 'The Barton', and 'Primrose Cottage', a small farm worker's dwelling of about the same period. On 'The Barton' lawn stood a pleasant red brick building of recent construction known as 'Red Wing' which I subsequently discovered had been disigned and built by Ben Belton, resident artist, potter and architect, to accommodate a small number of children together with their therapist.

What struck me was the cheerful domesticity and 'normality' of it all. The buildings were snug, intimate and welcoming, as full of cats, dogs and plants, it seemed, as human beings, and there was a total absence of those institutional sights, smells and sounds which can be guaranteed to inspire apprehention in a newcomer.

I spent a happy day. Over lunch Mrs Champernowne introduced me to Ben who, four years earlier, had given up a remunerative job in London as a deputy borough architect in order to run the pottery at Withymead for £400 a year and a small flat in 'The Barton'. His sister, Joanna Hogg, had already joined the Withymead staff before him, and her enthusiasm for the place first attracted him to it. 'It wasn't just the terrific physical attraction of Withymead', Ben later told me, 'but the emphasis placed on the arts. You see, I would never have bothered to become an architect if I could have afforded to paint or make pots, and I realized at once that the opportunities for self-expression at Withymead were too good to miss; and the personalities there struck me as astonishingly different from the ordinary run of people I rubbed shoulders with in local authority architecture.' In the light of these considerations he felt the big drop in salary was unimportant: neither Ben nor his wife Jean had much taste for luxury, and they were spared worry over the education of their two children since Leonard Elmhirt, one of Withymead's Trustees, offered them free places at Dartington Hall School. So Ben took the job and had no regrets.

I liked him immensely. A tall, loose-limbed man in his early forties with angular features and a rich sense of humour, he dressed and looked more like a builder's labourer than an architect. He radiated masculine reliability and it was clear to me even then that he made an important contribution to the community's stability and self-confidence.

After lunch Ben took me over to the pottery and showed me how to use the wheel: under his guidance I threw my first, rather wobbly pot. There I met Michael Edwards, an energetic man in his late twenties who lived with his wife and young children in 'Primrose Cottage'. Michael had trained as a painter as well as a potter before joining the staff at Withymead and he was later to become an important figure in the worlds of art therapy and art education.

From the pottery I climbed an outdoor staircase to the painting studio in the old stable loft. There I found Elizabeth Colyer with a group of five or six people sitting in front of easels, too absorbed by what they were doing to be much bothered by me. The walls were covered with unframed pictures, some naïve and childlike, some bizarre, some banal, but a number bearing unmistakeable signs of talent. I asked Elizabeth about her work and I remember she told me that it was not her function to 'interpret' the pictures that people painted but to create an atmosphere in which it was possible for them to paint whatever they wanted. She did not conceive of herself so much as a therapist as a midwife whose job it was to facilitate a natural process as it occurred. 'What you actually *say* about someone's painting doesn't matter as much as the spirit in which you *receive* it', she said. 'I try not to forget that each painting is a unique expression of the individual who painted it – no one else could have done it. It has to be honoured as a unique creation.' I was much taken with Elizabeth. I was touched by her gentleness and her sense of commitment to her work. I hoped I should be able to paint in her studio.

I went down the outdoor staircase to what I took to be the music room, which was set at right angles to the pottery. I entered and found myself in a big, attractive room with a beautiful view across the duck pond and river to the meadows and the Haldon Hills. To one side of the large windows was a grand piano, behind which sat the slim, elegant form of Molly Kemp, the Centre's music therapist. I introduced myself and said how much I had enjoyed the Mozart in the morning.

'Do you sing or play an instrument?' she asked.

'I play the piano,' I said. 'But only for my own amazement.'

She laughed gratifyingly. 'And what about your voice?'

'Oh, I can't sing.'

Molly grimaced ruefully. 'That can't be right,' she said. 'Everyone can sing. It is the natural human condition to sing. Which composers do you like?'

I told her of my love for Schubert, whose impromtus for piano I was working on with the organ scholar at my college.

'Good,' said Molly. 'When you come here to stay we'll have you singing lieder.'

I was dumbfounded by this suggestion. Left to my own devices such a thought would never have occurred to me, but now, thanks to Molly, I wondered if I could.

Not knowing what to say, I glanced round the room. I noticed the handsome, well polished parquet floor. On the wall my eye was caught by a slate plaque. It carried an inscription commemorating the life of Toni Wolff, C.G. Jung's friend and colleague. I wondered why it was there and Molly must have noticed my curiosity. 'Mrs C. analysed with Miss Wolff for several years and they were good friends,' she explained. 'We put up that memorial to her when she died three years ago.'

It's a lovely room,' I said.

'Yes, isn't it. Before Ben Belton joined us it was the garage. But he and the men's working group transformed it into what you see now. We call it the River Room, for obvious reasons, and we use it for music, movement and dancing, as well as for important community occasions like Christmas and Easter.' With a quick, graceful movement she closed the piano and got to her feet. 'It's tea time,' she said.

We crossed the courtyard and walked through the garden to the dining room, a modern extension built onto the front of the house – another of Ben's innovations, I learned. There I met Sylvie, Withymead's only nurse. A short, energetic person in her sixties, Sylvie was all bustle and loquacity. She made me very much at home and I found her instantly endearing. Before coming to Withymead a few years previously, she had worked hard all her life delivering babies in London, and I could tell that she liked the idea of me because I was a medical student. I liked her too, not because of her profession but because she was a dear.

Over tea I talked to some of the patients. Altogether there were about twenty-five of them. They were of all ages and, as is usual in psychiatric clinics, there were rather more females than males. On the whole, they seemed to be the sort of nice, intelligent people one would be pleased to meet anywhere, and only a few of them had any obvious difficulties. One man I noticed had withdrawn into himself and sat alone in a secluded alcove which Sylvie told me was called 'introverts' corner'. ('If ever you don't want to talk to us at mealtimes, you can go and eat there'.) The other occupant of 'introverts' corner' was a frail girl in her twenties who was slowly munching her way through a piece of cake. Periodically she threw her head back and in a loud but oddly dispassionate voice called 'MUM'. Everyone accepted this as if it were the most natural thing in the world.

Then, while I was attempting to talk to a boy with a crippling stammer, a stocky young Frenchman to whom I had just been chatting proceeded to have an epileptic fit, which impressed me because it was the first I had ever witnessed. Sylvie dealt with it with brisk efficiency and when the fit was over Ben gathered the unconscious figure in his arms and carried him off to his room.

The hubbub released by this incident subsided, and I turned to see a handsome, white haired man with glasses and a hearing aid coming very slowly down the hall stairs, leaning heavily on the bannister and a thick walking stick. It was something of a shock to realize that this must be Irene Champernowne's husband, Gilbert. When, eventually, he reached the bottom of the stairs, Sylvie called me over and introduced me to him. I liked his fine eyes and kind, gentle manner, but conversation was desultory between us at first because for some reason we were shy of one another. But then we discovered a bond that animated both of us. We had both been to the same school, and hated it. It was there, Mr Champernowne told me, that while fighting with another boy he had banged his leg against the iron frame supporting his desk. The wound turned septic and, in the absence of antibiotics, he developed severe osteomyelitis and the leg had to be amputated. He now had arthritis badly in both hips. And he was deaf, too. But these afflictions evidently did not prevent him from being involved in what went on around him. As we talked I felt that he was taking a kindly interest in me while at the same time pretty shrewdly summing me up.

I left soon after tea to return to my parents' home in Plymouth. I was elated. Not just because I had been treated so well but because I felt as if I had passed some kind of test, and that I had been accepted as a potential member of the community. By the time I reached home I knew there was nothing in the world I wanted more than to analyze with Irene Champernowne and become a part of Withymead.

The summer term at Oxford passed quickly with the laboratory practicals, lectures, tutorials, tests and examinations which torment all medical students, however idyllic their surroundings. There were parties, college balls and sunny afternoons punting on the Cherwell, which I enjoyed of course but, for all that, I was impatient for the term to end so that I could go to Withymead and start my analysis.

Money, however, was a worry because I could not afford the modest fee that Withymead charged for board, lodging and analysis. But during my interview with her, Mrs Champernowne had insisted – very characteristically, as I subsequently discovered – that such considerations should not be allowed to stand in the way. 'If it is right for you to come here,' she said, 'Life will make it possible'. As it turned out, she was right. Tipped off by a fellow undergraduate, I applied to the British Council for a vacation job acting as courier to a group of French school teachers attending a summer school at Exeter University. Just before the end of term I wrote gleefully to Mrs Champernowne telling her that I had been given the job. She responded by tackling the Withymead Management Committee on my behalf, arranging for me to pay analytic fees at what she called 'a reduced student rate' and it seemed that nothing could now stand in my way.

When the term was over I went home to see my parents and then, before going on to Withymead, I went to Dartington to spend a few days with my friends. The first evening there, my leg was broken in a road accident, and all my plans were ruined. With a badly smashed tibia and plaster up to my hip, the British Council considered, not unreasonably, that I should not make a very agile guide and wrote to say that they proposed to make other arrangements. From Totnes Cottage Hospital I wrote a miserable note to Mrs Champernowne saying that it looked as if we would have to cancel our plans. By return post I received an immensely encouraging reply: 'Whatever you do, don't lose heart; a way will be found.'

Again she was right. This time she approached the Withymead 'Grants and Loans Committee' and persuaded them to make me a 'student loan.' This would cover a substantial part of the cost. My hard-pressed parents, who were putting me through Oxford without benefit of a government grant (I had used my grant allocation in obtaining my psychology degree), found the rest of the money necessary and, excited but rather self-conscious, I moved into Withymead on crutches in time for my first analytic session.

This was the first of many stays in Withymead and it marked for me a major turning point, for, as the years of my analysis with Irene Champernowne went by, the quality of my life changed very wonderfully, and I became convinced that eventually I, in my turn, would be a psychotherapist, that I might do in some measure for others what Withymead and Irene Champernowne has done for me.

So settled and established did Withymead seem when I first went there that it came as a surprise to discover that the Champernownes had lived there for only fourteen years. They found Withymead soon after they had been bombed out of their London flat by the Luftwaffe in 1941, but did not begin to have patients to stay with them until the night after the Exeter Blitz in early May, 1942. Devon appealed to them as a refuge partly because of their friendship with Leonard and Dorothy Elmhirst, who felt that it could be useful to the Dartington community to have Irene's services close at hand, and partly because of Gilbert's family connections with the region.

Gilbert, born in 1884, was the nineth child of Arthur Champernowne, who was then Squire of Dartington. An ancient Devonshire family, the Champernownes lived at Dartington Hall for centuries, and there they had remained until the Elmhirsts bought the whole estate from them in 1925. Gilbert's childhood was, I discovered, unhappy and had wounded him psychologically and physically for life. But, as it was to find out for myself, it was out of these wounds that a rich compassion flowed, and it was because of them that he could be the committed and humane director of Withymead that he was.

That summer I came to know and admire Gilbert and as the weeks passed a friendship grew between us. This might well have been otherwise because we were both shy, introverted people; but initial contact between us was made easy by the number of things we had in common. Both Devonians, we not only went to the same school but to the same University and both of us had suffered traumatic leg injuries: although mine was less serious, I was, for the time being, more incapacitated than he. As our friendship developed he would often invite me to join him for coffee in his study, an extension built for him on the first floor by Ben, with a spacious view of the garden, river and the distant hills. We must have seemed an odd pair with out sticks and crutches and a fifty year gap between us in age, but the rapport we found eroded the years and we were able to discuss all topics as equals and as friends. I talked to him of my hopes, fears and ambitions and gave him the benefit of my undergraduate views on psychology, literature and life, while he listened attentively, commenting wisely and, with a little pumping from me, spoke of his own history, his family, and his bachelor existence before meeting Irene at the comparatively late age of 53. It was in this manner that I learned of his unhappiness as a child.

His father died when Gilbert was only three, leaving his widow with a great deal of responsibility and worry, which she bore ill. In keeping with the general deterioration of British agriculture at the time, the Champernowne fortunes were in decline. Dartington Hall and its large estate were in advanced decay and there was little money available to do anything about it. Gilbert's mother grieved bitterly over her husband's death and gradually retreated into the life of a chronic invalid. When she was not resting in her room she was preoccupied with law suits and family business. Not infrequently, the problems which Dartington presented became too much for her and she would rent a house somewhere well away from it all and go off to live there for months at a time. So it was that after the death of their father, the Champernowne children saw little of their mother, and their upbringing became the responibility of a succession of governesses and nannies.

Gilbert had but one recollection of his father and that was of playing lions and tigers with him in the back corridor of the Elizabethan wing where it joined the medieval courtyard. After his death no one seems to have adopted a paternal role in Gilbert's life, except for his elder brothers who abused their authority by bullying him. Three older brothers were separated in time from three much younger ones by four sisters, and the absence of any senior authority in the household meant that the older boys were free to persecute the younger ones whenever the whim took them – which it did, often. This sadistic triumvirate would form a pack and pass happy hours marauding through the ruined house and dilapidated grounds hunting the three frightened small boys. When they caught them, they tied them up, tortured them and locked them away in dark cupboards.

The incessant bullying, combined with the withdrawal of his mother's love, would probably had had more damaging consequences for Gilbert were it not for the close ties of affection which bound him to his sister, Eleanor, who became a substitute mother to him and was probably his salvation. She was particularly good to him when at sixteen he lost his leg – a shattering experience for a naturally athletic boy who loved cricket and riding and hiking over the moors. Despite Eleanor's loving attention, he suffered greatly in the months which followed his operation: the grief of irreparable loss was bad enough but with no antibiotics available his infection persisted and the wound proved extremely reluctant to heal. The artificial limb which he wore for the rest of his life was a source of constant discomfort and embarrasment to him

As a result to this misfortune he missed many months of

schooling, and when he eventually went up to Oxford he was a year older than his brothers had been. Like them he went to Christ Church, but he was not happy there: it was too large and too hearty for one of his retiring disposition. At that time there was in university life still a tremendous emphasis on sport and, possessing only one leg, Gilbert felt very much an odd man out. Nor did things work out well for him academically. His mother wanted him to enter the Church so that he might take over the living at Dartington and she persuaded him, rather against his wishes, to read theology. As he feared, he found it uncongenial and, to his mother's disappointment, ended up with a general arts degree.

Gilbert did, however, make two friendships at Oxford which proved to be lasting ones: with Bill Lane-Claypon, who subsequently became a Trustee of Withymead, and with Cuthbert Kelly, a musician. During the summer vacations these two friends would come down to Devon from Oxford and accompany the Champernownes on their annual migration by the wagon load from Dartington to a farm owned by the Coaker family in the heart of Dartmoor. There they would stay for many weeks, the men living in tents and the woman in the spartan farm buildings. These were memorably happy occasions and Bill continued to come for them after he and Gilbert had gone down from Oxford and, after his marriage, he would bring his wife, Frances, with him. When I met Frances many years later she remembered Gilbert as he then was 'a dear lovable man' who, for all his shyness, was a most agreeable companion. He had a pleasant baritone voice and, together with Bill and Cuthbert, he sang inexhaustably and with great enjoyment songs from Gilbert and Sullivan operas. Despite his artificial limb, he was very active, and would ride and walk over the moor as far as anybody.

To Gilbert, however, the presence of Frances was always associated with poignant memories, for he had once fallen deeply in love with her sister. He was never able to declare his love because he felt utterly unworthy of her and he went through a period of great unhappiness. It is a sad sign of how maimed he was, in spirit as well as body, by his loss of a limb. His suffering was further intensified when his younger brother, Edward, took advantage of Gilbert's reticence, quickly won the girl's affection, and married her himself.

Compassion born of suffering during these formative years determined the purpose on which Gilbert put his energies for the rest of his life. On going down from Oxford he decided that he wanted to do something to relieve the appalling conditions which existed at the turn of the century in the slums of the East End of London. Together with a small group of his comtemporaries, who possessed like him both a social conscience and a private income, he went to live and work at Oxford House in Bethnal Green. This university settlement existed for the purpose of bringing Oxford graduates, mostly churchmen, into touch with the poor of London, so that they might understand their problems and bring social and moral forces to bear on their solution.

At Oxford House Gilbert began to discover his own value. He realized that he had inner resources that could be mobilized in the service of others in such a way as to bring meaning and happiness into his life. There he developed strong ties of friendship with William Temple, Dick Sheppard and George Bell, two of whom subsequently became bishops and, in Temple's case, Archbishop of Canterbury. These men had a powerful influence on Gilbert's personal development.

Mostly, he spent his time doing the sort of things which nowadays are done by salaried social workers, but he was never slow to take on additional responsibilities. One job that gave him particular satisfaction was the secretaryship of the Children's Country Holiday Fund, which existed to give East End children, who would otherwise never have escaped from the slums, a holiday in the country every summer. Increasingly, he interested himself in the work of the Discharged Prisoners' Aid Society, eventually becoming secretary of this too. He regarded this as his most important job, for this society was the only organization in existence that did anything to assist people when they were discharged from prison. Throughout his long secretaryship (it lasted for twenty-five years) Gilbert struggled with the limited funds and manpower at his disposal to relieve the often terrible distress that he encountered. He worked closely with probation officers, who in those days were voluntary workers usually associated with religious organizations, to bring about the permanent rehabilitation of prisoners, and did his best to encourage them to put their energies into other than criminal activities. It was this concern with the rehabilitation of those who had fallen foul of society which, in July, 1937, brought him into contact with his future wife.

At that time, Irene was working in London as the colleague of an eminent analytical psychologist and friend of C.G. Jung, Dr Godwin Baynes. In the 1930s, 'Peter' Baynes, as he was known to his friends, was as important a representative of Jung in England as was Ernest Jones of Sigmund Freud. An energetic man with a powerful personality and a lively mind, Baynes had many interests, both personal and professional. One of these was the newly founded Institute for the Scientific Treatment of Delinquency, an organization with which Gilbert Champernowne was associated. A patient whom the Institute had referred to Baynes for treatment was a man who had been in and out of prison for the most of his life. His social and family circumstances were in a dreadful mess and in an attempt to obtain some practical help in dealing with them Baynes asked Irene to call in at the office of the Discharged Prisoners' Aid Society.

Many years later, when Irene and I had become close friends, I asked her about this first meeting with Gilbert. Apparently she had some difficulty in identifying the building and stopped to ask a cockney mechanic who was working at the roadside under a lorry. He was able to direct her. She thanked him, and as she walked off down the street, he called after her. 'I 'ope you gets yer aid, lady!' 'Well, I did,' commented Irene. 'I got financial help for the patient and eventually I got Gilbert for myself.'

Their courtship was slow to get under way, but gradually they began to see a lot of each other, going out to theatres and restaurants, and on excursions by train out of London for long walks in the country. 'He was such a keen walker,' Irene told me, 'that I had no idea at first about his artificial leg. He limped, of course, but I thought it might be a war wound. Then, one weekend, we were walking on the downs in Kent. We sat down to rest and a grasshopper landed on my skirt. I noticed that it had lost a leg. I pointed this out to Gilbert. He put his hand out to touch it, and it hopped off in a wide circle. Gilbert grinned and said, "He seems to manage all right with only one." He was silent for a while. Then, rather tense, he said, "I've only got one leg, you know. Do you mind?" And I said, "No, I don't mind at all." Nor did I mind. I'm not a woman to mind about that sort of thing. It never worried me.'

Through Irene, Gilbert met 'Peter' Baynes and was so impressed by him, that, in order to understand more about Irene's work and more about himself, he asked Baynes to take him on as an analysand. Baynes readily agreed and the analysis continued until the war separated him from the Champernownes in 1941.

As their love grew, Irene and Gilbert discovered that they had many qualities and values in common; but what delighted them most was the discovery of attributes which each possessed which were the precise opposite of the other's. On the face of it, they could not have been more different. Gilbert, a reserved, reflective introvert, conserved his energy for use in attaining carefully considered objectives, and seldom displayed much emotion. Irene, on the other hand, was a powerful extravert. A great talker, brimming with social vitality, ideas and insights poured out of her in torrents. As far as people were concerned, she was prodigal with her time, money, attention and love. Unlike Gilbert, she possessed a fiery temper and could, when roused, 'blow up' – sometimes to devastating effect.

But in these differences lay the strength of their relationship. Where Irene was incautious Gilbert was prudent, where he was shy and reticent she spun the wheels of social life, when she was inspired with plans for the future he could assess quietly those which were feasible and persuade her to drop those which were not. He was her head and her executor, she was his heart and his soul. Although at first sight they appeared an improbable couple, one did not have to know them very long to realize how well they complemented one another. I remember that within a few weeks of my arrival at Withymead it became clear to me the extent to which the whole atmosphere of the place was an expression of their personalities. The dignity of life there was a reflection of Gilbert's dignity and sense of form, whereas the warm vitality of Withymead was an extension of Irene herself.

No less disparate than their personalities were the backgrounds from which they came. Irene Broomhall was born in a manse in Islington in 1901, the elder of two daughters of a missionary who had seen arduous service in China. Although she was greatly loved by both parents and never knew deprivation of any kind, the financial circumstances of the family were modest to the point of hardship. She was educated at the City of London Girls' School and her adolesence was lived out in the terrible context of the First World War. Normally a time when one is being prepared for life, for Irene and her contemporaries adolescence was a period filled with the omnipresence of death. Irene's male cousins and their friends, on leave from the front, were always welcomed by the Broomhalls, and the tragic tales they told profoundly affected Irene, and the anguish of those years was indelibly printed on her life. Young though she was, she became preoccupied with the theological problem which the incalculable evil of the war presented. Children are religious by inclination until education and life turn them cynical, and it is not surprising that a girl growing up in a missionary's household should be absorbed with problems of this kind.

One of the young soldiers who visited Irene's home when he was on leave from Flanders was an attractive cousin, a lieutenant four years her senior. Before the war he had begun to study medicine and used to accompany the Broomhalls on holidays to the Western Isles of Scotland. Irene was greatly attached to him and longed for his visits; but as the war went on she found his leaves increasingly unbearable, for the horror of trench warfare was, she could see, slowly destroying him. When eventually he broke down, he was beyond cure and he spent the rest of his life in a mental hospital. To this tragic experience Irene owned her vocation: it convinced her that she must devote her life to the relief of mental suffering.

At first she thought she would become a doctor, but her medical ambitions received little encouragement from her school. Irene remembered the headmistress telling her mother that she should give up all idea of going to a university as she was 'not the right calibre'. Characteristically, she took no notice of this verdict and went off to Birkbeck College to enrol as a student in botany, zoology and chemistry, subjects which would qualify her to enter a medical school, should she be able to afford it, once she had obtained her degree.

It was to be a gruelling period. Her parents were in no position to pay for a university education and Irene had to contribute a large share of the cost herself. She found a job teaching biology and mathematics at a private school. Every morning she would teach until lunchtime and then go to Birkbeck to study and attend laboratories from 2 until 9 p.m. The strain was considerable and she suffered for it later. Telling me of this time Irene said, 'As you know, I am an intuitive feeling type, and at Birkbeck I was having to work all the time on my inferior function (sensation). I mean, can you imagine *me* having to do gravimetric analysis, weighing to point naught naught of a thing, whatever it was?' In fact, her gravimetric analysis was her undoing. When she sat her finals, she failed. She had done well enough on all the other papers but she had to repeat everything the next year. On that occasion she was successful and was awarded a second class honours degree. But the strain and worry of it all had exhausted her and in the months that followed she became quite badly depressed.

Irene always regarded that period as her 'night journey of the soul.' My parents had a bad time with me, I fear', she said. 'I cut right out on religion. I was in outer darkness. Life seemed quite meaningless to me. Everything was completely black. God was dead. When patients tell me that I don't know what it's like to be depressed, to feel that nothing has any value any more, I say "Yes I do", and I think of that time. It was indescribable: quite different from the experience of losing a loved person, because there your very sorrow is your love. The despair of spiritual darkness lies beyond that.'

Persuaded by her worried parents, Irene went to stay with three spinster sisters whom they knew, the Misses Pugh, who ran a field study centre in Kent, called Hill Farm. There, under the Pughs' gentle guidance, Irene was brought back into touch with meaning and value through daily contact with nature. It was an experience which had implications for Withymead, for Hill Farm was an inspiration to Irene: 'That old Tudor farm was so beautiful', she told me. 'I loved the simple country life and eating out under the trees in the orchard, just like at Withymead. I came to understand that interchange with nature makes you part of the total picture of life: you see that you belong. The Pughs were in touch with all that went on around them. They knew where everything grew and if a bird arrived it was no unhonoured happening. It was noted, discussed, greeted, if you like. It became part of your expanded life.' A similar attitude to nature prevailed at Withymead. As Irene explained, 'If anyone spots the otters the news spreads rapidly and we all go quietly to have a look. The same thing happens when red-throated divers or kingfishers visit our pond. This makes life rich for people who are shut in. It makes them more at home in the universe.'

Irene spent most of 1926 at Hill Farm. Towards the end of the year she returned to her teaching job. She had almost fully recovered her zest for life, but her 'dark night of the soul' had left her with a desire for greater psychological understanding. She took herself off to the Tavistock Clinic and as a result of this visit embarked on the first of her personal analyses. Her analyst, Leonard Brown, was a neo-Freudian, and the analysis went on for three years. 'He was a nice man and I learned a lot from him', Irene told me. 'But it wasn't nearly as important for me as any of the analyses I had later on. He certainly didn't do me any harm – I was too critical for that. Of course, he always put down my criticisms to "resistance". What I didn't like was all that remote thing of lying on a couch with him out of sight behind me, and I got bored with harping back continuously to the breast, the womb and the penis. After three years I got sick of it and gave up.

Her hunger for greater psychological wisdom still unsatisfied, Irene turned elsewhere. Through an old friend of the family, Dr Marjorie Edwards, a Harley Street gynaecologist, she became a member of the London Adlerian Society. She toyed with the idea of doing a degree in psychology at University College under the tutelage of J.C. Flugel and Sir Cyril Burt but she was discouraged by the atmosphere there. 'It just wasn't living', she said. Feeling that London could not offer the education she was after she decided to go abroad – 'to the home of psychology: Vienna'.

This was made possible by a lucky chance. Christine Pugh, who was Senior Lecturer in Biology at Gipsy Hill Teachers' Training College, wanted an assistant and offered Irene the job. As luck would have it, she was able to make a condition of her employment that she be allowed to spend half of each year abroad studying psychology. Since she was to be employed at the college for half the year, she was to receive, not unreasonably, only half the salary which the position carried, but this would be enough to live on. That the authorities at Gipsy Hill agreed to this helpful arrangement was due in no small measure to the good offices of Christine Pugh, who was very much in favour of Irene studying abroad.

Shortly before she set off for Austria, Irene was sent a ticket by Dr Edwards for a lecture given at the Royal Society of Medicine by Dr Leonhard Seif, an Adlerian from Munich. By a coincidence, an early love of Irene's, now a doctor, was chairing the meeting, and afterwards he introduced her to Dr Seif, who invited her to visit him in Munich. Irene was much taken by him and decided to accept his invitation.

She eventually left for Vienna in the summer of 1930. As soon as she arrived, she wrote to Alfred Adler saying that she was a friend of Dr Edwards (who had analysed with him) and a member of the London Adlerian Society, and asking if she could meet him. He replied warmly, and invited her to come to the hotel where he met regularly with his colleagues and students. She was fascinated by him, and the influence which he had on her was to be significant for the success of Withymead. Adler suggested that Irene should attend his famous 'open clinics'. There were thirty-two of these, each attached to a Viennese school, and nearly all of them were run by teachers who had been trained and analysed by Adler. There was one training clinic which was run by Adler himself, and it was this that Irene most frequently attended. What impressed her was the way in which he made use of his audience as a therpeutic group. 'He used us as a sensitive instrument for bringing the child, who was an outcast, back into the human fold,' she said 'It's always seemed strange to me that Adler called his approach "Individual Psychology" because he believed so strongly in the therapeutic importance of the community. Adler enabled me to make my extraverted relationship to groups. He taught me the value of working therapeutically through a community.'

Being a warmly extraverted person herself, Irene found

this aspect of Adler and his followers entirely sympathetic. 'It was very different from what I later experienced with the Jungians,' she said. 'Adler would say, "We meet at our café in the evening between eight and ten. Do come." Seif was the same in Munich: "You are always welcome. Come." Immediately you found yourself part of the group round the man. Whereas in London, the first time I went to the [Jungian] Analytical Psychology Club, I thought I'd never met a more distant, unwelcoming set of people in my life!'

Irene never analysed with Adler. Her contacts with him were confined to her attendances at his clinics and the informal gatherings of his adherents. On that first visit she spent six weeks in Vienna before moving on to Munich to see Seif. There she made friends with an interesting group of people. Among them were Mrs Forbes-Dennis (better known as Phyllis Bottome, the biographer of Alfred Adler) her husband and her ward, Ian Fleming, who at that time was not yet in the grip of his James Bond phantasies.

Seif deeply impressed Irene. 'I admired his integrity and his erudition. He was steeped in German philosphy, particularly Nietzsche. I remember his eyes well: deep, dark eyes, introverted and full of passion, full of a strange energy which I've seen in other men of that kind – like my own dear Gilbert.' Although she learned a lot from Adler, Irene was sure she absorbed far more from Seif, not only through her personal analysis with him but through the group that formed round him. She found Seif more cultivated, more wise and more lovable than Adler. He was also a stepping stone to C.G. Jung: 'I don't think I would ever have started to read Jung's books if I hadn't been put onto them by Seif,' she said.

From 1930 to 1936 Irene spent half of each year in Munich, with occasional visits to Vienna, just able to manage on the half pay she drew from Gipsy Hill. 'The pound did pretty well in Germany in those days, but even so I lived very frugally and it was difficult to get much fun.' She lodged with a sculptor and his wife and ate at the *studentenhaus*, where meals were extraordinarily cheap. Seif was understanding about her circumstances and charged her low fees for her analytic sessions, a piece of generosity which she was to repay manyfold in later years when her own patients were unable to pay the going rate.

Two years after Irene started at Gipsy Hill, Christina Pugh died, and Irene was appointed as her successor. On the strength of her increase in salary, Irene moved out of her rooms in college into a flat in Handel Mansions, Bloomsbury, which she shared with Marjorie Sanders, a fellow teacher. It was a quiet, comfortable flat and she found it conducive to study. A voracious reader, Irene complemented the knowledge she acquired in Munich and Vienna by hard work on her own. Her psychological understanding grew steadily, but she realized that if she was ever to make professional use of her experience she would need more academic qualifications. Accordingly, in 1935 she once again visited University College and, struggling with her repugnance at the 'dead atmosphere' of the department run by Flugel and Burt, enrolled for a two year B.Sc. course in psychology.

By this time, life for her friends in Munich was becoming disagreeable, and Irene was forced to recognize that Nazi oppression would soon stamp out the activities that took her there. She dreaded the vacuum which this loss would create in her life and she wondered how she would be able to fill it. Happily, the problem did not bother her for long, for the vacuum was filled almost as soon as it was made by the growth of a new personal and professional relationship, which was to prove one of the most significant of her life. It was through the ever-obliging Marjorie Edwards that she met Godwin Baynes. 'He struck me at once as a colossal figure,' Irene remembered. 'I didn't understand what he was talking about at first, because he was the first Jungian I ever knew, but we clicked from the very beginning.' Under Seif's influence, her reading had already carried her in Jung's direction; her relationship with 'Peter' Baynes now took her all the way. Knowing that her days with Seif were over, she began to analyze with Baynes, believing that it must be an essential part of training to experience the process at first hand. She came to him for two sessions a week and this continued for years.

During her last visit to Munich in the summer of 1936 Irene took a momentous step. She wrote to C.G. Jung. She had just read *Modern Man in Search of a Soul* and she sensed that her spiritual quest had ended: she had, so to speak, come home. 'I felt that Jung filled the gaps I needed to fill. I was not satisfied with Freudian psychology, nor with Adlerian, although I had learned a great deal from both. Yet neither had a corpus of theory or a *Weltanschauung* that I could really go along with.' In her letter she told Jung all this, describing the course her psychological training had followed, and asking if she could come to meet him. She received an immediate reply telling her to come to Ascona, where Jung was attending the annual Eranos meeting. Irene set off at once, leaving Munich never to return.

At Ascona, Jung received her in the garden of the villa of Frau Kapteyn. It was evening, and Jung was sitting under a palm tree. 'To me,' said Irene, 'he looked like God Almighty sitting there. He was very welcoming and I confess I was overwhelmed. I was such an insignificant creature, who had been wondering round Europe searching for something I didn't really understand. We had a long and very warm talk, but I can remember only one thing that he said to me. I was in my thirties and still perhaps a bit naíve. I told him that I felt as if I were in the Garden of Eden with God Almighty in the cool of the day beneath a palm tree, and he said, "Miss Broomhall, we've been driven out of the Garden of Eden. There's an angel with a flaming sword at the gate, and we can't go back." You see, I was an idealist and I thought the world could be put right quite easily but Jung's comment brought me up sharp against my own naívety.' Jung suggested that once Irene had obtained her B.Sc. in psychology she should come regularly to Zurich in order to analyze with him and collect material for a Ph.D. thesis. Greatly encouraged by this interview, Irene returned to London to tackle her final examinations and to continue her analysis with 'Peter' Baynes.

For his part, Baynes was clearly as impressed with Irene as she with him, for he valued her enough to pay her the highest compliment that an analyst can pay to one of his analysands: he invited her to become his assistant, and offered her the use of a consulting room in his house in Mansfield Street. Understandably, she jumped at the offer. She resigned from her biology lectureship at Gipsy Hill, installed herself in Mansfield Street, and began treating her first patients. It was an auspicious beginning to her career as a psychotherapist.

Through working as a colleague, Irene continued to learn avidly from Baynes. There was never any formal teacher-pupil relationship between them, but they were forever popping in and out of each other's rooms to discuss patients and regularly had working lunches at the Bolivar Restaurant, just round the corner. Irene always believed this to be the best way for young analysts to learn their job, and it was the way that, much later in our relationship, I was to learn to use what skills I possess as a therapist from Irene.

When Irene started working with him, Baynes was writing *Mythology of the Soul*, and they spent many hours discussing the paintings on which this work was based. This experience had important consequences for Withymead, as Irene acknowledged: 'From Baynes I learned the essentials of art therapy – how to enter into the drama of the painting with the patient, how to drop right into the individual's own myth. He taught me how people can create their myth by dreaming, painting and modelling. He used to tell me about how Jung had done this himself, for he knew all about the "Red Book"'.

Irene obtained her B.Sc. in June 1937, and went to Zurich for the winter semester of 1937–38. She began at once to have regular analytic sessions with Jung. She did not find it easy. 'I was disturbed by his directness and, at times, his ruthless-

Gilbert and Irene Champernowne

A moment musicale on the River Room terrace

ness. He could be very harsh. I was utterly convinced of the great integrity and spiritual capacity of the man, and I would not have given up under any circumstances, but I'm a feeling type, and his extraverted feeling was his weakest function. So for me, an extraverted intuitive-feeling type, this was difficult. It meant that one of us had to meet the other on another plane. I think intuition was where I really found my contact with him.'

The most vivid recollections Irene had of her sessions with Jung concerned his attitude to the work. 'I was deeply impressed by the way he was so utterly *present* with you', she said. 'While you were there you were for him the only important thing in his world. I used to feel that his research was being continued through *my* life, through what *I* brought to the session, and I believe that this was his intention. He wasn't doing it for me alone. This gave me enormous confidence because I felt that he was there for his own reasons, that the psychology of the whole situation was part of the scientific material on which he was working with total commitment. I had never met anyone who was so completely *there*. He was no outside observer because he was experiencing all the time. That so impressed me – the way he gave one honour. He affirmed one's life. And yet, if you were in any way weak or stupid he could be sharp and relentless.

'I remember once leaving him and walking along the shore of the lake of Küsnacht on a grey winter day, feeling stripped to the bone and thinking, "Why, I can't tolerate this! It's just too awful!" And when I got back to England later that winter I said to Peter Baynes, "Either I'm a hopeless person or he's terribly cruel". But Peter said, "Rene, he must think you are worth it or he wouldn't take the trouble to treat you like that." That rather consoled me to go back for more.'

In addition to seeing Jung, Irene spent that first semester working academically with Dr C.A. Meier, collecting material related to Jung's word association test for her Ph.D. thesis, and having analytic sessions with Toni Wolff. 'I think

I really got more of Jung's psychology from her than I did from Jung himself. She was totally absorbed in his work and always in touch with him, and whenever I was analyzing with Toni I never felt I was out of analysis with Jung. In fact, it was in Zurich that I learned the secret of working with two people and saw how creative it could be – provided that they were close to each other and worked in the same sort of way, it didn't interfere with the analysis at all. I felt free to move from one to the other. Toni might be struck by one of my dreams and say, "I think you ought to take this one to Dr Jung. I'd like to know what he makes of it." So I would arrange an appointment and go. It was invariably extraordinarily revealing: he focused things in such an astute way. He always saw the point.'

Irene left Zurich just before the coming of spring: for one thing, Jung had departed on a trip in India and, for another, she had an important event to prepare for in England. On April 9th, 1938, she was to marry Gilbert Champernowne.

As soon as they were married, Irene and Gilbert moved into a large, comfortable flat in Bedford Square, where they were free to indulge their talent for hospitality. Their handsome drawing room became a regular meeting place for their friends and colleagues, and for members of the Analytical Psychology Club, now grown somewhat more friendly having been thawed by Irene's personality. They also accommodated the Club's guest speakers, including Emma Jung, who they loved. But the approach of war meant that their delight in their first home was to be short-lived.

As the international crisis worsened, Irene continued to see patients during the day and work on her thesis at night, and she managed to make one more protracted visit to Zurich. She eventually obtained her Ph.D. just before war was declared. A few months earlier, the London section of the Discharged Prisoner' Aid Society was amalgamated with its parent national association and the two secretaryships were combined. The national secretary was much younger than Gilbert and so Gilbert stood down in his favour. After some months of rest, during which he read widely and continued his analysis with Baynes, he went to work as an occupational therapist at Mill Hill Military Psychiatric Hospital, doing pottery and woodwork with the patients.

When the bombing started, Irene and Gilbert continued to live and work in London, despite almost nightly visits from the Luftwaffe. At the weekends, however, their need for some respite from the bombardment took them out into the peace of the Hertfordshire countryside where, early in 1941, they found and rented a cottage not far from Irene's sister, who lived in Harpenden. As it turned out, this arrangement was more fortuitous than they realized, for, one Saturday night just after they had begun to use the cottage, the house in Bedford Square was wrecked by blast. The Regency glass dome over the staircase well was blown in, the windows and much brickwork shattered, and the flat was rendered uninhabitable. Even before this disaster Irene and Godwin Baynes had been finding it increasingly difficult to practice in London. Many patients had evacuated themselves to various parts of the country, while those who remained were often unable to keep their appointments because of transport failures. The bombing of Bedford Square was the last straw, and they agreed that the time had now come for them to join the exodus from London.

Since Gilbert could not at once drop his work with the psychiatric patients in North London, Irene went down to Exeter on her own and put up at a guest house in Paris Street run by Biddy Twyford, daughter of the Champernownes' old gardener at Dartington. Irene began house-hunting right away, assisted by Gilbert's brother, Edward. Her main concern was to find a house with enough room to accommodate painting and pottery studios. She was not at that juncture thinking in terms of running a residential centre, but as a result of the influence of Baynes and Jung she was determined that art therapy should form an integral part of her work, and that her patients must be provided with all the necessary facilities to paint and use clay.

At first she and Edward looked at an attractive eighteenth century house in Southernhay, but they decided against it on the grounds that it was not large enough – a fortunate decision as it happened, for six months later it was completely obliterated by German bombs. They looked at a number of other houses but something was wrong with all of them. Then, by chance, Irene discovered that the preparatory school which she had attended as a child before going to the City of London Girls' School, from which she had been expelled for beating up a fellow pupil ('She asked for it, she was a bully'.), had been evacuated to Exeter, and was now housed for the duration of the war in the old Clock House at Countess Wear. She had a hunch that she should call on the headmistress and, characteristically, she acted on it. 'I just walked in and presented myself to her', said Irene. 'It was the same headmistress who had expelled me, very ancient by that time, and I told her who I was. She was suitably impressed!' In fact, the elderly headmistress received her delinquent ex-pupil with surprising conviviality, and became quite animated when Irene told her she was looking for a house. Apparently the Clock House was bursting with young ladies, and the head was badly in need of overspill accommodation. There was, she announced, an attractive Georgian house only a quarter of a mile away with no less than fourteen rooms and the old lady who lived there would not allow the school to use a single one of them as a classroom. 'Why don't you go down and see her, my dear,' she said, 'and persuade her to sell it to you. Then you could let us a couple of rooms till the end of the war.' Irene thought this a good idea. She asked how to get to the house, and set off down the road to the river's edge to look at it. And there was Withymead.

Irene could never remember how much Withymead cost, but thought it must have been somewhere in the region of £3,000 or £4,000 – a considerable sum in those days. Rather than borrow the money from a bank, they poured their own funds into the purchase and restoration of the house, and when, at one point, their resources ran dangerously low, they borrowed £1,000 from a member of Gilbert's family. With this they just managed. During the whole of the winter of 1941–42, while Irene was building up a practice in Exeter, Gilbert redecorated the interior, helped by a girl who had run away from home to become a patient of Irene's, and by a small band of superannuated workmen, too decrepid to be called up for military service. By early spring they had finished the kitchen, dining room and sitting room on the ground floor, and the four bedrooms and bathroom on the first floor, and had made a start on the four bedrooms at the top of the house. Though they did not realize it, they had completed as much in the nick of time. On May 3rd a large formation of German planes attacked Exeter and much of the centre of the city was razed to the ground. 'Early the following morning we went up onto the roof', Irene remembered. 'The whole city seemed to be in flames. We expected to see scores of people trekking out, but it was uncanny – there wasn't a soul – just a few terrified cats and dogs, running.'

Fortunately, Withymead was unscathed. There was no water or gas and the telephone would not work, but the electricity was turned on for a few hours a day and they were able to cook primitively on an upturned electric fire. Although a number of rooms were still unfurnished, camp beds and blankets were found and when the refugees finally began to emerge from the city later that day, Gilbert and Irene were ready for them. 'That night the house was full,' said Irene. 'We must have put up fifteen at least. Most of them were patients of mine – not that we discriminated in their favour, but they knew where we were and they were the first to reach us. Many of them left after a few days when life in Exeter began to return to normal, but several stayed on.' Thus the residential community began. The sanctuary which offered refuge to the victims of war was, when the bombing stopped, to continue to shelter the victims of life.

Chapter II
The Historical and Social Context

When I look back on Withymead as it was in the 1950s, I do so with hindsight gained by spending two decades in the practice of psychiatry, and I realize what an incomparable place it was. After all, Withymead was a residential clinic for the mentally ill. Normally such places are bleak, inhospitable institutions, full of sad, dilapidated people, where no one in his right mind would ever want to stay. But Withymead was different: I, like many others, found it hard to keep away. In fact, at that time, there was nowhere in the world where I would rather be – not even Oxford, which I loved. Nowhere as attractive, as interesting and as exciting as Withymead existed. Nowhere, before or since, have I had such talks with people, nowhere have I felt so completely accepted as an individual in my own right, and nowhere else has given me such an opportunity to discover and live out my own reality. At Withymead something was always happening, either in the community or in oneself, that one would never want to miss. It was the richest *temenos* of the human spirit I have ever known.

Of course, a Jungian analysis can in itself be a life enhancing and transformative experience, and for me it certainly was so. Whether this was due to Irene's natural gifts as a therapist or because of the effectiveness of analytical psychology itself I was not sure, but that my horizons widened, that my capacity to understand myself and others grew, that my ability to share love deepened, that I felt personally enriched, was as evident to me as it was to my friends and my family. But my delight in Withymead was due to more than my analytic sessions with Irene, vital to my development though these were. It had to do with finding myself part of a community of people whom I liked and who were all committed to living and working as creatively as they could. Thus, I discovered that indeed I *could* sing, and several times a week I would rehearse a song from *Die Schöne Müllerin* with Molly in the River Room. One of these comes back to me now as I write, with a sweet pang of nostalgia:

Ich hört' ein Bächlein rauschen wohl aus dem Felsenquell,
hinab zum Thale rauschen so frisch und wunderhell.

I can still hear in my mind's ear Molly's vivid reproduction of the burbling brook in the piano accompaniment to this enchanting song. With Elizabeth Colyer I rediscovered my childhood talent for painting and achieved some likenesses of my Anima which are still a source of astonishment and pleasure to me. I worked in the pottery with Ben and Michael, producing some reasonable pots and one memorable piece of sculpture. In the River Room we did Laban movement with Carole Paul-Jones, and rehearsed plays and danced reels under the guidance of Guida Swann. With the mens' working party I learned to mix cement and build walls, after which we would have coffee and sit for an hour working together on one of Jung's books. Then invariably in the studios, in the dining room, in the gardens, by the stream, there was the endless, fascinating talk. Not chat, but good, long, ernest talk about anything and everything that mattered. I would not have missed those years for the world. In a life which has not been short of blessings, the times that I spent at Withymead are among those which I treasure most.

Yet there was something essentially accidental about it all, as if it had never been planned, worked out, or intended. The casually haphazard way in which Withymead came into being was typical of the manner in which its affairs continued to be conducted. Efficient organization and careful administrative planning were incompatible with Irene's volatile temperament and although Gilbert was more capable in these matters he approached them with gentle unobtrusiveness and never questioned Irene's fundamental assumption that people must come first. Withymead, therefore, had all the unpredictable characteristics of a natural phenomenon: the Centre grew like a tree, putting out a limb here, bearing fruit there, and seeding itself somewhere nearby through a process which, at first sight, appeared capricious but which, nevertheless, owed its development to a hidden organization emanating from the character of the founders and their sensitivity to the needs of the people who gathered round them.

When Withymead first opened its doors to residential patients, Irene and Gilbert had little conception of the extraordinary demands which would later be made on them, but life had well equipped them for what was to come. Irene's perception of evil and suffering, experienced with clairvoyant intensity during a childhood permeated with religion and later dominated by war, had driven her to embark on a course of preparation for life which was destined to bring her into even closer relationship with the priest and healer archetypes active within her. The breakdown which she suffered in her twenties gave her an awareness of mental anguish that rendered her capable of absolute empathy with the sufferings of her patients, while the cure of her breakdown through her stay with the Pugh sisters at Hill Farm provided her with the paradigm of a community which heals by encouraging participation in a natural cycle of life transcending the plight of the purely personal condition. Moreover, years of extensive study and personal analytical experience of the three major schools of depth psychology had furnished Irene with the weapons, the insight and skill to attack mental illness at its intrapsychic roots.

If Gilbert lacked Irene's formal training, his personal understanding of suffering was, if anything, more profound. The early loss of his father and the emotional withdrawal of his mother, the sadistic bullying he endured at the hands of his elder brothers, and the amputation of his leg as a schoolboy, sowed seeds in his childhood which later blossomed into a rich compassion for anyone in genuine sorrow or distress. As with his wife, compassion was no mere sentiment for Gilbert but a potent spur to action, and his dedicated work at Oxford House, the Discharged Prisoners' Aid Society, and at Mill Hill Hospital, together with the insight he gained through his analysis with Godwin Baynes, left him with a fund of practical wisdom from which he gave unstintingly to those who looked to him for help. His knowledge of the world combined with his integrity to make him the indispensable father of the community, capable, as it turned out, of surmounting that universal difficulty of institutions, the problem of combining administration with humanity.

A striking feature that distinguished Withymead from any conventional nursing home or residential institution was the degree to which the directors were prepared to be involved with their patients. For Gilbert and Irene Withymead was home, and anyone who came to stay was accepted as a matter of course as a member of the family. This meant that they had very little privacy, which was more of a burden to Gilbert than to the strongly extraverted Irene. To many of their visitors it seemed incredible that the two of them could survive the emotional strain of living in such close proximity to a group of psychologically disturbed individuals. One regular visitor to Withymead was the analyst, Doris Layard, wife of the anthropologist, John Layard. 'I couldn't imagine how they put up with it,' she told me. 'To begin with they didn't even have a sitting room to themselves, and it must have been a ghastly strain. Toni Wolff was very concerned about it and used to advise Rene to get away more often. She told Rene she ought to have a room of her own which people couldn't expect to come into uninvited. Of course, if they'd had children it would have been different, and they couldn't have given themselves in the same way.' But Gilbert and Irene did not have children and in many ways their patients formed a surrogate family for them, and they felt that the stress of close proximity was a small price to pay for the emotional and therapeutic advantages it seemed to bring to all concerned. Moreover, they were proud of their bold innovation, born of the exigences of war, of providing facilities for patients undergoing analysis to reside in the same houshold as their analyst and to pass their extra-analytic hours in creative activities. No one else had ever tried this, and they felt that the results justified whatever strain it caused them.

From the small number of residents who sought refuge at Withymead in May, 1942, the community grew through the 1940s and 50s, acquiring neighbouring properties, to accommodate about forty-five people, consisting mostly of patients, but with a hard core of psychotherapists and art therapists to give the community security, permanence and shape. Despite the material and labour shortages and the bureaucratic hindrances of the postwar period, the dilapidated out buildings which the Champernownes originally purchased had been converted into the attractive, business-like studios which I found on my arrival, each adapted and equipped for painting, modelling, pottery, music, movement and dance, and all staffed with personnel expert in their own artistic disciplines. This profusion of facilities and talent made Withymead, without question, one of the major pioneers of art therapy in Great Britain. Yet this was not Withymead's sole claim to distinction, for in the course of its development it came to apply entirely new concepts to the residential care of the mentally ill, concepts which were notably at variance with those which prevailed at the time and which, with certain laudable exceptions, have prevailed since.

Up to the time that Withymead was established, the model on which residential care for mentally sick patients was based was essentially custodial – the model of the lunatic asylum, prison, workhouse, orphanage, remand home, or 'home' for the aged and destitute. One has only to look at a photograph of conventional mental hospital buildings to know what life in them was like, for their architecture speaks eloquently of the attitudes which informed their construction: huge, impersonal fortresses, they stand in isolated locations, surrounded by high spiked walls. Inside them, the unfortunate inmates were provided with the basic essentials of life – clothing, shelter and food – but they had no say over the circumstances of their incarceration and little choice whether to stay there or not. Certainly, no conviction possessed the administrators of such places that they might have a creative or therapeutic function. On the contrary, they were clearly viewed as repositories where people who were an embarrassment to society could be kept out of sight and out of mind.

In the early 1940s, mental hospitals throughout Europe and America were still much as they had been since the nineteenth century. Modern social psychiatry and its daughter therapeutic communities had yet to be born. Seen in the context of its time, therefore, Withymead represented a remarkable and original achievement. Indeed, Irene and Gilbert Champernowne merit comparison with the charismatic figures of psychiatric history who had the imagination to reject the limited, often cruel conceptions of mental illness current at their time and the courage to try new, more humane methods in its treatment. The Champernownes were of the same stamp as the Tukes who, horrified by the brutal squalor characteristic of mad houses at the end of the eighteenth century, founded the Retreat at York, 'a place where the unhappy might obtain a refuge, a quiet haven in which the shattered bark might find a means of reparation or of safety.' (Account of Mrs Henry Tuke).

The Tukes had themselves been influenced by another great innovator of the late eighteenth century, Philippe Pinel, the French mathematician, philosopher and physician, who assumed responsibility for the Bicêtre and Salpêtrière Hospitals in Paris in the early 1790s. Sustained by the Revoluntionary spirit of liberté, égalité, fraternité, he liberated his patients from the fetters which had restrained them, in some cases for as long as thirty or forty years, and inaugurated a system of treatment which he called *moral management*. Like Pinel, the Tukes were able to prove that even the most insane patients responded to kind treatment and that violence, fetters and chains were not only repugnant and unnecessary but hostile to all therapeutic endeavour. They provided their charges with clean, comfortable accommodation, pleasant surroundings, good food, kind, sympathetic attendants, plenty of exercise, interesting and amusing activities, and generally ran the hospital as if it were a large family home. They published accounts of the success of their methods and advocated an approach to mental illness which was based on Christian principles and simple humanity.

During the nineteenth century others followed the example of Pinel and the Tukes, and gradually the principles of non-restraint and moral management were applied to larger populations of patients, thanks to the efforts of such people as John Conolly and Lord Shaftesbury in England and Benjamin Rush and Dorothea Dix in America. That the new humane approach succeeded was due to the personal investment which its advocates put into it. The same was true of the success of Withymead. Like Philippe Pinel, William Tuke and John Conolly, Gilbert and Irene Champernowne were *enthusiasts*: they believed with passionate conviction in what they were doing. They loved their patients, hated cruelty, and believed that kindness could cure. That they achieved the measure of success that they did was due to the unusual energy and dedication they put into their work. They knew that what mattered above all was the *attitude* one adopted to the mentally ill. If one denigrated them, treating them as subhuman, they became brutalized, helpless, and 'incurable'. What these reformers all had in commom was the determination to treat the mad as worthy of respect as human beings.

Unfortunately, people with this degree of enthusiasm are in short supply, and, as a consequence, the impetus behind the spread of moral management petered out in the second half of the nineteenth century. Rapidly growing populations and the social conditions induced by the Industrial Revolution resulted in the bureaucratic institutionalization of mental illness and its treatment in Western society. Asylums grew in size, many were overcrowded and understaffed. The doctors and nurses who worked in them were of indifferent quality and displayed little imagination and less compassion in the manner in which they carried out their duties. Increasingly they conceived their role as custodial and saw no moral objection to the use of strait jackets and padded cells. The outstanding achievements of nineteenth century medicine, such as anaesthesia, asepsis, inoculation and the improvement in public hygiene, attracted the best people into surgery and medicine and away from psychiatry, which became the Cinderella it has since remained, its practitioners relegated to a lowly status in the eyes of their colleagues – a status which their patients were compelled to share. Mental hospitals ceased to be the havens of enlightenment and humanity that the Tukes advocated and became instead concentration camps ruled by apathetic, regimentalized custodians. Such they remained until 1950s, when a revolutionary development occurred which was to prove similar in many ways to the non-restraint moral movement of the nineteenth century: the mental hospitals began to open their previously locked doors.

The 'open door' movement which swept through Western psychiatry like the Pentacostal wind coincided with the introduction of the major tranquillizers (the phenothiazine drugs) in the treatment of psychosis and with the post-war shift in Western society from a 'patrist' to a 'matrist' culture with its permissive morality, anti-authoritarian attitudes, welfare institutions, and increased public tolerance of deviant behaviour. Before the advent of phenothiazine drugs and the permissive society, it required great courage to countence the opening of asylum doors, although here too enthusiasm and charismatic leadership had, on occasion, prevailed. Thus, in 1881, Rutherford threw open the doors of Lenzie Asylum. In the 1930s, Saxtby Good attempted to emulate Rutherford's example at Littlemore Hospital, an experiment which was repeated in 1949 by Mc Donald Bell at Dingleton Hospital, Melrose in Scotland. In the social atmosphere of the time, and in the absence of effective psychotropic drugs, these were quixotically brave revolutions, but, like those of the nineteenth century, they seldom outlived their originators. But in the 1950s the situation was dramatically transformed, and by the late 60s no less than 90 per cent of the psychiatric patients in England and Wales were living in unlocked wards. Withymead, which admitted psychotic as well as neurotic patients, was of course ahead of this movement, since the only doors ever to be locked there was the front door at night.

The open door policy coincided with more than the introduction of effective drugs: it was in harmony with the development of a new approach in psychiatry which placed emphasis on the social context in which mental illness occurs – an approach dignified by the name of *social psychiatry*. The principles of social psychiatry were worked out in England during the latter stages of the war by two military psychiatrists, Tom Main and Maxwell Jones. At about the same time, W.R. Bion and S.H. Foulkes were developing the use of group methods in psychoanalysis. The work of these four men gave rise to a further concept which was to have a significant influence on postwar psychiatry – the so-called *therapeutic community* concept. The essential feature of this concept was that the social environment to which a mental patient was admitted should itself function in such a way as to be a therapeutic agent. The first working example of the concept were established in Surrey – by Dr Main in 1946 at the Cassel Hospital, Richmond, and by Dr Jones in 1947 at Belmont (later Henderson) Hospital, Sutton. These communities operated on a small scale. The first successful attempt to extend the concept to the work of an entire mental hospital was not made until ten years later, when it was undertaken at Claybury hospital by Dr Dennis Martin.

Although in no manner connected with these developments, Withymead was in many ways a model therapeutic community, though there were important differences which will be discussed in chapter IV. Thus, by opening Withymead in 1942, Irene and Gilbert Champernowne anticipated the innovations at the Cassel by four years, at Belmont by five years, and at Claybury by fifteen years. It was, in fact, the first therapeutic community in the modern sense to be founded, though this is never acknowledged in the extensive therapeutic community literature. And it was achieved with a tiny fraction of the resources available to Doctors Main, Jones and Martin.

Since Withymead was the original creation of two unusual people, it is hard to find parallels to it in the history of mental care. To some extent, its origins bore a resemblance to those of Spring Lake Ranch, a community founded by Wayne and Elizabeth Sarcka. In 1932, this couple bought an abandoned farm in Vermont. It was the time of the great depression and they had very little money with which to do up the buildings and restock the farm, and the only help available was provided by two emotionally disturbed young men sent to them by a friend who was a psychiatrist in New York. The work was hard, especially in view of the severities of the Vermont climate, but the farm was made sound and the two patients improved remarkably. As a result, the Sarckas decided to extend the experiment. They took on more young patients and developed the facilities of the Ranch. Gradually a form of therapeutic community emerged, based on the Sarckas' belief that the best way to treat mentally sick people was not to incarcerate them in institutions but to take them into one's home, treat them as members of the family, accept them as they are, and encourage them to share fully in the responsibilities of living together and the hard work of running a farm. The idea was clearly a good one, for it worked. It was not, however, altogether new. It had been put into practice for centuries at Gheel in Belgium, where in the Middle Ages there had been a shrine famous for its ability to heel distempered minds. Many who made the pilgrimage there were taken into the homes of local farmers and remained to live and work in the locality. In a sense, this was the first example of 'community care', and the tolerant hospitality of the good people of Gheel has continued up to the present time.

Twenty-eight years after they had started it, the Sarckas turned to Spring Lake Ranch into a private, tax-exempt, charitable foundation, so as to ensure that the community would outlive them and continue to do its work when they were no longer able to run it. By the mid-1970s, the community consisted of approximately fifty people, of whom thirty were residents and the rest staff and their families. Spring Lake Ranch has been variously described as a therapeutic work community, a halfway house, a transitional residence, and an intentional community, and these terms could roughly be applied to Withymead. Certainly, the Champernownes shared the Sarckas' enthusiasm for the therapeutic value of community life, but they differed in placing more emphasis on participation in the arts than participation in manual work, and they believed that people need analysis if lasting improvement was to occur.

Another more distant parallel to Withymead can be traced in the development of the Richmond Fellowship by Elly Jansen. Writing of her experience, Elly Jansen says, 'it was possible for a private individual to take initiatives which were unthinkable for formalised authorities. A number of accounts have been given of the origins of the Richmond Fellowship; what can never be adequately conveyed is the temerity of launching, in isolation, a non-medical therapeutic community, on an experimental egalitarian basis, in a rented house in the heart of a genteel residential suburb.' (1980). Precisely the same could be said of the origins of Withymead, except that it was not rented. But there the parallel ends. The Richmond Fellowship had done magnificent work in providing accommodation and support for mentally ill people in sheltered surroundings, but its main objective is to sustain them in the community at large. The purpose of Withymead, on the other hand, was to give sanctuary to those who could no longer cope with life in the wider community and to provide them with psychotherapy and art therapy until such time as they have achieved mature independence and were capable of complete social rehabilitation.

Somewhat closer to Withymead are small hospitals where analysis is combined with intensive care provided by a team of dedicated therapists. Like Withymead, these are invariably started by charismatic enthusiasts. Examples are the unit at the Sheppard and Enoch Pratt Hospital in Maryland, built up during the 1920s by Harry Stack Sullivan, the 'Orthogenic School' founded much later by Bruno Bettelheim under the auspices of the University of Chicago, and Tom Main's Cassel Hospital. In such residential centres the aim is to produce a warm, intimate atmosphere in which everything is done to help the patient feel both accepted and valued, while he is treated through the medium of analysis combined with intensive social interaction with the staff. They differ from Withymead, however, in being hospitals rather than homes and cannot provide the inestimable advantages of natural community life.

Withymead, then, may at first glance seem to bear a resemblance to a few other residential centres for the mentally ill established before and after it, but on closer scrutiny one must acknowledge it as a unique phenomenon, true only to itself and based on no other model. In addition to pioneering the concept of the community as a potent therapeutic agent, alone among residential centres Withymead placed great emphasis on the arts and granted high status to art therapists within the therapeutic team, giving their contributions as much weight as those of the analysts and psychiatrists. The success of this policy depended on two factors: the first was that all members of the staff were in personal analysis and many of them had extensive analytic experience; secondly, there was a continuous interaction between the psychotherapists and the art therapists as they lived and worked together. The therapeutic effectiveness of this interaction owed much to the formal *staff meeting* which was held every week. At this meeting the progress of each patient was carefully reviewed, and any dissentions arising between individual members of the staff were worked through, if necessary late into the night. This meant that a broader, more unified view of each patient could evolve and that any staff conflicts which happened to centre on him, which might otherwise have a divisive influence in his own psyche, could be brought to some kind of resolution.

The crucial significance of the staff meeting for group consensus and cohesion was recognized by Irene Champernowne, who often referred to it as 'the ego of the community'. Amongst other things, it provided a regular opportunity for 'the shadow of the community' (i.e., the negative feeling and disruptive notions which might be current at any particular time) to be confronted and analyzed. The correctness of Irene's view was born out by a study published in 1954 of staff-patient relations in a small, private analytically-orientated hospital in Maryland, called Chestnut Lodge. This study was conducted over a three year period by Stanton (a psychiatrist) and Schwartz (a social psychologist). They described a number of characteristic patterns of behaviour in these relationships and in particular drew attention to what they termed the 'triangular conflict'. This conflict arose when two staff members disagreed over the proper way to treat a given patient – invariably a demanding and difficult one. The investigators found that the triangular conflict developed when the staff members kept their disagreement to themselves, failing to have it out in the open in an effort to find some form of resolution. Each would come to feel that only he or she *really* understood the patient and knew what was required. Increasingly one or other would become involved with the patient and begin to suffer from anxiety, agitation and insomnia. Characteristically this would culminate in a crisis when the staff member attacked the patient – either verbally or physically – and then broke down with guilt and remorse. Stanton and Schwartz argued that in order to prevent this it was essential that staff members should confront each other *early on*, work their differances through, and evolve a plan of treatment which both could endorse and which defined the role which each would perform. They advised that whenever it looked as if a patient were becoming a 'special case' it was important for staff to examine their own attitudes to him and ask each other where any covert disagreements between them might lie. The comparison between this advice and the importance attached by Withymeadians to the staff meeting is clear, yet Irene did not know of this study until I drew her attention to it in 1974.

In the same study, Stanton and Schwartz reported their observation that the psychiatric symptoms exhibited by many patients reflected the organization and structure of the institution in which they were treated. They went on to suggest that large mental hospitals were anti-therapeutic in the sense that they were impersonal and encouraged apathy in both patients and staff. This view was supported by the publication in 1959 of Dr Russell Barton's book *Institutional Neurosis*. Barton was the first psychiatrist to attempt a systematic description of the iatrogenic condition induced by custodial care in a mental institution. 'Institutional neurosis,' he wrote, 'is a disease characterized by apathy, lack of initiative, loss of interest, especially in things of an impersonal nature, submissiveness, apparent inability to make plans for the future, lack of individuality and sometimes a characteristic posture and gait.' Though this is seen commonly as part of the clinical picture of chronic schizophrenia whatever the enviromental circumstances, Barton noted that it also occurred in non-schizophrenic patients who had been in a conventional mental hospital for any length of time, and in the inmates of non-psychiatric institutions such as prisons, orphanages and tuberculosis sanitoria. Barton believed that the features of mental hospital life which caused the condition were the loss of contact with the outside world, the loss of personal friends and possessions, the loss of prospects outside the institution, bossiness on the part of the staff, and enforced idleness and loss of personal responsibility. As the 'moral management' people knew, the abolition of squalor, chains and cruelty is not enough. Patients need intellectual stimulus, social interaction, creative activity, intimate relationships and personal respect. At a time when the vast majority of people in mental hospital had few of these things, residents at Withymead had them in abundance, and cases of institutional neurosis were unthinkable there. The traditional mental hospital was a good example of what Max Weber (1948) described as 'rational bureaucracy' – a form of social organization characterized by a hierarachy of offices, each with its own functional specification, a unified disciplinary system with chains of command, all based on a well defined body of rules and regulations. The purpose of such an organization is to ensure that its functions can be performed in a routine manner so as to save time and effort and provide standard solutions for any problems which might arise. It may be appropriate to an army, a police force, or a ministerial department, but when applied to the care of the mentally sick it results in the 'total institution' so vividly described by Erving Goffman in his book *Asylums*. Goffman lays bare the manner in which total institutions make use of 'trimming' and 'programming' procedures in order to strip the 'inmate' of self-esteem and personal autonomy, turning him into an object which can be fed into the administrative machinery of the establishment, to be worked on by its routine operations.

Withymead, like the therapeutic communities that came after it, was fundamentally anti-bureaucratic in spirit and organization. It was as far from a 'rational bureaucracy' or 'total institution' as it is possible to be. When I first went there, rules and regulations just did not exist, there were no chains of command, no disciplinary system and no 'inmate subculture'. Everything proceeded on the basis of intimate personal contact between staff members and residents, with Gilbert and Irene co-ordinating the activities of the community through the influence of their 'charismatic' leadership. From the very beginning, the Champernownes were aware of the anti-therapeutic nature of large institutions and were determined that, however successful, the community must be restricted in size and never allowed to exceed about forty-five people.

Public recognition of the anti-therapeutic milieu afforded by traditional mental hospitals did not become apparent until the 1960s, but when it came it led to a movement of which the 'open door' policy and the therapeutic community movement were only a part. Some people began to argue that mental hospitals should be done away with altogether and replaced with much smaller psychiatric units attached to general hospitals, where patients could be admitted for comparatively brief periods at times of crisis, their long term care being undertaken by specially created services in the community at large. In Britain this became official policy when Enoch Powell was Minister of Health and in 1962 revealed his 'Hospital Plan for England and Wales.' This proposed to reduce the number of mental hospital beds from the level of 2.91 per thousand members of the population (as it then was) to 1.8 per thousand in 1975. In 1971 the Department of Health issued a memorandum suggesting a further reduction in beds to 0.5 per thousand, the phasing out of all large mental hospitals, and the completion of 230 psychiatric units attached to general hospitals through the country. From these units psychiatric teams would work both in the hospital and in the community, each team covering a population of 60,000 people. These units would be backed up with community services provided by local authorities and they would include social workers, hostels, homes for the elderly, and accommodation in supervised lodgings.

Similar policies were espoused in the United States, where a deliberate programme of running down the state mental hospital system was adopted in 1957 with the eventual intention of 'deinstitutionalizing' psychiatric patients and treating them in Community Mental Health Centres.

But both in Britain and America these intentions proved hard to implement and produced more problems than they solved. Since the Hospital Plan was published in 1962, only one large mental hospital had been closed in England and Wales, and for all the effort that has gone into 'deinstitutionalizing' America's psychiatric population, 40% of all hospital beds in the U.S.A. continue to be occupied by the mentally ill. During the last two decades, it is true, mental hospitals everywhere have been closing down wards and reducing the numbers of beds available, but this has not been balanced by any adequate provision of community services to care for the patients thus denied treatment in hospital. Instead, the wards remaining open have become overcrowded, it has become increasingly necessary for patients actually to 'break down' in order to obtain a hospital bed, and there has been a steady rise in the number of poorly housed and homeless chronic mental patients, an increasing number of whom end up in prisons already disastrously overcrowded with criminals. Thus, a policy which has humane and enlightened objectives has for many people, particularly the large population of chronic schizophrenics and their families, resulted in real hardship. 'Community care' which was to have provided the lasting antidote to 'institutional neurosis' has proved inadequate to meet the needs of people deprived of hospital care. The reason for this failure is the brute fact that, in a very real sense, the community does *not* care – certainly not enough to invest money in the services required. For all their faults, the old mental hospitals kept their patients in greater comfort and provided them with more essential facilities than the community does now. In fact, it can be convincingly argued that as a result of all the efforts of those responsible for national psychiatric services since the late 1950s, mentally ill people on both sides of the Atlantic are actually in a worse plight than they were before. In Britain, the National Schizophrenia Fellowship has been effective in calling attention to the widely disseminated suffering that these policies have caused, claiming that many chronically ill patients have no wish to leave hospital and have to be forced out against their will. A large proportion of these deteriorate because they cannot handle community life and yet, once discharged, it is virtually impossible for them to gain re-admission. (*Bulletin of the Royal College of Psychiatrists*, March, 1985).

The shift from hospital care to 'community care' has had two further consequences: one is an ever greater emphasis on physical methods of treatment, such as the use of drugs, and the other is the abandonment of the ancient idea of 'sanctuary' or 'asylum'. The success of drugs such as the phenothiazines and the antidepressants in treating acute psychiatric symptoms has encouraged mental health authorities in many countries to argue that their widespread use can serve economy by reducing the time that a patient has to spend in hospital and the energy that a doctor has to devote to dealing with his case. As a result, these authorities have become as 'drug dependent' as their patients.

If the health authorities are satisfied with this state of affairs, however, their patients and their families most certainly are not. One much publicized report which appeared in 1974 in *Mind*, the journal of the British National Association for Mental Health, revealed that a majority of patients complained that when they approached doctors or psychiatrists for help, they were given drugs and nothing else. They felt they needed someone kind and sympathetic to whom the could tell their anxieties and problems but instead, they complained, they were treated like objects and were quite unable to find a doctor willing to listen to them. This criticism is as justified now as it was at the time of the report. When confronted with a psychiatric patient, it would appear that the main concern of many doctors is to stem the torrent of anxious words with a presciption and get the patient as quickly as possibly out into the street. Many practitioners defend such conduct by arguing that chat is ineffectual and drugs do more good. Some have even maintained that the drugs we now possess are of such therapeutic potency as to be capable of annihilating most of the mental ills that man is heir to. But it is hard to reconcile their complacency with the knowledge that at least half of the patients admitted to psychiatric hospitals every year are not new cases but previously treated ones who have again broken down. The *Mind* report suggested that this appallingly high readmission rate was at least in part due to the readiness of psychiatrists to treat symptoms with drugs rather than tackling the underlying problems from which the symptoms were derived. The report concluded that there was an urgent need for psychiatrists to provide their patients with more 'talking treatment' instead of relying so heavily on physical methods like drugs and E.C.T (electro-convulsive therapy).

In marked contrast to contempory psychiatric units, the therapeutic goal of Withymead was to provide healing which lasted. While Irene Champernowne was not against the use of therapeutic drugs if a psychiatrist whom she respected prescribed them, she felt that their benefits were primarily cosmetic, making the patient's illness easier to live with, both for himself and the community. She was not concerned, however, with the economics of 'rapid turnover', 'intensive use of beds', of the quick removal of symptoms. She believed that if healing was to endure it could occur only through an organic process which must be permitted to proceed as its own inherent pace. At Withymead, she aimed to provide not just a retreat for those needing to withdraw from the stresses of ordinary life, but a wholly therapeutic environment in which disturbed people could, in their own time, come to terms with their plight, seek some solution to their problems, and prepare themselves for new, more fruitful initiatives in the world outside.

The intellectual atmosphere of Withymead reverberated with Jung's ideas, and none was shared with greater conviction than his belief that mental illness possesses rich subjective meaning, in that it represents an individual's solution to the problems of his life at a particular stage in his personal history. The conventional notion of mental illness as a wholly pathological process to be constrained with drugs and electric shocks was unreservedly rejected. Following Jung, Irene and her colleagues regarded the human psyche as a homostatically controlled, self-regulating system which was capable, given the appropriate conditions, of healing itself. They believed that in any mental illness a potentially creative process was at work which, provided it was understood and assisted, could enable the patient to evolve towards a more satisfactory solution of his circumstances than the neurotic or psychotic solution that his illness represented. At Withymead, the individual who was accepted and taken on by the community was himself encouraged to accept and take on the unique meaning of his illness, so that with the community's help he could find his own way out of sickness and into health.

Jung believed that the inherent goal of human psychic activity was *individuation* – the quest for wholeness. As Jung himself put it: 'Individuation means becoming a single, homogeneous being, and, in so far as "individuality" embraces our innermost, last, and incomparable uniqueness, it also implies becoming one's own self. We could therefore translate individuation as "coming to selfhood" or "self-realization"' (*CW* 7, para. 266). Irene and Gilbert Champernowne conceived their therapeutic purpose to be the provision of the environment and the facilities most likely to promote the individuation process in anyone who came to Withymead. They aimed to stimulate the whole individual by giving him rich possibilities for self-expression and self-discovery. What they wished to foster was nothing less than that ultimate Jungian achievement, the constellation of the Self. This was why Withymead was an exciting place and why one always felt privileged to be there.

In the light of modern advances in brain chemistry, which have given us partial insights into the mode of action of the major tranquillizers and antidepressants, Irene's rather condescending attitude to the use of drugs may seem naïve, particularly when it came to treating the small minority of psychotic patients in the Withymead community. For it seems increasingly likely that psychosis is due to genetic and biochemical factors as well as to emotional and social ones. The condition is notoriously unsusceptible to analytic treatment, whereas drugs can often satisfactorily modify psychotic behaviour disturbances, hallucinations and delusions. However, unlike many Jungians at the time, Irene was not against the use of drugs on principle, and, as we have seen, modern psychiatric opinion agrees with the proposition that psychotic patients do better in intimate groups where people take an active interest in their welfare than in large institutions where they are ignored. Schizophrenics were clearly better off taking their Largactil at Withymead than in a conventional mental hospital ward.

But the majority of patients who came to Withymead were not psychotic. Most of them suffered from that large group of psychiatric disorders collectively known as the neuroses. These can be severely incapacitating and can profoundly disturb the well-being of people, while in no way depriving them of their reason. It is these patients who are most prone to seek psychiatric help and who, when close to breakdown, express a desire for sanctuary in order to 'get away from it all' and find 'peace of mind'. And it was these people whom Withymead was outstandingly well equipped to treat.

The longing for sanctuary, Irene saw as a striking example of Jung's self-regulating principle at work. The desire to withdraw from those environmental circumstances which have caused neurotic suffering is as evident an expression of the insinct for self-preservation as the desire to leave a sinking ship. It is a necessary preliminary to survival.

Just how many neurotics there are in the population is not possible to assess with any accuracy: those statistics which do exist are almost certainly underestimates since they are derived from patients who actually present themselves for treatment. Even so, on the most conservative estimate, neurotics account for at least a third of all patients consulting general practitioners. Whether, as is often said, this vast neurotic population is growing, it is impossible to be sure; what is certain is that the demand for treatment of the neuroses has been growing steadily for years, and it is a demand which the mental health services in Europe and America conspicuously fail to meet. These services have their work cut out dealing with the huge population of psychotics, alcoholics, drug addicts and old people suffering from senile dementia; they have few resources left over to help those who are merely anxious, miserable or obsessed. Advances in pharmacology have resulted in the production of drugs capable of relieving neurotic insecurity and despair, but drugs are seldom what neurotic patients ask for: they want understanding, reassurance and advice – in other words, they want psychotherapy.

Although psychotherapy may be defined quite simply as the treatment of one mind by another, there exists, in fact, a host of different psychotherapeutic techniques which have been developed over the last hundred years. In addition to the classic analytical approaches devised by Jung and Freud, there are various forms of 'supportive' psychotherapy, counselling, group therapy, casework and family therapy, to name but the commonest of them.

Yet it is extraordinary that in spite of the variety of relatively sophisticated techniques available, very few psychiatrists receive training in any of them. Most psychiatrists hold, in addition to an ordinary medical degree, a postgraduate diploma qualification in their speciality, but this can usually be obtained without any training in psychotherapy. Moreover, in Britain no experience of any form of psychotherapy is required to become a member of the Royal College of Psychiatrists. This curious omission is usually justified by the argument that psychotherapy is an 'unscientific' proceedure, in that its results are hard to evaluate using objective criteria.

Scientific or not, the demand for psychotherapy is huge, and those comparatively few men and women who equip themselves to provide such treatment are inundated with work. Irene Champernowne had little patience with the criticisms of psychotherapy made by 'scientific psychologists' like that hammer of the analysts, Professor Eysenck of London University. In common with the majority of her colleagues, Irene felt she could not sit about waiting for the scientists to evaluate what she did, because the human need that daily confronted her was too imperative. 'Who do they think they are?' she demanded, with some heat, when I discussed these issues with her. 'What have they contributed to the relief of human suffering? All they can do is make destructive criticisms of those of us who are trying to do something about it.' Though a harsh judgment, it contains more that a grain of truth. Working in the Olympian seclusion of their university departments, academic psychologists have not, it must be admitted, been much help in the quest for methods to relieve mental anguish. Apart from the introduction of certain diagnostic tests of questionable usefulness, and the development of the conditioning techniques of 'behaviour therapy', academic psychologists have tended to sit on the fence, playing a role in the evolution of psychiatry and psychotherapy which has indeed been critical rather than innovative. Their preoccupation with the technological aspects of human perception, information storage, and so on, has too often meant the exclusion from the psychology laboratory of the human mind: indeed, under the blight of orthodox behaviourism, 'mind' has been stigmatized as a four letter word, on which scientific puritanism, the only form of puritanism left to us, has, for most of this century, placed a strict taboo.

A similar taboo has served to exorcise the 'psyche' from the consulting room, augmenting the fear that has always haunted the psychiatric establishment of seeming disreputable in the eyes of its medical and surgical mentors. This desire for professional respectability has manifested itself in a determination to cling to an essentially 'medical' approach to patients, and in a refusal to regard mental distress as anything but a social and biochemical problem to be solved by social and pharmacological means. One great advantage of non-medical therapists like Irene Champernowne is that they are not intimidated by this taboo and are able to share in the psychic reality of their patients without the constraints or preconceptions imposed on psychiatrists by the prejudices of their profession.

However, whether psychiatrists choose to recognize it or not, the patients entering their consulting rooms have continued to bring their psyches with them; but since the inauguration of the National Health Service in 1948, a faceless multitude of unhappy men and women has waited interminably on the hard benches of Victorian out-patient departments in search of wise counsel only to receive, when their turn comes, a bottle of pills.

Unfortunately, the national failure to provide adequate treatment for neurosis is by no means confined to the out-patient sphere. The Health Service is no less insensitive to the plight of the 25,000 neurotics who each year require treatment as in-patients. Instead of finding peace in a welcome sanctuary, these unfortunate people usually end up in the acute wards of the vast mental institutions which, despite Enoch Powell's intentions, are still scattered plentifully throughout the country. Not infrequently, the majority of their fellow patients are psychotic, often suffering from delusions and hallucinations of the most florid kind. Since one of the commonest fears of the neurotic is that he might be 'going mad', it does not require much imagination to realize that this practice is both anti-therapeutic and inhumane.

The situation has not improved with the provision of small psychiatric units in general hospitals, since the number of beds they contain is very limited and it is the practice to use them as intensively as possible in the interests of 'high turnover'.

Thus, the organisers of the nation's psychiatric services have turned deaf ears to the pleas of neurotics for asylum, preferring to adopt a policy specifically designed to patch them up with drugs and 'get 'em in and out quick'. It is an *Alice in Wonderland* predicament with tragic overtones, for it has bred a new generation of psychiatrists who behave as if they were constantly muttering to their patients the words of the old Yiddish proverb: 'Sleep faster, we need the pillows!' If the present trend continues, more and more of these 'instant repair' units will be opened, to be staffed by doctors who, in the shortest possible time, will, to paraphrase Voltaire, pour drugs of which they know little, to treat diseases of which they know less, into human beings of whom they know nothing.

It is against this depressing background that the true value of the Champernownes' achievement can be appreciated. Withymead stood, as no other institution, for values largely antithetical to those prevailing in orthodox Britain psychiatry which, since its annexation by the National Health Service in 1948, has been dominated by the imperative to cater for large populations of mentally sick people as economically as possible. It has attempted to do this by championing methods designed to erase the symptoms of mental illness while neglecting the existential meaning of the individual's suffering and the possibilities it affords for personal growth. Increasingly, the National Health Service conceives patients as commodities to be processed efficiently through the Service's limited facilities. Treatment means drugs and electric shocks, admission means rapid discharge, progress means the suppression of symptoms, cure means return to work with a medical certificate naming the illness from which a benevolent state has granted deliverance. The whole purpose of the excercise is to achieve what Jung called 'the negative restoration of the persona' – i.e. to restore the patient to the state he was in before he became ill.

The Champernownes, on the other hand, regarded a neurotic breakdown not so much as an 'illness' as an existential crisis which was rich in implications for individual development. The provision of time and sanctuary was necessary not only to distance the patient from the outer pressures responsible for his distress but to give him a chance to take stock of his circumstances and to reconsider the principles on which his life had hitherto been lived. The neurotic's need to abandon, for the time being, his social and economic responsibilities they understood as a *reculer pour mieux sauter*, a hiatus in the routine compulsions of ordinary living which was vital if he was to turn inwards, to re-establish some real and lasting contact with the Self, and to allow the homeostatic mechanisms of the psyche to perform their natural functions of healing. They criticized conventional psychiatry for being too bureaucratic, too extraverted, too organic, and too materialistically orientated for the patient's good. They saw clearly that what was so catastrophically lacking was an intimate approach which took seriously the patient's own account of his condition and which provided him with the support and understanding he needed if he was to transcend his ills.

By providing a secure sanctuary, a compassionate community, a team of gifted therapists, and a creative atmosphere, Irene and Gilbert established a model centre for the treatment of neurotic illness which has been unsurpassed in the annals of psychiatric care. To be sure, the number of people who found their way to Withymead was tiny in comparison with the great population of neurotics as a whole, but statistics are irrelevant when applied to individuals or to the question of optimum care. Statistics give no indication of the suffering that individual neurotics endure when they are inadequately treated or which, indirectly, they inflict on their families. Mental disorder invariably receives less sympathy than physical illness, not only from relatives and friends, but often from family doctors as well. It is also the misfortune of the neurotic that his symptoms are usually no more comprehensible to himself than to his immediate circle; irrational fears and phobias, pointless obsessional ruminations, unaccountable attacks of despair, all are capable of overwhelming him with a sense of hopeless vulnerability, made all the more terrible if he knows of no one to whom he can turn for help.

It was these neglected and misunderstood people whose need touched the compassion of Gilbert and Irene, and it was to them that they dedicated their lives of admirable service. Withymead was the result.

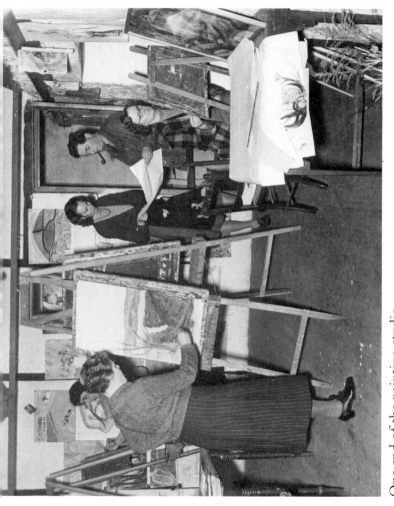

One end of the painting studio . . . .

. . . and the other

Chapter III

The Human Factor

The quality of life in a community depends on the quality of the people who are its members. Most of all, it depends on the quality of those who are its leaders, for they carry the 'culture' of the community: they sustain its ethos and determine its atmosphere. Withymead's success, however, depended not only on Gilbert and Irene and the talented staff they gathered round them to form what Irene referred to, somewhat mystically, as the 'therapeutic ring', but also on the kind of people they attracted as patients. These came from all walks of life, but they were predominantly drawn from the culturally more advantaged sections of society. Thus, of the 240 adults who were admitted between January 1942 and October 1954, 151 were connected with the professions or the arts, while only 47 belonged to a miscellaneous group of occupations such as secretaries, clerks, domestic workers, etc. The remaining 42 were women who were full-time housewives, married, for the most part, to professional men.

That working class patients were not more in evidence was due to Withymead's private status. It had to charge fees in order to survive. To be sure, the Champernownes were generous to the point of improvidence and, as in my own case, frequently admitted people who could not afford the full fees, but economic necessity dictated that Withymead should receive the majority of its residents from among those who could meet the cost. Within the social context of the time, however, the therapeutic reputation of the Centre benefitted from this enforced selection. It meant that the general educational level of the community was high, and it is well known that people of good cultural background, ready verbal facility, and above average intelligence are those who are best suited to analytic treatment and most helped by it. But it is only fair to bear this limitation in mind when comparing Withymead with state run institutions, which must accommodate patients of much more diverse social origins.

People came to Withymead for all sorts of reasons and in all kinds of ways. Most were sent with a doctor's blessing, but many were self-referred, either they or their families having heard of Withymead, or having known someone who had been treated there. Whether or not they had been medically referred, new patients were always seen soon after admission by one of the Centre's doctors, it being a rule never to treat anyone without full medical cover and consent.

Although Withymead was best equipped to treat neurotics, its therapeutic efforts were not confined exclusively to such patients. For those interested in labels, it is true to say that practically all diagnostic categories of psychiatric disorder were represented, with the exception of mental subnormality and the organic psychoses (mental illnesses due to physical changes in the brain). The diagnoses made by the doctors either before or after admission included the 'functional' psychoses (schizophrenia and manic–depressive psychosis), as well as the neuroses, personality and psychosexual disorders, drug and alcohol dependencies, and vaguely defined 'problems' in the working, social and marital spheres of life. The majority of psychiatric referrals came from London. Thus, of the 46 doctors referring patients up to 1955, no less that 25 practiced in the capital, and included such eminent members of the profession as Dr. E. A. Bennet, Dr Michael Fordham, Dr Gilbert Russell, Dr David Stafford-Clark, and Dr D. W. Winnicott.

Admission to Withymead was accomplished with a tactful informality which totally eschewed the 'mortification rituals' described by Erving Goffman as characterising the admission of patients to mental hospitals (i.e. the history taking, listing of personal possessions and next of kin, undressing, bathing, examining, tabulating, issuing with insitutional clothing, instructing as to rules and regulations, and so on) all of which have the function of stripping the new arrival of his past supports and preparing him to live as a member of the inmate subculture. At Withymead, no one thought of admission as a formal procedure but as a delicate process of grafting the new member into the community. Irene Champernowne set great store by this. 'The staff would weave the new one in,' she told me, 'handling them from one to another. We always shared news about someone who was coming so that we were ready to welcome them. They would come for a couple of days to see if they liked it and wanted to stay. I would see them and the doctor would see them and then they'd be handed on to a member of staff. At the first interview I'd make up my mind who would be the best therapist for them. Then they'd go off to coffee or tea, and be introduced first to one and then to another, and so on.

'After the two days were up, we'd discuss the person and all say what we felt. We usually knew whether it would work or not: it was almost invariably unanimous. The patient usually knew quite decidely too. Like that they became members of the family. In those first days they were hitched on to somebody and then became part of the body of the community – as a sick bit – and the healthy blood stream of the body helped to heal them as well as the analysis.' Another Withymead therapist, Inge Allenby, expressed a similar idea, if somewhat less mystically, when she described Withymead as 'a community of sick people shot through with normality, a community characterised by sickness but tempered by health.'

To the newcomer, therefore, Withymead was both physically and socially welcoming. 'My first impression was one of warmth and sunshine,' wrote one ex-patient. 'I stood there, after the taxi had gone, looking up at the blue sky and the flowers growing in the gardens above the lane at the edge of Redwing lawn. Irene gave me a marvellous welcome, and I had dinner with her that first evening at her own table in the dining room. She told me I no longer needed to bear my burdens alone now that there was someone to share them with me. I felt gratitude, though I couldn't bring myself to say anything at the time. I shall never forget her kindness, any more than I shall the loveliness of the place: the mill pond and the stream, the ducks, the orchard full of primroses in the spring and dandelions in the early summer.' 'Above all else', another ex-patient told me, 'I remember the quiet warmth of welcome one always received on arrival at Withymead. It gave one the feeling that life there went on in an orderly, creative cycle, irrespective of individual comings and goings. One always felt received as a welcome addition to the community, while not being expected to fill any particular function against one's inclination.'

Not everyone who came to Withymead was ill. Some had nothing wrong with them at all. For instance, it was not uncommon for interested members of the teaching or 'helping' professions, without any pressing personal problems, to stay for a period at the Centre in order to experience its methods at first hand, in order later on to use the fruits of this experience in their professional work. Such visitors invariably expressed enthusiasm for what they found, but, unlike those who had actually been ill at Withymead, they did not always realize that the community gave hope and security to many more people that those who happened, at any one time, to be residing there. The centre considered it had a clear responsibility to provide this vulnerable and widely dispersed collection of people with a central point in their lives to which they might return in time of need, and whose very existence would give them security when they were far away. Many ex-patients have told me how helpful this was to them. 'When I was away from Withymead,' wrote one, 'it comforted me to know that members would follow the daily and seasonal pattern of their lives in my absence, so that it was always possible to imagine from miles away what might be happening just then at Withymead. At the same time, I could always be certain that I should not be forgotten, even though there might be no specific communication before my next visit.' The mother of a large family who had been nursed through a breakdown at Withymead, told me that, as a result of this experience, she felt she belonged to the community as a full member. 'And when we went abroad to live as a family, this fact remained – Withymead was there and always the same. I could write or telephone and, although I was disappointed if Mrs C. wasn't available, really it didn't seem to matter who I spoke to, the contact was there; the life-line was being firmly held at the other end, and so one felt reassured and the feeling of safety returned. This was vital to me, and it never let me down: it was always THERE.'

That it should not be allowed to let people down was a constant concern of the Withymead staff, and very early in the Centre's history they came to recognize several conditions that needed to be fulfilled if the life-line was to go on 'being firmly held'. In the first place, it was important to avoid any rapid turnover among the key figures, especially the parental figures round whom the Centre had grown. It was essential that a hard core of staff members should remain unfailingly at Withymead over the years. Inevitably, these figures became intimately identified with the place, and loss of any one of them could result in strong feelings of insecurity, even despair, in patients both past and present. Secondly, the physical no less than the social characteristics of the Centre needed to remain relatively unchanged. When unavoidable changes did occur, the staff took care that they should be gradual and organic in their development. They believed that the domestic arrangements of the house, the layout and use of the studios and gardens, and the daily life of the entire community must possess a basic and evident unchangingness, so that however long Withymeadians may have been away, they would feel on their return that they had 'come home'.

Despite the life-line, people did occasionally return to Withymead because of a further breakdown, but more usually they returned for succour in order to keep going in the outside world. The staff were sensitive to this need and never shed the belief that a crucial function of Withymead must be to afford sanctuary to those who were beginning to find life more than they could cope with. Their attitude contrasts vividly with that prevailing in mental hospitals, where it is virtually impossible to get patients admitted unless they have completely broken down. In the view of the National Health Service authorities, it seems, mental hospitals exist to patch up psychiatric disasters when they have occured rather than to prevent them in the first place. Withymead, on the other hand, managed to sustain a large number of psychologically fragile individuals by arranging periodic visits to the Centre and encouraging them to continue functioning in their professional and social lives. Teachers came and went during their holidays while holding down a job during term time; social workers came on their off-duty weekends; and parents and children returned to the Centre for varying periods of time when family pressures became too much for them at home. Readmission to Withymead was not a sign of therapeutic ineffectiveness but a preventive technique designed to replenish the individual's personal resources and enable him to deal satisfactorily and more consciously with new situations which had arisen in his life.

Withymead's willingness to allow patients to return and to stay on until they felt strong enough to face the outside world was construed by some of the Centre's critics as a serious weakness. Such critics tended to be doctors, social workers and teachers who subscribed to the view that neurotic patients should be encouraged to be 'independent' and 'self-reliant', that they should give up their 'immature dependence on others' and 'stand on their own feet'. They attributed Withymead's alleged failure to appreciate the importance of these aims to the maternal possessiveness of Irene Champernowne, arguing that her patients were surrogate children of her whom she could not bear to see go out into the world.

Irene, however, had no patience with these criticisms. To her they represented a grossly limited view of neurosis and psychotherapy, for they failed to take into consideration the need that we all share, even the most mature of us, for what she called 'healthy dependence', namely, the security of having people and places in our lives that we know we can depend on. 'People criticized what they saw as our weaknesses,' she said, 'but it was out of our weakness that we worked. I'm all against people trying to be too independent, unless they have reached the point where they *have* to be independent. Instinctively, I know it. I find it so pathological when people say "I ought to be able to stand on my own feet" because it is just an idea off the top of their heads. People stand on their feet when they are able to.'

Irene's 'instinctive' knowledge of the need for 'mature dependency' has since been amply corroborated by Dr John Bowlby and his followers who have demonstrated the fundamental importance of attachment bonds for the maintenance of emotional security. The need for attachment figures is, indeed, an instinctive need, an *a priori* fact of human nature, and it persists throughout the entire life-cycle – like the need for oxygen, warmth, shelter and nourishment. Once we have established a bond with an appropriate figure – whether it be mother, spouse, therapist or close friend – that person functions as a 'secure base' and, as a consequence, our sense of well-being depends on that person being available and accessible to us. A healthy person, Bowlby believes, is one who can recognize suitable attachment figures willing to function as a secure base and who can collabarate with them in maintaining a mutually rewarding relationship. 'Paradoxically,' he writes, 'the healthy personality when viewed in this light proves by no means as independent as cultural stereotypes suppose. Essential ingredients are a capacity to rely trustingly on others when occasion demands and to know on whom it is appropriate to rely.' (Bowlby, 1979).

As Bowlby has shown, neurosis is largely a consequence of disturbed attachments formed in the course of personality development. Thus, the majority of neurotic patients are found, on examination, to have a history of deficient parental care – deficient in the sense that the quality of the care provided was such as to frustrate those archetypal imperatives inherent within the personality which are concerned with the formation of attachment bonds, the establishment of 'basic trust' in life and in people, and the development of a secure ego conceiving of itself as being acceptable to others and capable of coping with the eventualities and vicissitudes of ordinary living.

The characteristic patterns of parental deficiency which Bowlby has described include absence or separation from the child (i.e. one or both parents may go away and leave the child, or put him in hospital or an institution; the earlier the loss and the longer or more frequent the separations, the more serious are the consequences for mental health), unresponsiveness to the child's attachment needs (i.e. one or both parents are persistently unresponsive to child's care-eliciting behaviour, and they may indeed actively disparage or reject him), parental induction of guilt as a disciplinary technique (i.e. assertions are made that the child's behaviour will be responsible for the illness or death of one or other parent), parental threats to abandon the child if he does not behave (i.e. threats are made to withdraw love, abandon the family, commit suicide or even kill the spouse or child), and parental 'clinging' on to the child, exerting pressure on him to be the primary care-giver in their relationship, thus inverting the normal pattern, and forcing the child to be responsible and grown up beyond his years.

Any one of these forms of distortion of the parent-child relationship can result in anxious, insecure individuals who complain of lacking confidence, of being shy, inadequate and unable to cope with the ordinary demands of life. They often have difficulty in forming and maintaining lasting relationships and are characteristically described by psychiatrists and social workers as 'over-dependent' or 'immature'. Under stress they are prone to break down and develop frank neurotic symptoms, such as persistent anxiety, depression, obsessive-compulsive phenomena and phobias.

The actual kind of distortion which a neurotic patient may have suffered in childhood can sometimes be deduced from the way in which he relates to emotionally significant people in his environment – especially his therapist. The commonest consequence of pathogenic parenting is what Bowlby describes as *anxious attachment* – a nagging anxiety that one's attachment figures may either be lost or prove inaccessible. Typically, such patients become extremely anxious when their therapist goes away on holiday, or if they fear they may have displeased or annoyed him in some way. Moreover, all forms of deficient parenting are liable to release anger in the child as a result of repeated frustration of his basic emotional needs. However, since the parents are infinitely more powerful than the child, and since the care and protection they provide is essential to his survival, he usually feels obliged to control his anger and inhibit its expression. The largely unconscious resentment which this induces tends to persist into adult life as a 'chip on the shoulder'. At the same time, such people often have a strong unconscious *yearning for love* which may reveal itself in some aberrant form of care-eliciting behaviour which, as often as not, is modelled on the aberrant form of care-giving behaviour displayed by the parents (e.g. half-hearted suicide attempts, threats to leave, malingering, hypochondria, guilt-induction, and so on). This does not make them easy to live with.

The approach adopted at Withymead to these psychodynamic issues was a mixture of pragmatism and theoretical ingenuity. The Champernownes were, of course, aware that by providing a family atmosphere they would inevitably reactivate conflicts originally experienced by the neurotic patient in the course of his own family history. They accepted the emotional storms and tensions this would induce as a necessary part of treatment. For only when these conflicts were activated could their pathology be analyzed and some degree of resolution achieved. At the same time, the community's provision of willing parent and sibling figures went far towards fulfulling the attachment longings which had remained unsatisfied often since childhood. The patient also tended to experience this new family group as being considerably more tolerant and insightful in dealing with his problems than the family into which he had been born. Gradually, as bonds of attachment formed, Withymead itself became a secure base where, relieved of anxiety and despair, he could examine his present circumstances in the light of his past, develop his creative potential in the studios, and fashion a new image of himself as an integrated, valued and effective personality.

The period immediately after admission was frequently one of psychic regression and extreme emotional dependency. This is only to be expected in demoralized people who, finding their lives impossible to manage, have been forced to seek asylum among professionals willing to assume responsibility for their care. The severity of the patient's distress determines the extent of his regression to childish modes of dependency and the amount of care and attention he will need if he is to find 'basic trust', grow towards emotional maturity and develop a capacity for reciprocal relationships. Regression is a phenomenon which, like most psychotherapists, Irene Champernowne understood as a necessary preliminary to therapeutic effort, and she knew that a patient's subsequent growth to a more mature stage of personal development is a process which cannot be hurried and which must be permitted to go forward at its own pace. Any attempt to force the pace in the interests of economic efficiency would result in pseudo-maturity and the state of false independence which Dr Colin Murray Parkes (1973) has appropriately termed *compulsive self-reliance*. Critics of

Withymead who misconstrued Irene's intuitive understanding of these facts as evidence of her 'overprotectiveness' and a
penchant for 'clinging onto the beloved child' did so through
ignorance of the indispensable part played by attachment
formation in the development of basic trust and in the
successful treatment of neurosis.

This policy was both humane and therapeutically effective.
But it took a heavy toll of Irene and Gilbert both financially
and emotionally. The time needed for a patient to grow 'at
his own pace' from the stage of anxious attachment to mature
attachment, from basic distrust to basic trust, was often
much longer than the patient could afford to finance out of
his own pocket. Yet such was the determination to see him
through once he had been taken on, that his personal financial
concerns became the concern of the community – a state of
affairs which the world, as it is at present constituted, would
be unwilling to tolerate unless it were organized through the
bureaucratic machinery of the state. The supreme value of
Withymead was that it managed to remain intimate, personal
and unbureaucratic, and it was characteristic of the place that
whenever human considerations had to be weighed against
financial ones, humanity invariably prevailed. To anyone
who knew the community, and the personalities round
whom the community evolved, it was not hard to trace the
source of this splendidly unmercenary attitude. There are
some people who, by the wildest stretch of the imagination,
could never be thought capable of running a business for
profit. One such person was Irene Champernowne. Her
heart ruled her head in most matters, but never more than
when dealing with money. To be sure, Gilbert was usually
able to exercise some restraint over her pecuniary impulsive-
ness, for much as he appreciated her passionate humanity, he
was sufficiently a man of the world to know that if the
Centre was to survive, the generosity of its founders must be
tempered by certain fiscal constraints. Meticulous book
keeper that he was, Gilbert had too much integrity to
countenance the running up of debts. When Irene's warm

heart looked as if it were about to gallop away with her, he would note the signs and, gently but firmly, bring her up short. In this way he did the community an important service. There were other people whose financial advice Irene would listen to, it is true – Leonard and Dorothy Elmhirst, for example, and their accountant, Frank Walters – but, when she had set her heart on doing something which could prove financially imprudent, only Gilbert had enough influence with her to make her change her mind. Irene would take guidance from Gilbert as from no one else, not just because she respected his judgement, but because she knew that his sensitivity to the human problems they daily encountered in their work was as acute as her own.

Despite Gilbert's wise influence, however, Withymead persistently erred on the side of generosity. Each year he made determined efforts to keep the balance between income and expenditure in credit, and each year he just failed to do so. The trouble was that he was no more a hard-headed businessman than Irene: invariably they permitted Caritas to triumph over Mammon, and, try as they would, there seemed to be no way of stemming the slow but incessant haemorrhage which afflicted their small exchequer. Increasingly, money was a worry to them, and as the 40s drew to an end, they were compelled to acknowledge that Withymead had become a financial liability which they could not hope much longer to sustain, and that nothing short of a miracle could save them from having to close it down.

But Irene believed in miracles, and as so often in her life her faith was justified. The miracle occurred one weekend in the summer of 1950, when Irene and Gilbert were staying with Leonard and Dorothy Elmhirst at Dartington. Many years later, Leonard Elmhirst told me about it. 'We had the greatest admiration for Irene and Gilbert and what they had built up at Withymead,' he said. 'We thought they had wonderful ideas, and it was extraordinary how they'd managed to put them into effect with hardly any financial resources to speak of. Dorothy and I were entirely in sympathy with their work, and, like them, we were convinced of the fundamental importance of creativeness and intuition. When we settled in the wilds of Devon, we gave priority to providing facilities for the creative use of leisure – we saw the escape from routine and from intellectuality as an essential need. We must never allow ourselves to be led down the drain by the academics! We have to use and understand intuition. Dorothy and I saw Withymead as a fight by Rene and Gilbert for the creative side of human beings, and we decided we *must* give them our support.

'We thought Withymead was absolutely the right centre for their activities. What appealed to us was the idea of a small, intimate unit capable of gradual but organic growth. We realized that our best way to help was not by any flashy expenditure right at the beginning, but bit by bit over the years, so that they could slowly accumulate all that was needed for a small community within an attractive, compact area.'

As a result of the Elmhirsts' timely intervention, the Withymead Trust was born, the cherished daughter of the much richer Elmgrant Trust, whose maternal bounty was to continue unstintingly throughout the 1950s. This inaugurated a period which was to prove the heyday of Withymed: it was a time when all the promise of the early years reached maximum fulfilment, and when the community brought rich possibilities for health and personal growth into the lives of many hundreds of people.

For years, Irene and Gilbert had recognized that if Withymead were to survive it needed to expand. Now, with the foundation of the Withymead Trust, they were in a position to do something about it. They were fortunate in their three Trustees – Leonard Elmhirst, Maurice Ash (Leonard's son-in-law, later chairman of the Dartington Trust) and John Trevelyan (a friend of both the Elmhirsts and the Champernownes, who was to become well known as the Chairman of the Board of Film Censors). Gilbert was not a Trustee, but, as Secretary of the Trust, he was involved in making and implementing all policy decisions. From the outset, all four men agreed that their chief objective should be to make Withymead self-supporting by increasing the Centre's capacity to accommodate patients and thus raise more revenue.

As luck would have it, only months after the new Trust came into being, the seventeenth century farm house just across the lane from Withymead was put up for sale. It had great charm and was exactly the right size to accommodate the increase in numbers that the Trustees were considering: it would provide twelve comfortable bed-sitting rooms, one of which was a large double room, and two tiny rooms in the attic. This was enough for at least fifteen additional residents, and it was thought that the revenue which these would bring in would be sufficient to put the Centre's finances on a sound basis.

Seeing that the opportunity was too good to miss, Leonard declared his willingness to make a personal, interest-free loan to the Withymead Trust to cover the purchase of the house. Unfortunately, the old lady who owned it and who had lived there for many years, so disapproved of the idea that it should become a 'mental home' that, despite good offers and entreaties, she insisted on selling to someone else. Not to be outdone, however, the Trustees approached the new owners who, to everyone's relief, agreed to re-sell – though at a substantially increased figure.

Everyone at Withymead shared in this happy turn in the Centre's fortunes. The new property was christened 'The Barton' (barton being the Devonshire word for farm house) and the whole community set to work scrubbing, scraping and painting, and making curtains, quilts and covers. Meanwhile, the Management Committee began to consider the logistic problems which the increased numbers of patients would bring in their train. It was clear that the relatively small dining room, which had accommodated the old family group with such cosy intimacy, would no longer be adequate, and that a new dining room would have to be built onto the old. Such an extension was now financially possible since Leonard's personal loan left the Trustees free to raise the necessary money against 'The Barton' as security.

Increasingly, children were being brought into the Centre, both as residents and as day patients, first under the care of Ruth Allen and later Mary Pye (both ex-school teachers), and they needed somewhere to live and play where they could be free to enjoy themselves without disturbing the rest of the community. It was agreed that the large garage occupying the whole of the lower floor of the barn facing onto the river would, when converted into the handsome 'River Room', make an admirable play area, and in the garden to the East of 'The Barton' there existed an ideal site for a new Children's Wing (later christened 'Red Wing'), if only the money were forthcoming and the Ministry of Works could be induced to issue the building permits still necessary at that time of post-war reconstruction.

In fact, the money proved easier to come by than the permits, for as with most bureaucratic procedures the way to success was strewn with red tape. The Ministry of Health would do nothing to help things along, although several times invited to do so: they declined to sponsor Withymead's applications on the grounds that the Centre did not supplement the work of the National Health Service – despite the fact that N.H.S. doctors were increasingly referring patients there rather than to Health Service hospitals and clinics.

Only when Ben Belton arrived on the scene in 1952 and exercised his professional skill in manipulating ministries did the permits begin to come through and it was not until 1955 that the necessary reconstruction was completed. In the meantime, as the community grew, its members had no alternative than to make the best of things in very over-crowded circumstances.

It was a difficult time for the staff. The increase in population which followed the acquisition of 'The Barton' made ever greater demands on their patience and skill, and the one who bore most of the strain was Irene. While it is true that both she and Gilbert functioned as 'parent surrogates' to the whole community, it was nevertheless Irene, passionate, energetic figure that she was, who held the community together and gave it its emotional direction and strength. Many people who knew Withymead had spoken of it as a matriarchy. They saw Irene in the guise of Queen Victoria and Gilbert as her Prince Consort. There is little doubt that the role of consort suited Gilbert's retiring disposition. While the influence of Irene's personality was everywhere in evidence, Gilbert remained an *éminence grise*, a power behind the throne, a counsellor to whom the Queen turned for advice and who alone possessed the influence to curb her head-strong passions.

Like Queen Victoria, Irene's presence radiated comfortable maternity. She never disguised how deeply she cared for each member of her 'family', watching benevolently over their growth, arbitrating between them in their squabbles, giving praise and blame where they were due, encouraging their endeavours and succouring their ills. She also mediated executively between her 'children' and the outside world, playing to the full her role as Withymead's external repre-sentative, while at the same time guiding the fortunes, hopes and aspirations of the family as a whole. As a loving, devoted mother, striving on all fronts for the welfare of her sons and daughters she was indeftiguable, and the loyalty and, on occasion, the hostility that she inspired was correspondingly passionate. Irene seemed to possess an inexhaustible cornuco-pia of maternal love which flowed out abundantly to those whom she had taken on, so that once they had arrived at Withymead, the lonely, insecure and rejected felt valued, safe and accepted in a way that they had not known, many of them, since their infancy and often not even then. Thus it was that for many Withymead became home, giving a family to those who felt they had none and restoring the mother to those who had lost her. And it was in this family configura-tion that Withymead possessed the secret of its stability and therapeutic power, for it provided a living context clearly more appropriate to the inherent social nature of mankind than the anonymous, sophisticated society outside. Through its *ad hoc* mixture of the generations Withymead afforded just that kind of 'extended family' within which men and women have traditionally lived out their days and on which they have depended for their sense of identity and personal security.

Irene was always wholehearted in everything she did and in performing her role as mother and 'secure base' she often drove herself to the point of exhaustion. So robust did she appear, however, that few people knew just how much she demanded of herself. In the interests of community security she would allow only Gilbert and Dorothy Elmhirst to know the extent of the emotional tax that Withymead imposed on her. For months at a time, her only escape from these pressures was the one night she spent each week at Dartington after working a session at the nearby Crichel Hostel for Children, where she held a visiting consultancy. After one such visit in August, 1950, she wrote to Dorothy: 'I have had such a terrible sense of my back to the wall recently . . . but Dartington always gives me a feeling of refuge and, however low I am, something always comes in again from you and Leonard and your family – and from the place itself.'

For her part, Dorothy could see the toll that Withymead was exacting on Irene's energies and encouraged her to get away for a few weeks every year to Zurich, where contact with Jung, Toni Wolff, Barbara Hannah and others, and hours spent in peaceful reflection, doing 'active imagination', painting and writing were always a source of spiritual regeneration to her. These regular visits to Zurich enabled Irene to carry on as the mainstay of Withymead, and they were made possible by Dorothy's personal generosity. Without this help Irene would not have been able to afford to go: incredible though it now seems, for all her industry and dedication, she drew from the Withymead Trust a salary of only £450 a year (i.e. £9 a week).

In Zurich she found peace, and time to introvert on the crucial issues of her life and of Withymead. She invariably stayed in the friendly Sonne Hotel at Kusnacht, a short walk along the lakeside from Jung's house. Her letters from there to Dorothy reveal just how large a burden those who run a community like Withymead must be willing and able to carry. 'There is a tremendous price to be paid in maintaining a place like Withymead,' she wrote. 'It is a small collective unit, trying to live by community laws, which also respects fully and primarily the individual value. This means that the amount of work that goes to helping each individual is enormous. In cases of psychic sickness, especially where the patient is sunk very low in the unconscious, one has to allow oneself to drop down and touch those levels of madness, suicide or despair and *take on* the evil to a certain extent, and by virtue of the healthy psychic quality, if one has it, deal with the sickness. It is akin to a blood transfusion or the taking over of a load; but one must only take the load for which one is psychically fit and able. Keeping one's soul free and ready, and having time to go away and deal with the evil one is carrying, is essential or it means death.

'Already the restructuring of Withymead is demanding so much, with the minimum of free time for us all, and the psychic burden increases with the necessity of making Withymead an economic unit of the 'right' size. I did not realize how spiritually and psychically in danger I was until I got here. And the letters which come [from Withymead] show me the way the load falls when I am not there. The young members of the staff are often hours on end with people in a pathological state, sometimes to the point of danger. The thing is, it isn't noticed until much later, and then only by those of us who have had more experience.

'But if this work is to be done, and the psychic and spiritual sickness dealt with, we have to risk something. Or else we must shut up these valuable people in mental hospitals to be policed by jailers who are too thick-skinned to be infected – that is, not infected enough to understand what the disease is, let alone how to heal it.'

The load which the Withymead staff had to carry was composed not only of sickness but also of the intense emotional demands invariably made by patients who have broken down and regressed to childish modes of dependency. Such regression customarily results in the misperception and overidealization of key figures like Irene and Gilbert who have 'transferred' to them deep seated attitudes and expectations derived from early life experiences as well as legitimate attachment needs. Subtle nuances in the quality of the relationship with these figures tend to become exaggerated out of all proportion in the distressed individual's mind, and he may devote much time to futile preoccupations, such as whether their intentions towards him are good or bad. He may show extraordinary sensitivity to their behaviour towards him, over-reacting to imagined slights or becoming suicidal when out of touch with them. Such reactions are, of course, the hourly lot of the practicing analyst treating patients individually, but when they are encountered as group phenomena, as they were at Withymead, they are at once more formidable and difficult to manage, and it is unlikely that even a therapist of Irene's stature would have been able to cope with the experience she had not the unflagging support of her band of trusted colleagues on the Withymead staff. Even then, the strain could be almost intolerable, as her letters to Dorothy Elmhirst make clear. Leadership of a community like Withymead requires not only compassion, insight and skill, but strength, determination and deep inner resourcefulness as well. It is not a job for spiritual light-weights.

In discharging their responsibilities as valiantly as they did, the Champernownes relied as much on the Elmhirsts' friendship as on their financial support. After a visit to Dartington in 1952, Gilbert wrote to them saying that their material help, great as it was, meant little in comparison with their personal affection and their warm encouragement of the work at Withymead. 'I really think it is wonderful,' he wrote, 'that in the midst of your many preoccupations with personal affairs and the immeasurable problems which Dartington must present, you should be able to give so much of *yourselves* to us and to our work . . . I do hope that we and Withymead may be able to give an increasing return for all you have brought us, both spiritually and materially.'

But the relationship between the two couples was far from one-sided, as the following letter from Dorothy makes clear. It was written on Good Friday, 1952.

> Dartington Hall,
> Totnes,
> Devon.

Dearest Irene,

As Easter approaches I realize with great joy that new life has come to me, and it has come from you. I tried this morning to think of all the ways in which you have helped me, but I saw behind all the particular things you have done, and the enlightenment you have brought, lies the tremendous quality of what you are yourself. I think I have never known in anyone such love and such power combined. It is, of course, your knowledge that gives strength and direction to the driving power of your love; it is the greatest force for life I have come across. And Easter will be for me a day of infinite gratitude for knowing you, and for being able, here and there, through my contact with you, to glimpse something of the Holy Spirit.

> Bless you always and for everything.
> Dorothy.

Irene and Gilbert needed friends of this quality if they were to carry on, for their concern for individual patients invariably led them into commitments which carried them way beyond the call of duty.

'The most important single factor in the efficiency of the treatment given in a mental hospital,' reported a W.H.O. Expert Committee on Psychiatry (1953), 'appears to the committee to be an intangible element which can only be described as its atmosphere.' This was unquestionably true of Withymead where, as one resident said, the atmosphere was one of love and acceptance. 'That was the thing about Withymead,' she told me, 'the loving acceptance of people *as they were*. They got better because they were loved and accepted.'

Chapter IV

The Therapeutic Community

Withymead was, as we have seen, the first therapeutic community to be established in Britain. We may agree that this is an important achievement and that it justly represents one of Withymead's most significant claims to fame. But it raises the question of what the term really means. What is it about a community that makes it therapeutic? And how did community therapy at Withymead actually work?

The fairly self-evident notion that the environment in which psychiatric patients are treated may itself play a part in making them better is a current psychiatric cliché which has been elevated to the status of a *movement*. And in the years since Tom Main, Maxwell Jones and Dennis Martin first published accounts of their achievements in this field an extensive literature has grown up explicitly centred on this so-called therapeutic community movement. Yet, for all the millions of words that have been printed there is still no consensus about what precisely a therapeutic community is or how it should normally function. To propose a formulation that would receive general consent is therefore extremely difficult. However, a reasonably thorough perusal of this literature encourages me to believe that few commentators would disagree with the suggestion that what most therapeutic communities seek to achieve – whether they realize it or not – is a reversal of those characteristics of the traditional mental hospital which Dr Russell Barton deemed responsible for inducing the unfortunate condition he termed *insitutional neurosis* (see page 43 above).

In the effort to reach a more precise definition, Zeigenfuss (1976), a man of impressive stamina, read no less than 270 papers, all relating to therapeutic communities and all published between 1970 and 1975. Unfortunately, this labour yielded little reward. Zeigenfuss complained that the therapeutic community concept was so vaguely defined and used to cover such a multitude of practices that he could come up with no more helpful conclusion than that, on the whole, therapeutic communities are based on a 'social approach' to psychiatric treatment.

To my mind, the most serviceable definition of the term remains that of its originator, Tom Main (1946), who spoke of it as 'an attempt to use a hospital not as an organization run by doctors in the interests of their own great technical efficiency, but as a community with the immediate aim of full participation of all its members in its daily life and the eventual aim of the resocialization of the neurotic individual for life in ordinary society.' This still stands as a concise statement of the basic intent behind the therapeutic community and it has the virtue of clarity, being uncluttered by the trendy terminology beloved of many contemporary advocates of the 'movement', whose writings sometimes read like the 'on-going situations' column in the satirical magazine *Private Eye*. Indeed, Main's unashamed use of words like *doctor* and *neurotic* dates the passage and would shock many of today's practitioners. Maxwell Jones, the St Paul of the movement, has proscribed such terms in the interests of egalitarianism, as he thinks the notion of staff treating patients is bad for the staff and degrading for the patients. Jones, nevertheless, finds it impossible to avoid using them altogether, and when he does so he salves his conscience by putting them in inverted commas! Thus, when he defines the therapeutic community, it is 'treatment based on social organization and using the social environment of the "patient" to effect change.' This practice in piety savours of a Victorian hostess using frilly trousers to cover the indelicacy of piano legs.

The contemporary flight from medical terminology, together with recent attempts to drop the concept of mental illness altogether, fosters a retreat into jargon, euphemism and hypocrisy. As I read some of these authors, I am reminded of the exchange between Gwendolen Fairfax and Cecily Cardew in *The Importance of Being Ernest*: irritated by Gwendolen's London manners and superior airs, Cecily observes, 'When I see a spade I call it a spade'. Gwendolen replies sweetly, 'I am glad to say that I have never seen a spade. It is obvious that our social spheres have been widely different.' Miss Fairfax would find herself at home in the therapeutic community movement.

The truth of the matter is that institutions reflect the assumptions of the society which creates them: the reaction against the hierarchically organized mental hospital and its replacement by the egalitarian therapeutic community is a direct expression of the cultural shift which has taken place in our society from the *patrism* and *tradition-directedness* of Victorian times towards the *matrism* and *other-directedness* of today. It is necessary to be clear about this shift for it throws light on the historical position of Withymead in relation to the therapeutic community movement and helps us to judge the status of its achievement.

The terms patrism and matrism I owe to Taylor (1972) and tradition-directedness and other-directedness to Riesman (1952). Taylor's distinction rests on the anthropological observation that peoples who believe in father gods living in the sky tend to have a father-dominated social structure, in that their social institutions, behaviour patterns, customs and values embody characteristics of the father archetype, while peoples who believe in mother goddesses inhabiting the earth tend to have a mother-dominated social structure, in that they reflect the characteristics of the mother archetype. Examples of patrist cultures are to be found among traditional adherents of the Jewish, Christian and Muslim faiths, while examples of matrist cultures are thought to have existed in the Mediterranean region among the devotees of

Ceres, Astarte, Cybele, Demeter, and the Magna Mater.

Patrist cultures are prone to be puritanical in sexual matters, to assign low status to women, and to have an authoritarian political structure; they set great store by social hierarchies, law and order, discipline and efficient organization, and they devise rules and regulations to cover everything. The basic model of a patrist culture is the social pyramid, and the Army and the Catholic Church are obvious examples. Matrist cultures on the other hand tend to be permissive in sexual matters, to assign high status to women, and to embrace a democratic social structure; they are less coercive than patrist cultures, place fewer constraints on individual freedom, and encourage creative self-expression and spontaneity.

At times of political upheaval or religious crisis, it is clearly possible for a culture of one sort to transform itself into the other, for this is precisely what has happened in Western society during the past sixty years. At the end of the nineteenth century our society was still unequivocally patrist, but now, as a result of two World Wars and the loss of faith in Our Father which art in Heaven, it has lurched rapidly in the matrist direction. As yet, it is true, no goddess has arisen from the terrigenous depths to sanctify this transition, but when she does it will presumably be from the mineral deposits on which our material-worshipping culture is based: Our Great Mother of the Oil Fields.

When one thinks about it, the evidence for this swing to matrism is, as Taylor suggests, overwhelming: the increase in sexual permissiveness, the progressive improvement in the status of women, the prevalence of egalitarian attitudes, the rejection of class distinctions in dress, speech and behaviour, the political impetus to dismantle hierarchical institutions, the orgiastic pursuit of euphoria through rock music and the use of drugs, the self-evidently maternal concern with the provision of nurturant welfare services to ensure that everyone is nourished, clothed, housed, and given medical care, together with the notion that everyone has a right to these things (as a child has a right to them from his mother) whether he helps to pay for them or not, the importance attached to *fairness* and *sharing*, the emphasis on consent and consultation between government and governed, employer and employee, teacher and pupil, 'doctor' and 'patient', the belief that crime is the fault of society rather than the criminal and the progressive abandonment of the use of punishment as an appropriate means of dealing with him, and so on. The most dramatic move towards matrism occurred in the two decades which followed the end of the second World War, whereas the war itself witnessed the last flicker of patrist assertion. By championing matrist values while the war was still on, Withymead was clearly ahead of its time, while the therapeutic community movement coming years later was essentially of it.

The other sociological distinction which is relevant to Withymead is made by David Riesman in his book *The Lonely Crowd*, where he designates three types of culture, which he terms 'tradition-directed', 'other-directed' and 'inner-directed' respectively. Since our earliest cultural beginning most members of our species have lived in tradition-directed cultures. Such cultures tend to be stable and to persist relatively unchanged throughout long periods of time. Their customs, values and beliefs are handed on unquestioned from generation to generation, and their members share a profound sense of historical continuity.

In recent times, practically all tradition-directed cultures, including our own, have been overwhelmed by other-directed values, which reject the traditions of the past as suffocating and oppressive and seek after new meanings in modern ideas, fashions and movements. In these cultures, the centre of gravity shifts backwards along the life cycle from old age to youth, from senex to puer. The emphasis is on rebellion against the tradition of the fathers and on solidarity with the peer group. Instead of respect for the old institutions hallowed by the gods, a restless passion arises for revolutionary notions which change with each new generation, basing their currency not on what has 'always been' but on what 'everybody thinks'. Hence the rapid spread of popular mass movements like the Campaign for Nuclear Disarmament in the '50s, the revolutionary student movement in the '60s, the Womens' Liberation and Gay Liberation movements in the '70s, the successive generations of Teds, Mods, Rockers, Hippies and Punks, the popularity of subversive drug cultures, Maoists, Trotskyists, and so on. The therapeutic community movement is an example of the same trend.

Unfortunately, a life of undiluted other-directedness is deeply unsatisfactory because the obsession with ephemera promotes alienation of the ego from the centre of the total personality which Jung termed the Self; it encourages the adoption of a pseudo-identity, distracting the 'with it' individual from the development of a mature character structure securely rooted in the reality of his own nature. A more satisfactory alternative is Riesman's third orientation, which he terms 'inner-directedness'. The inner-directed person does not derive his sense of value or identity from tradition or from conformity to peer group fashions, but from the resources inherent within himself. This third orientation is the most difficult to attain because it requires courage and determination and can only be achieved by each individual in the course of developing his own character. The most original, creative, and outstanding men and women are often of this type, for their centre of gravity resides not in society but in the Self. Yet it is no élitist condition, for it represents a mode of adjustment which is potentially available to every human being. It is the way of life that takes individuation, or Self-fulfilment, as its goal.

While tradition-directed cultures tend to be patrist in character, other-directed cultures incline to the matrist pattern. Inner-directedness, on the other hand, provides a means of transcending both these cultural forms through awareness of the fundamental characteristics of the creature that we are, the essence of which is crystallized in the Self. It is possible for a culture to display more than one of these orientations. Ancient Greece, for example, was both patrist and matrist, the Greek pantheon combining sky gods with earth mother goddesses. Another example was Withymead. For as long as it functioned successfully, Withymead represented a unique combination of all three propensities: it was midly patrist, strongly matrist, and it was inner-directed as well. The patrist component was upheld by Gilbert Champernowne: with his gentle, dignified manner and his respect for form and decency, Gilbert was a gentleman in the traditional and very best sense of the word. His was the ultimate political authority in the community, and on those few occasions when it was asserted everyone deferred to it, including Irene. Withymead's matrism was, as we have seen, a direct expression of the powerful personality of Irene, who, for many, seemed to embody the archetype of the Great Mother herself.

The inner-directedness of Withymead was evident in the central position given to individual analysis and the practice of the arts. In strict contrast to the psychiatric clinics of the time (and of the present), the therapeutic regime at Withymead had little to do with behavioural manipulation, social adjustment or symptom removal, but focused on Self-discovery and individual creativity. The aim was not so much to confront problems head on (as in contemporary therapeutic communities), but to help the patient, through personal growth, to transcend them. Because of the respect which everyone shared for the creative potential of the Self and its capacity to engender healing in the total personality, the attitude to art therapy at Withymead was very different from that prevailing in occupational therapy departments elsewhere. At Withymead one felt the strength of peoples' commitment to work in the studios, whereas in more conventional psychiatric units one finds that patients often reject 'O.T.' as an exercise in futility. For example, Anne Crozier (1979) describing her experience in the 1970s of being a patient at the Marlborough Day Hospital, a well known therapeutic community in London, wrote 'Patients . . .

never attended work groups regularly: only when there was a specific project, e.g. making stuffed dolls for a bazaar, producing a magazine, etc., was anything done. We felt that it was "useless work", doing something for the sake of doing it only, doing meaningless repetitive things which did not even constitute learning a skill . . . Work groups seemed only to emphasize the difference between ourselves and the staff, who had real work to do, were so busy they did not even have a proper lunch break, and patients who had nothing real to do, and were unable to get on with their lives.' At Withymead the situation was in marked contrast. There everybody felt that artistic creation was *real* work, for it, like analysis, was working on the Self, and staff did that as much as patients.

Another salient difference between Withymead and other therapeutic communities is to be found in the theoretical foundations underlying their work. The analysts on the Withymead staff, Irene Champernowne, Florida Scott-Maxwell, Inge Allenby, Joan Macworth, and, later, Doris Layard and Eve Lewis, were all thoroughly schooled in the Jungian tradition, and this gave a sense of confident assurance to their analytical formulations and to the way they went about their work. By contrast, conventional therapeutic communities display a relative conceptual vagueness and a degree of uncertainty in the manner in which they conduct their affairs. Indeed, a fundamental problem encountered in defining the modern therapeutic community – let alone in organizing and running one – has been pointed out by Tom Main himself (1980) for he declares that no 'adequate general theory of psycho-social development' exists on which the therapeutic community concept can be based. In other words, contemporary therapeutic communities lack the archetypal/explanatory dimension which permeated all activities at Withymead and which provided a ready understanding of the psychic needs characterizing different stages of the human life cycle, both in the individual and in the group. As Main confessed thirty years after becoming clinical director of the Cassel Hospital, 'much of our work is still at the level of pragmatism and intuition'. Much of the work at Withymead was pragmatic and intuitive too, but it was based on firmer theoretical foundations.

Maxwell Jones gets round this central weakness in the movement which he started by characteristically making a virtue of necessity: he tells us that when he assumed clinical responsibility for his population of psychopaths at Belmont Hospital, 'we knew of no effective "treatment" for this condition and had to turn to the patients for help. Thus started the chain reaction of daily community meetings with all "patients" and staff present (approximately 100 people) information sharing, identification of problems, setting priorities, and shared decision-making, if possible reaching a consensus.

'One could say that this experiment was forced on us by the very fact of our ignorance, but might one not extrapolate and suggest that all "treatment" units might follow this pattern and attempt a fresh start, questioning all their preoccupations and prejudices, and involving the "patients" as people from the start?' (Jones, 1979).

Thus, out of ignorance was the therapeutic community movement born and in ignorance it has remained, for all the conferences, heated debates and learned papers on the subject. Maxwell Jones is as much a product of his time as a shaper of it. His blanket rejection of past attitudes as 'preoccupations and prejudices', his abandonment of the tradtional view of mental and behavioural disturbance as 'illness' requiring 'treatment', his reliance on the spontaneous utterances of the peer group rather than the knowledge and clinical experience of the staff, his insistence on the preeminent importance of *communication*, 'information sharing' and 'shared decision-making', all are symptomatic of the matrist, 'other-directed' rebellion of the present against the patrist, 'tradition-directed' past. That 'communication' and 'sharing' should be elevated to such a high status is typically to be expected of a peer-orientated society which has lost respect for traditional values and has experienced the progressive relativization of all canons and ethics. When authority is no longer ordained by the gods, one citizen's opinion becomes as good as the next, nothing can be known for certain, and communications ('The Media') emerge as the only means by which a culture can sustain itself. In the therapeutic community movement the importance of communication is a primary article of faith, whole therapeutic community pantheon being ruled by the god Mercury. Commenting on this contemporary obsession, de Mare (1972) writes: 'Marxism, Gestalt psychology, field theory, communication theory all have in common that it is neither the individual nor the group, neither the part nor the whole which is primary but it is the interstices of intercommunication, interaction and interrelation which play the primary part.' As Marshall MacLuhan, the high priest of the communications cult, put it, 'the medium is the message'. In some ways this is like saying that it is not the people on both ends of a telephone that matter but the lines connecting them together. As Dr J.K.W. Morrice (1979), himself a consultant at a therapeutic community in Scotland, dryly observes, 'Often, what we need is not better communication, but rather something better to communicate.' When, early in the history of communications technology, the first transcontinental telephone line was inaugurated in the United States, it was proudly boasted that now California could speak to Maine. 'Good', commented a wag, 'but what has California to *say* to Maine?'

While belief in the importance of communication is shared by most proponents of the therapeutic community movement, there are several other factors which are thought to be equally important; and in the absence of any 'adequate theory of psycho-social development', several attempts have been made to study therapeutic communities in action with the objective of defining their structure and function and establishing a systematic body of evidence and theory on which the movement may be based. One of the best known of these studies was undertaken by Rapoport (1960) and his colleagues at the Henderson Hospital in the late 1950s. They described four fundamental principles as characterizing the Henderson approach, and these have become hallowed with time. These are as follows:

(1) *Democratization*: an egalitarian attitude prevails together with a determination to 'flatten the hierarchical pyramid of power' and give patients more say in their treatment and a sense of greater responsibility for their lives.

(2) *Permissiveness*: rules and regulations, sanctions and constraints are minimized, and deviant behaviour is tolerated in the hope that it can be examined and its causes understood. As a result of this, 'social learning' is thought to occur which is believed to be beneficial both to the individual patient and his peers.

(3) *Reality confrontation*: as patients pass their days together their socially inept patterns of behaviour emerge. These are studied and analyzed by the group and reflected back to the patient in the hope that he will learn from the experience and develop more satisfactory modes of social adaptation.

(4) *Communalism*: emphasis is placed on 'sharing' and participating in all the activities of the community. Staff and patients mingle in a free and easy way, addressing one another by their christian names, eating together and taking it in turns to do duties and chores.

Another influential theoretician is Dr David H. Clark, who for many years has run a therapeutic community at Fulbourn Hospital, Cambridge. In his book, *Administrative Therapy*, Clark lists six characteristics which he believes should be present if a community is to be therapeutic:

(1) *Freeing of communications*: in traditional mental hospitals information flowed predominantly downwards from the top of the authority pyramid, from the Physician Superintendent through the doctors, matron and nurses to the inmates at the bottom. In a therapeutic community information must flow up the pyramid as much as down, and laterally as well.

(2) *Analysis of all events*: 'every happening is relevant,' comments Clark, 'and everyone may be able to gain something of value from understanding it better.'

(3) *Provision of learning experiences*: not only groups but workshops, outings, dances and parties are used as opportunities for identifying neurotic or ill-adpted modes of social functioning and for encouraging more appropriate modes.

(4) *Flattening of the authority pyramid*: this goes hand in glove with the 'democratization', 'information-sharing' and 'shared decision-making' generally agreed to be indispensable to the therapeutic community concept.

(5) *Role-examination*: 'all members of the community are called on to examine what they are doing, why, and how it affects others.'

(6) *The community meeting*: this is believed by Clark, and many other writers, to be the most important institution and instrument of the therapeutic community. 'Regularly, preferably daily, all members of the community assemble, usually for an hour. All matters of general concern are discussed. The general pattern is of great informality; anyone is free to speak, and the less direction by the nurse or doctor the better.' Invariably, a staff meeting should follow the community meeting. 'This is essential to allow the staff to work through the material and their own aroused feelings and also to work out policy problems'.

In a later book (1974) Clark reduces these six charateristics to three fundamentals: *activity* ('People kept unoccupied regress . . . Almost any activity is good; but purposeful, socially valued, rehabilitative activity is best.'), *freedom* ('Every bureaucracy will tend to limit people's freedom "for fear of what may happen", and the more this extends, the more people are crippled.'), and *responsibility*. To these he adds Maxwell Jones' concept of the therapeutic community as a 'living-learning situation': 'This is the idea that people learn best from the things that they experience and that the incidents of everyday life should be constantly used to allow people to learn a little more – about themselves and their emotions, about other people and their reactions, about what is possible and what is unacceptable in society.' This incorporates the idea popularized by John and Elaine Cumming in their influential book, *Ego and Milieu*, that, properly understood, crises, and the resolution of crises, provide opportunities for personal development.

It will be seen that there is a fair measure of overlap between these concepts and that, taken together, they represent the antithesis of Max Weber's 'rational bureau-cracy' with its hierarchy of offices, discipline, chains of command, and rules and regulations on which the traditional mental hospital was based. But, as a result of their influence, can it be said that mental hospitals have become more liberal, more humane institutions than they were? And, above all, have they become more truly *therapeutic*?

These questions are difficult to answer. To take the latter question first: various attempts have been made by social psychologists and psychiatrists to assess the efficacy of community therapy, but it has to be admitted that the results are entirely inconclusive. The problem is that a therapeutic community cannot be assessed like a drug. To begin with, it is not possible to design a *double-blind trial* (in which neither doctors nor patients know whether they are using the therapeutic agent to be tested or whether it is a pharmacolo-gically inert substance designed to look like it – a placebo) since everyone except the most severely psychotic patient knows whether or not he is in a therapeutic community. In the second place, there are too many variables which are difficult or impossible to control, such as the training and theoretical orientation of the staff, the tensions which may arise between individual doctors and nurses, the sort of atmosphere they create, their degree of commitment to the therapeutic community ideal, their personal ability to relate to patients, their sense of professional vocation and their enthusiasm for their work, and so on. Finally, there are inherent problems in assessing the progress of mental illness itself: it usually follows an unpredictable course, characterized by relapses and remissions which seem, as often as not, to be spontaneous and capricious in that they may not be related to any obvious changes in the patient's outer circumstances or in the treatment prescribed. Drug trials reveal most conclusive evidence of therapeutic efficacy when applied to a physical illness which has a known course and a predictable outcome. Since mental illness satisfies neither of these criteria it is not possible to establish beyond doubt whether a given psychotherapeutic approach is effective or not. On the face of it, the proposition advanced by Stuart Whiteley, Maxwell Jones' successor at the Henderson, that 'treatment milieu has important influences on treatment outcome' and that 'patient participation' in the treatment process is related to 'patient improvement' would seem unexceptionable, but no one has been able to prove it. Thus, at the present state of knowledge, for a psychiatric hospital to set up a therapeutic community is more an act of faith than of scientific wisdom.

However, in a number of hospitals this act of faith has been made. Have they become better, more humane institutions as a result? Here again the answer must be uncertain. Not many psychiatrists working in large institutions have followed Dennis Martin's example and turned their whole hospital into a therapeutic community. In most cases, one part of the hospital, a ward, or a 'villa' in the grounds, has been designated a therapeutic community while the rest of the hospital has continued to be run on conventional lines. These therapeutic community 'units' have varied greatly in quality depending on the training, experience and abilities of the people running them. Some of them are therapeutic communities in no more than name. Others have succeeded in implementing the basic principles and, despite ups and downs, have functioned approximately as their founders intended. But a number have disintegrated into anarchy and ended in disaster. All of them have tended to cream off doctors and nurses from other parts of the hospital, leaving these already understaffed areas, where the majority of patients are accommodated, worse off than they were before. Moreover, the influence of the therapeutic community ideology has spread beyond the confines of the officially designated 'unit' and has come to influence the way in which the administration of all mental hospitals is conducted. Thus, in the interest of 'democratization' and 'flattening the authority pyramid', the position of Physician Superintendent has been abolished and government by committee has been put in its place. This erosion of central medical authority has been associated, in a frighteningly large number of cases, with a decline in the quality of management and a breakdown in discipline; and this has resulted in a frank abuse of patients' welfare.

Overall, the evidence suggests that mental hospitals have not become the congenial centres of communal living-and-learning that the community therapists envisaged. On the contrary, something seems to have gone badly wrong with them. Before the impact of social psychiatry was felt, mental hospitals may have had an authoritarian structure, but they seldom gave rise to scandals involving staff in the gross ill-treatment and neglect of patients. Yet, the unpalatable fact is that in the past decade and a half no less than 16 psychiatric hospitals in Britain have been the subject of public inquiries provoked by serious allegations of cruelty and fraud against members of staff. In a number of instances the allegations have been upheld. (Rollin, 1981)

The long reports published after these expensive inquiries (e.g., the inquiry into the scandals at Normansfield Hospital, Middlesex, in 1978, cost £500,000 and processed nine million words of evidence) make dismal reading, filled as they are with nauseating details of mentally ill people being assaulted, robbed and forceably drugged by members of staff, who usually blame 'poor management' and 'lack of resources' for their crimes. These published examples are terrible enough, yet they probably represent but the tip of an iceberg. As one authority has commented: 'For every inquiry we have had there have probably been another half dozen hospitals which were just as bad.' (Yates, 1982). So endemic has this squalid problem become that a research team at the N.H.S. Management Centre at Birmingham University has been monitoring data recieved for all 212 of Britain's mental hospitals in an effort to detect by computer analysis those institutions where the next scandals are most likely to occur. According to a report appearing in *The Times* on April 6th, 1982, the team had selected the names of 15 hospitals where patients were in immediate danger of physical brutality, fraud, or wilful neglect at the hands of their protectors. It is not without irony that during the period that psychiatrists have extolled the therapeutic virtues of freedom, democracy and permissiveness, so many of their patients have been subjected to treatment that would appal the inmates and shame the custodians of a Dickensian workhouse.

To understand this paradox one must take into account the wider social forces by which psychiatry has been influenced since the second World War, when the struggle against fascism and the Hitlerian *Führer-prinzip* brought the father archetype into disrepute. The consequent increase in power of the mother archetype has resulted, as we have seen, in a rejection of authoritarian, puritanical values and their re-placement with egalitarian, permissive ones. A number of spokesmen gave eloquent testimony to this cultural swing, particularly in the 1960s when it was at its height. These included R.D. Laing, Herbert Marcuse, Thomas Szasz and Maxwell Jones, all of whom influenced the development of the therapeutic community movement. Laing himself foun-ded an idiosyncratic therapeutic community at Kingsley Hall in the East End of London, which was a direct embodiment of the self-indulgent, hippie drug sub-culture of the time: it was not concerned with social responsibility, adjustment or rehabilitation, but with the provision of an environment in which deluded and hallucinated individuals could have their 'trip', on the basis of the highly questionable assumption that it was good for them to do so. Herbert Marcuse's brand of

'Freudian Marxism' was particularly influential, tied up, as it was, with the student revolution of 1968. Marcuse declared our social ills to be caused by a failure to throw off the puritanical work ethic which had characterized the rise of capitalism and which still held our libido in chains. At the peak of the 60s' economic boom, he argued persuasively that drudgery and self-denial were no longer appropriate in an affluent society where the problem was not how to maintain subsistence but how to stimulate demand. Marcuse's message – to reject work and liberate Eros – was ideally suited to an adolescent, peer-orientated culture, with its collective wish to be indulged, looked after and kept irresponsible by an all-providing matrist state.

Marcuse's ideas were enthusiastically taken up by the younger social psychiatrists, some of whom began to express self-righteous views about the sickness of society and the need to overthrow the establishment. They came to regard the therapeutic community as a political instrument whose purpose should be to *convert* clients to the 'correct' liberated views in order to *change society*. The therapeutic community, they believed, must establish itself as an 'open system' in marked contrast to the 'closed system' operating in the wider community outside. As Maxwell Jones (1979) himself put it: 'By and large, everyone grows up in a relatively closed hierarchical system, and an attempt to create an open system strikes at the very roots of our culture.' A number of his followers argued that this should indeed be the objective of their movement – that it should actively seek to strike at the every roots of our culture. Their aim should be not only to destroy the power structure of the mental hospital but to subvert the established institutions of the state so that the whole nation could be turned into the great Therapeutic Community.

Not everyone took a sanguine view of these developments, however. Stuart Whiteley (1979), for example, maintained that the therapeutic community had become the victim of its own success: 'As the 1960s came to an end the freedom of expression and the increased tolerance for deviant behaviour, disinhibition and the general throwing-off of authoritarian controls resulted in a near anarchy in some European countries, and instituted a generalized threat to the stability of many societies. The therapeutic community, with its well-known goals of freedom of expression and replacement of authoritarian direction by democratic process, has come to be seen as a similar threat to the established order of the health services as perhaps never before. The myths of anarchy and loss of control have been resurrected, and there have been instances in both Germany and Holland where links between therapeutic communities and anarchist groups have been alleged and dealt with by police intervention.' Others have deplored the attack on the notion of leadership which the therapeutic community movement has fostered. As Dr J.K.W. Morrice (1979) observes: 'in the flight from authoritarianism, from medical dominance, and oppressive bureaucracy, many have called the whole idea of leadership into question. But it is a paradox worth remembering that a democracy needs good leadership and can be effectively maintained only from a position of power. The task of leadership in a therapeutic community is burdensome and exposed. But abdication or the "killing off of the father" solves nothing.' Morrice also has grave reservations about the over-enthusiastic adoption of permissiveness: 'even in our context of social learning, it is all too easy for permissiveness to drift into licence, self-indulgence and neglect, unless it is conscientiously linked to reality confrontation. Instances are not hard to find where a community's authority structure has been eagerly dismantled in the unrealistic expectation that a sense of responsibility would prevail and new oppertunities for therapy arise. But the result has been a descent into confusion and discontent, followed by a painful struggle for survival. Because power and authority have been widely abused (and not least in hosptials, schools, and institutes of correction), it does not follow that they can be abandoned. Nor is it true that the less authority we use and the more permissive we are, the more effective become our treatment methods. Much of the misunderstanding of so-called "progressive" methods stems from a reluctance of practitioners to acknowledge the importance of limit-setting and the necessity of sanctions. While discipline, to have any significance, must finally be self-discipline, it has to be learned.'

One fact which is often overlooked is that the preoccupation with democracy and the rejection of authority is not only congruent with the egalitarian notions of our time, but is also a consequence of the circumstance that the first serious presentation of therapeutic community principles (Rapoport, 1960) was derived from a community of psychopaths, who by the very nature of their condition invariably have severe problems with all forms of authority. Moreover, the prevalent obsession with establishing democracy at the expense of medical authority means that the business of the community too easily descends from therapy to politics, often with disastrous results. Anne Crozier (1979), writing of efforts to achieve greater democracy at the Marlborough Day Hospital, reports: 'There were several weeks of violent arguments with no one seeing anyone else's point of view, and some people disrupting the meetings by walking out, feeling that the decision would be taken against them anyway, without their views being taken into account. Finally, the dissenters did not come at all, and although the handful of people who did come all agreed with the motion [that committee meetings should be open to all patients who wished to participate] we felt we could not push it through without more support from the community.' It seems that an anti-authority bias, combined with an insistance on equal rights at all costs can induce more stress and more insecurity than the exercise of a benign oligarchy, such as that exercised by loving parents over their children or clinicians over their patients. As Plato insisted, preoccupation with an ever greater extention of democratic procedures is the road that leads to anarchy. Yet in those therapuetic communities that survive, the preoccupation persists: whatever the topic at issue, be it clinical, culinary or managerial, it is considered essential that every member of the community, be he doctor or patient, domestic or nurse, porter or odd-job man, should have an equal right to expound and expostulate. This guarantees an extraordinary waste of time and often gross managerial and clinical inefficiency.

The difficulties of running a therapeutic community, therefore, are formidable and there is serious reason to doubt that the movement has contributed much to the welfare of patients or staff in psychiatric units throughout the land. Nick Manning (1979), a sociologist and an authority on therapeutic community research, writes in a review of the evidence: 'It seems that staff dissatisfaction may be higher in the permissive atmosphere of a therapeutic community. There is also some agreement that therapeutic communities are exhausting for their leaders, and indeed have resulted in the breakdown of those in such positions.' Another authority, Dr Robert Hobson, who for years ran a therapeutic community called Tyson West Two at Bethlem Royal Hospital, goes further than Manning: 'The existence of Tyson West Two was maintained at a cost – a cost many of us are no longer willing or, indeed, able to pay . . . Serious psychological breakdowns occur, especially in prominent members of staff . . . Recurrent disturbances occur within the group, often with the extrusion of members, patients or staff, or by "acting-out" the unresolved persecution and destructiveness in diverse ways such as violence, suicide attempts and secret sexual relationships. Relief follows the departure of irritant members – but only for a time. The ritual of the "scapegoat" needs to be repeated.

'One, amongst many other less obvious but perhaps more serious effects, is a chronic state: a narrowing of the lives of staff members as well as long-stay patients, who become devoured by the dragon unit. Then, they remain relatively out of touch with the rest of the world in a state of what can be termed an "exclusive incestuous regression".

'There can be profound effects upon the families of staff,

who can either suffer intolerable involvement or, alter-
natively, envious exclusion.'

As a result of all he has been through, Hobson is
understandably critical of 'the current "progressive" fashion
in English mental hospitals, where so-called "community
methods" are being introduced widely. He is singularly
unimpressed by the results of research into the efficacy of
therapeutic communities: 'It is not merely a matter of
technical and methodological difficulties; we lack coherent
psychological theories which are needed to guide useful
research.' We just do not know what we are trying to do, he
says, for all that has been written about the subject: 'There
are too many words and too few facts.' The shattering
experience of running Tyson Ward Two, combined with his
knowledge of other such disastrous experiments, had led
Hobson to diagnose what he calls the *therapeutic community
disease*. Near the beginning of his paper describing the
condition he makes the shocking statement: 'My main
message is that we do harm. Much of what I have to say is
about failure and damage.'

Hobson is not alone in his disillusionment – though his
avowal of it is more frank than most – and it is not altogether
surprising that the enthusiasm which sustained therapeutic
communities throughout the 60s and 70s has begun to show
signs of flagging. Indeed, it seems likely that the whole
movement may go the same way as 'moral management' in
the nineteenth century, to be replaced by the conventional
doctor-patient relationship based on diagnosis and the
prescription of pills. If this is so it would be a sad outcome,
for there is much about the therapeutic community ideal
which is valuable and humane, and at least community
therapists allow people to talk about their sufferings and take
seriously what they have to say. The trouble is, as we have
seen, that the therapeutic community is as much a victim as it
is a product of its time. The permissive society too readily
becomes the lax society – loosening the ties of discipline can
result in self-indulgence and greed. The tolerance that

permits deviant behaviour to emerge within the therapeutic group has parallels with that which permits violent, anti-social behaviour to occur in the community at large.

Thus, at the heart of psychiatric progress during the last twenty years there lies a bitter irony: the very movement which came into existence to cure a medically induced illness has resulted in the production of another no less insidious process – 'institutional neurosis' has been replaced by the 'therapeutic community disease'.

Where does Withymead stand in relation to this irony? To what extent did it suffer from the therapeutic community disease? The answer is that for as long as the Champernownes remained firmly in control it did not. The reasons for the comparatively healthy state of Withymead were, I believe, as follows: (1) acceptance of the authority of Gilbert and Irene as charismatic leaders of the community, (2) the absense of all therapeutic group and community meetings (except the crucially important staff meeting), (3) the renunciation of any 'radical political intent', and (4) the fact the Withymead was a genuine community and not a synthetic one.

Although the *spirit* of Withymead was democratic – there was an absence of formality (though people were polite and considerate), christian names were used by everybody (though many habitually referred to Gilbert and Irene as 'Mr and Mrs C.') and one was unaware of any divisions of rank – the Centre was not run as a democracy. It was in fact an oligarchy ruled by Irene and Gilbert with the full co-operation of the staff. Administrative decisions were taken by the Trustees and the management committee, and clinical decisions by the staff meeting. Irene and Gilbert were privy to all deliberations; patients were privy to none. Yet, the kind of political battle that went on at the Marlborough Day Hospital to decide whether patients could attend staff meetings could not have occurred at Withymead as long as the Champernownes were in control because such matters were simply not open to dispute. This does not mean that the needs and wishes of patients were ignored. On the contrary, they were at the heart of the Centre's concern. But the staff believed that their knowledge, training and clinical experience qualified them to carry full responsibility for the welfare of their patients, and that to politicize these functions in the pursuit of democracy would be counter-productive, both clinically and administratively. It was of course inevitable that disputes should arise from time to time and that, on occasion, there should be major rows, but as long as the Champernownes were in charge the system worked well, largely because of their intimate and sensitive relationship with the community as a whole. While they did not deliberately seek to adopt a parental role within the community or to turn its members into their 'children', they nevertheless understood that the archetypal configuration on which Withymead was based was that of the extended family and that people would inevitably project the parental archetypes onto them, whether they wished it or not. They were careful, however, not to become devouring parents who sought to control their children in order to prevent them growing up. Instead, they tried to be good parents who wanted the children to get big and strong and go out into the world and make good. This sensitive use of authority guaranteed the community's stability, cohesiveness and ability to survive.

The most obvious difference between Withymead and other therapeutic communities was the absence of group therapy and daily community meetings. The Withymead community naturally gathered together every day in the dining room on five occasions – for breakfast, 'elevenses', lunch, tea and dinner – but these were informal occasions when people were free to talk about whatever they liked and to sit wherever and with whomever they pleased (except at the Champernownes' table, which was by invitation only). That formal group meetings never occurred – except for staff and management meetings – was deliberate policy. Irene was aware of the importance attributed to groups elsewhere, but she believed this to be fundamentally misguided, arguing, with Jung, that once an individual submerged himself in a group he 'rendered himself obsolete'. She was particlarly opposed to the mass community meetings held daily in therapeutic communities in hospitals, for she regarded them as thoroughly destructive, again quoting Jung in her support that 'the bigger the crowd the more negligible the individual becomes.' (*CW* 10, para. 503).

As the therapeutic community movement developed, Irene remained severely critical of it, comparing it with 'socialism, fascism, and the National Health Service' because she considered that it saw ultimate value not in terms of the individual but of the group. She was deeply suspicious of the whole trend of psychiatry in the mid-twentieth century because she saw it as compatible with the very *Zeitgeist* that was making people ill – namely, the view of the individual which conceived him as a statisical anomoly about which it is not possible to make any scientifically valid statement. She shared Jung's regret that 'we are all fascinated and overawed by statistical truths and large numbers and are daily apprised of the nullity of the individual personality, since it is not represented and personified by any mass organization.' (*CW* 10, para. 503).

The therapeutic approach practiced at Withymead was wholly opposed to this trend. What Withymead sought to promote was consciousness of one's own identity as a growing personality in one's own right, as distinct from conceiving oneself as a mere performer of a socially sanctioned role. Not that there was any hostility to the notion of social adaptation *per se*, but it was a question of correcting the balance. As Jung put it: 'I am fully aware that the individual must adapt himself to society, but I must stand up for the inalienable rights of the individual, because he alone is the carrier of life and because today he is perilously threatened by the levelling-off process. Even in the smallest group only that is acceptable which is accepted by the majority . . . a real and fundamental change in individuals . . . can only come from the personal encounter.' (*CW* 10, para. 516).

To Irene, the therapeutic community movement was essentially wrong-headed in its determined extraversion, its trendy anti-authoritarianism, and its view of individual men and women as being no more than the sum total of their social interactions. She knew that patients needed a secure environment in which to examine their inner lives and that this security depended on the community possessing structure and stability, with responsible authority clearly vested in Gilbert and herself, backed up by the staff and Trustees. She believed that this authority and structure protected the culture of the community, and that without these things culture must degenerate into barbarism. Marcuse's blanket rejection of the superego she saw as a subversive invitation to the barbarian in all of us to rise up and destroy civilization.

Certainly, Marcuse's equation of the superego with the puritan work ethic of early capitalism is fallible because possession of a superego is by no means confined to puritans and capitalists: it is a universal possession of all men and women and, as I have argued elsewhere, must have an archetypal basis in the collective unconscious of us all (Stevens, 1982). Its function in all cultures is to control the impulsive actions of the individual in order to preserve the social cohesiveness of the group. To blame puritanism and capitalism for individual libidinal restraint is an extreme form of cultural parochialism. Moreover, if the Freudian incrimination of the superego as the manufacturer of neurosis was correct (i.e. that it caused symptoms by repressing legitimate libidinal demands) then the remedy advocated by Marcuse (that of overthrowing the superego in the interests of complete libidinal freedom) would be worse than the disease, for it would lead to collective anarchy and individual despair.

The language of the therapeutic community movement was no less uncongenial to Irene than many of its ideas, particularly when it used the terminology of cybernetics and 'social engineering'. She found discussion of individual patients as units in a cybernetic system repugnant, as she did the notion that a residential centre for the mentally ill should be conceived as an 'open system' which 'exchanges materials with its environment' and has a 'human throughput' ('Like Himmler talking about Auschwitz') – the approach which Mansell Pattison (1976) has dignified with the uneuphonious term 'psycho-social systems therapy'. Conceptualizing their work in such terms, she believed, could only brutalize therapists and dehumanize their patients.

Furthermore, clinical experience had taught her that there were many patients who could never do well in an 'open system' where emphasis was on treatment in a group – i.e., introverts, the inarticulate, and those who, by virtue either of the nature of their illness (e.g. severe depression or psychosis) or the nature of their personality, cannot take an interest in other peoples' problems or allow them to take an interest in their own. But her main objection to group treatments was that they focus attention on processes going on outside the individual patient rather than inside the psyche, on the behavioural manifestations of his neurosis rather than its intra-psychic roots. She caricatured the activities of group therapists as 'Persona-fudging', arguing that time spent manipulating personality traits and neurotic symptoms was time wasted because it could be better spent in treating the unconscious processes from which the traits and symptoms were derived. This is not to say that she devalued the therapeutic potential of a group. On the contrary, she held it in high esteem; but she believed that it could be most successfully utilized when the group was permitted to exert its healing influence *indirectly* as at Withymead, the individual participating intimately in the life of the community whose therapeutic responsibility was vested in the staff meeting. This had the added virtue of protecting the confidentiality of clinical information which Irene thought far too readily abused in the conventional group therapeutic setting. At

Withymead, personal details relating to patients were strictly confined to the psychotherapists and art therapists who attended the staff meeting, thus ensuring that only those in a position of professional responsibility to the patient were acquainted with confidential material relating to his private life. As a result, leaks were unlikely to occur and patients could rest assured that their confidences would not be betrayed. When it became necessary to 'feed back' information to the patient as a therapeutic exercise it was done individually, never in the presence of other patients, and with considerably more tact than is customary in therapeutic communities.

Withymead's renunciation of any political intentions was in line with Irene's view of the therapeutic role of the community and was a further point of difference from other therapeutic communities. Naturally, Irene considered that society played a role in making people mentally ill, but she considered that Withymead could best help to get them better not by 'changing society' but by compensating for society's deficiencies. By providing the patient with more therapeutic milieu than other social conditions afforded, Withymead hoped to bring about developments within his personality which would help him to cope more effectively with those conditions when he returned to them. The deficiencies of Western society were, of course, numerous and profound, but it was the only society we had, and instead of 'striking at its roots' one should provide people with a therapeutic alternative where they might learn to live more creatively within the prevailing social context.

This was surely a more realistic approach than that adopted by those idealists who wished to transform the nation into One Great Therapeutic Community. Indeed, the history of a number of therapeutic communities, Withymead included, suggests that political activity is incompatible with the successful practice of psychotherapy. I am aware that this view will be anathema to those who see politics as the central issue of all human affairs, including mental health, but the psychotherapist needs to create an atmosphere of loving acceptance and trust if he is to facilitate the individuation process in his patients. Political action, on the other hand, creates factionalism, partizanship and an atmosphere of mutual hostility and recrimination which is less conducive to the quest for wholeness that it is to the quest for influence and power. Wholeness is about integration not schism and dissent. It is about transcending opposites rather than forcing them apart. Whereas politics demands inflation of the ego, individuation grants supremacy to the Self.

Thus, in its apolitical way, Withymead sought, within the confines of its territory and the limits of its resources, to reverse the titanic forces at work in our society which serve to induce that sense of 'alienation' in individual existence which Jung termed 'the general neurosis of our age' ('About a third of my cases are not suffering from any clinically definable neurosis, but from the senselessness and aimlessness of their lives. I should not object if this were called the general neurosis of our age.' (*CW* 16, para. 83). In place of the vast organizations which submerge modern men and women, the huge cities, the inhuman architecture, the enormous corporations and bureaucracies which regiment the lives of whole armies of unrelated and largely anoymous individuals, Withymead offered a homogeneous group consisting of a small number of people, all engaged in creative work in close association with each other. In the intimacy of its social organization, Withymead resembled not only an extended family but a small tribe or clan of the type of human beings have lived in since our species began. Withymead thus satisfied the archetypal nostalgia that all of us share for life in such small, intimate associations of people, and this goes far to explain its compelling attractiveness. It was the same nostalgia as that whose pervasive influence led many young people in the 1960s to 'drop out' of the wider social structure to form small communities of their own, a phenomenon which writers like Buckmaster Fuller and Marshall McLuhan described as a more towards 'retribalization'.

The power of this nostalgia is not hard to understand when one considers that for 99 per cent of our existence as a species (i.e. right up to the discovery of agriculture and animal husbandry), we lived in small tribal bands consisting of between 50 and 100 individuals. The size of these communities could never have grown much bigger than this for economic reasons, for their members had to support themselves by hunting and by gathering roots and berries over considerable distances. To feed the population of even a small town by these methods would have required a huge territory that pre-agricultural men had no means of patrolling, exploiting or defending. Farming and the domestication of animals began only 10,000 years ago – a matter of days in terms of the life span of our species – and it inaugurated the most dramatic ecological revolution in the history of our planet. It is this portentous event that Judeo-Christianity has symbolized as The Fall. From being dependent on what God provided, we now discovered His secrets and began to provide for ourselves. From being small tribal bands in a state of ecological balance with all other species of flora and fauna, living off relatively large portions of territory, we now began to form much larger communities – villages, towns, cities and nation states – sustained by much smaller, intensively farmed patches of territory. As a consequence, the ecological balance tipped increasingly in our favour to the detriment of our fellow occupants of the planet.

But what determines the archetypal structure of the contemporary human psyche, no less than that of our pre-agricultural forebears, is the state of affairs which prevailed at critical moments in our evolution – what ethologists call the 'environment of evolutionary adaptedness'. Towns and cities represent entirely new modes of adaptation for our species: they formed no part of our 'environment of evolutionary adaptedness', and we are less at home in them, archetypally speaking, than in intimate communities no more than 50 or 100 strong. There can be little doubt that an essential part of our archetypal endowment comprises a powerful imperative to live as a bonded member of such a community, and that our urban ills of crime, violence, psychopathy and neurosis are directly attributable to frustration of this basic archetypal need.

It seems reasonable to conclude, therefore, that for a community to possess therapeutic influence it needs to go some way towards fulfilling the archetypal demand for intimate relationship within the context of a small and enduring group. The success and importance of Withymead lie in the fact that it went further in this direction than any other foundation bold enough to claim the name of 'therapeutic community'.

Chapter V

Man, Woman and Creativity

Irene maintained that the survival of Withymead depended on balance – balance between authority and freedom, between therapists and patients, between old and young, between income and expenditure, and, above all, between what she invariably referred to as Man and Woman, by which she meant more than mere sexual equality, believing that the community itself inhered masculine and feminine principles which had to be kept closely related and in harmony with one another. Once when Robert Hobson was lecturing in London about his own therapeutic community, Tyson West Two, Irene was in the audience. In the discussion which followed, the question of balancing freedom with authority was raised. Suddenly, Hobson turned to Irene and said: 'Do you believe that someone has to have the last word in a community?' Her reply was immediate: 'Yes, I do,' she said. 'And the last word should be from a man.' This caused an outcry from some of the women present but, unperturbed, Irene waited for the hubbub to subside and went on: 'There is a big "but" to this. The man must be a very special kind of man, one who is deeply related to the community and capable of listening to its soul, which is feminine.'

Reporting this exchange in one of her own lectures, Irene continued: 'The man's outer authority will only destroy the community if his anima does not catch the deep feminine rhythm and inner authority by which the group lives and moves and has its being. The basis of community life is feminine and organic. The group is an organism and man can only administrate creatively if he listens with his inner ear to the soul of the community as to a woman.'

The 'very special kind of man' Irene had in mind, of course, was Gilbert, whose sensitivity admirably equipped him for this role. Though he may not have defined his position in the community in quite the same terms as Irene, he certainly shared her belief that 'woman is basically different from man biologically, psychologically, historically, socially, and personally' and that a man and woman worked most harmoniously together if they divided and shared their labours in a manner best suited to their natural gifts. As Irene's description of his function makes clear, he was no male chauvinist: like her he was a sexual egalitarian. But they did not commit the current fallacy of confusing equality with sameness: both believed in an equality which respected the essential differences between man and woman and which celebrated the rich way in which these different qualities complement one another. And both agreed that it was the polarity between the masculine and feminine principles at work within the community which produced the tension and released the energy essential for creative life.

In sharing these views, Irene and Gilbert displayed themselves as good Jungians. Contrary to the assertions of some critics, Jung did not hold that the masculine principle was in any way 'superior' to the feminine: he saw both as complementary, interdependent, and homeostatically balanced, and he belived both to be at work in every individual, regardless to his or her biologically assigned sexual identity. Sigmund Freud was of a similar opinion: 'All human beings,' he wrote, 'because of their bisexual constitution and crossed inheritance, unite male and female characteristics.' It is a view which is justified by experiments which demonstrate that both male and female behaviour patterns are 'programmed' into individual members of a number of different species and that either pattern of behaviour may be elicited by manipulating male or female hormone concentrations at critical periods of development. It also coincides with the Taoist concepts of Yin and Yang, those fundamental masculine and feminine principles which the ancient Chinese held to permeate all reality and to be present and active in both men and women. As a biologist Irene was in no doubt that the essential differences between man and woman were directly attributable to their different evolutionary history: woman the home-maker and life-giver, committed to the 'Eros of relationship', man the hunter-warrior, defender and provider, ruled by the 'Logos of experience'. This was one of the central convictions of her life. Although it was an unfashionable view to espouse, and sometimes got her into trouble with feminists, it is nevertheless one which has a sound basis in biological fact, which I have attempted to demonstrate elsewhere (Stevens, 1982). Irene was in broad agreement with generalizations about sex-typical functions made by the great American anthropologist Margaret Mead, who also attributed them to a biological foundation. Mead maintained that in all cultures a woman's activities are characteristically centred on her own person and her immediate environment: she is concerned with making clothes and utensils, with preparing and dispensing food, and so on. The man, on the other hand, uses his superior strength, aggression and visuo-spatial abilities to cooperate and compete with other men and animals and to manipulate materials, such as stone, wood and metal, to further his fascination with the external environment and his desire to exploit it. In the evolutionary history of our species, man has depended for his security and sustenance on the environment; woman for hers (and for that of her children) on man, and this crucial differentiation of function has engraved itself on culture no less than on our genes. Mead's distinction is in accord with the receptive, centripetal, gestative qualities of Yin and the aggressive, out-going, dynamic attributes of Yang. It is also broadly in line with the distinction made by Talcott Parsons (1955) between the *instrumental* role of fathers and the *expressive* role of mothers. Parsons argued that in practically all human cultures the father has a centrifugal orientation (i.e. towards society and the outside world) in contrast to the mother's centripetal concern (i.e. with home and family), and that our culture is no exception, despite attempts in some quarters to change it. Through his instrumental function the father represents society to the family and his family to society, he encourages the development of skills necessary for successful adult adaptation, and facilitates the transition of the child from home to the world at large. Through her expressive function, on the other hand, the mother continues to provide the emotional support and security which enables the child to go out and meet the world's challeges.

That men and women are constitutionally geared to perform different social and emotional roles does not rule out the possibility that men can display expressive capacities or women instrumental ones. Thus, Irene sometimes took the initiative in Withymead's practical affairs while Gilbert, as I discovered, was capable of forming warm, intimate relationships with members of the community. But the distinctions made by Jung, Mead, Parsons and others refer to *typical* dispositions and modes of functioning which are the hallmarks of archetypal expression. It is undeniable that women can perform the same roles as men, but that is not necessarily what they are best equipped to do. Irene was sympathetic to the egalitarian aspirations of the woman's movement, but she considered that feminists of the more militant kind did their sex a disservice by their strident assertion of the Animus (Jung's term for the masculine component in women) and their insistence on the need for women to compete with men on masculine terms. She saw that women had to find their own *feminine* way forward socially, intellectually and in the professions and the arts, that it was inappropriate for them to conform to masculine patterns of behaviour. And she believed that the way forward could only be discovered if women turned inwards and took the lead from their own feminine unconscious. 'We women at present have to tread a path to a great extent prepared by man in a masculine world.'

she said. 'We often lose our way. Only after patient receptive work with the unconscious can we rediscover and relive at the more conscious level the deep symbols of woman's essence of "being", related to the masculine side of our personality.'

This was no mere piece of rhetoric. Irene saw herself in the vanguard of this advance. She believed with Jung that 'modern woman stands before a great cultural task which means perhaps the beginning of a new era.' On her visits to Zurich she worked intensively on her dreams, phantasies and spontaneous paintings with Toni Wolff and has recorded the result in her memoir (Champernowne, 1980). She saw her work at Withymead as the sort of achievement that a modern woman could accomplish through the use of feminine understanding and the feminine genius for relationship and the formation of intimate community, thus correcting the souless anonymity which masculine technology had produced in the world. She lectured about this in Zurich at the C.G. Jung Institute: 'It is in the creation of the conscious community with man that I believe woman will find her new and satisfying destiny, a community small enough to support individual consciousness but large enough to give her scope for life.' She argued that if, through her desire for emancipation and equality, the modern woman loses touch with 'the archetypal woman within herself' then she will inevitably fail in her primary function as founder of family and community and all humankind will be impoverished: 'inside ourselves we belong to the generations and to the creating of community, and we must not seek the logos principle as isolated, emaciated pseudo-men, working in the outer world and returning to bed-sitters or empty flats. We must find a way to relate to the outer world as full-blooded women within ourselves.'

Irene saw woman's major biological need as the need to settle, to root herself, to found a home – preferably with a man's assistance: 'It is by the creation of new life at a fixed point that woman in her native femininity creates a centre, a small community, a family. If it is successful other families adhere to it, and a larger community or social group appears for purposes of protection and work. And the original rootedness of the core of this larger community and its success lies also, I think, in the fact that the feminine life is continuous: mother, daughter, daughter, mother, both in one – past, present and future. Man's relation to it is the factor that relates it to the bigger world and prevents it from growing in on itself in a destructive and psychologically incestuous way. There is instability in a home with little feminine influence. But there is deadness if there are only women, as well as outer insecurity.'

Her understanding of feminine psychology was fundamental to her understanding of the nature of the community which she and Gilbert founded: 'Woman starts life, unlike man, with one of her own kind – her mother. She is born into a primary feminine community of two, which is homogeneous and continuous, the woman being at one and the same time daughter to her mother and mother to her daughter.' Into this continuous stream of feminine life 'man comes almost as an intruder' and woman has to come out of this feminine stream 'in order to meet man in her lover or husband and create man in her son'. Forty years of analytic work had taught her that if a woman 'is rooted in her feminine matrix at the archetypal level . . . from there she is able to meet man on the right terms, secure enough in herself to leave him free and to be a free woman.' Woman, therefore, must become conscious of her own ground and unashamedly stand on it: 'the woman's base must be fully under her control and she must have the right to say "no admittance without permission" to the man and his world . . . We must retain our feminine intergrity and plan our community life so that we can retain it, even in a home.'

Although many people saw Irene's role at Withymead as that of matriarch, it was a view which she did not share, for she believed that matriarchies had never existed and could never survive. Here again she would appear to be in agreement with Margaret Mead who has declared: 'all the claims so glibly made about societies ruled by women are nonsense. We have no reason to believe they ever existed . . . men everywhere have been in charge of running the show . . . men have been the leaders in public affairs and the final authorities at home' (quoted by Goldberg, 1973). Irene accepted that this state of affairs was not due to 'male chauvinism' but represented the archetypal order of things. 'Men are better at authority than women,' she said. 'They always have been and they always will be. And that is why the last word in a community should rest with a man. I have no difficulty in recognizing masculine authority, provided it is tempered with feminine wisdom.'

At Withymead, the 'continuous stream of feminine life' was represented by Irene and the intimate bonds she formed with her younger and most trusted colleagues like Joanna Hogg, Molly Kemp, Elizabeth Colyer and Mary Pye. During the 1950s, Joanna became particularly important in the life of Withymead. An intelligent woman of deep integrity, Joanna joined the community soon after the formation of the Withymead Trust and a year or so before the arrival of her brother, the architect Ben Belton. Following the break-up of her marriage in her early thirties, she had moved to Exeter to work as a children's officer and train as a psychiatric social worker while analyzing with Irene. Always an adept talent spotter, Irene recognized her quality and encouraged her to join the Withymead staff as soon as a vacancy occurred.

To begin with, Joanna worked as a PSW, but it was not before she found herself slipping into a therapeutic role in relation to her patients. Irene did nothing to discourage this, for she realized that Joanna was a natural psychotherapist. In other institutions this would have been considered reprehensible, but at Withymead Joanna's psychotherapeutic contribution was appreciated while, at the same time, it was monitored by the staff meeting.

Gilbert and Irene found Joanna a source of great comfort

and support. They came to love her dearly and, as time wore on, to regard her as a daughter. Increasingly, Irene saw her as a possible heir apparent, as one who could carry the 'feminine stream' of the community's life on into the next generation. It worried Irene that Joanna had no formal analytic training, but she felt sure that this could be corrected in the future, if the necessary money could be found.

For her part, Joanna revered Irene and Gilbert and was utterly committed to the Withymead way of life. Like Irene, she was childless, and agreed that 'this cheating of the body' as Irene put it 'must be compensated for somehow', but in a way that did not betray the archetypal reality of feminine life. She agreed with Irene that there was such an entity as 'feminine consciousness' and that this could be best expressed within the context of community.

What did they mean by 'feminine consciousness'? Essentially, they believed the awareness of a well individuated woman to be more intuitive, more empathic, more touched by feeling than the consciousness of men, which they saw as more dispassionate, more objective, abstract and emotionally detached. They shared the Jungian view of masculine conciousness as being ruled by the Logos principle and feminine consciousness by Eros: as Jung put it, 'It is the function of Eros to join whereas Logos cuts and clarifies'. The masculine principle, with its penchant for abstraction, differentiation and division, is exemplified by the famous definition advanced by Rene Descartes (1596–1650) of his own existence in terms of his thinking function ('Cogito ergo sum') and by his division of the universe into two seperate entities, mind and matter. Karl Stern, a writer who had a profound influence on Irene's thinking in later years, has argued that the energy released by Descartes' great fission made modern science and technology possible. In his remarkable book, *The Flight From Woman*, Stern writes: 'as a *methodological basis* for the exact sciences, Cartesian dualism was a prerequisite. Where it goes beyond that, however, it develops into a disastrous fallacy. For one thing, it implies a fearful estrangement. Just think of nature as nothing but a huge, vastly extended soul-less machine which you can take apart experimentally and analyze mathematically, which you can run – but with which you have lost all oneness!' (Stern's italics). Like Stern, Irene believed that 'feminine consciousness' alone was capable of restoring this oneness.

In my book, *Archetype: A natural history of the Self*, I have suggested that the Cartesian split was an expression of the evolutionary tendency which has characterized our species in recent centuries to make increasing use of the left side of our brains at the expense of the right. Neurological research has established that the left cerebral hemisphere is primarily concerned with the use of language and abstract, analytical thinking, while the right hemisphere is more involved in synthesizing sensory data into percepts. In line with these findings, Arthur Deikman, of the Austen Riggs Medical Centre, has characterized the left hemisphere as 'active' inasmuch as it is concerned with *doing*, with manipulating the environment and 'making a dent', whereas the right hemisphere is 'receptive' in that it monitors events as they happen, and perceives the world as it is rather than subjecting it to some purpose or design. Broadly speaking, therefore, the left hemisphere would appear to mediate the Yang functions of Taoist philosophy while the right hemisphere is the mediator of Yin. The Californian psychologist, Robert Ornstein, has made a comparable distinction between the 'rational' functions of the left hemisphere and the 'intuitive' functions of the right, arguing that the thought processes characteristic of Western culture (i.e. logical, analytic, directed thinking) predominantly make use of the left hemisphere, while Eastern thought (which is more diffuse, synthetic and tolerant of paradoxes) is more dependent on the right. Another authority, Joseph Bogen (1969), has attributed 'propositional' thinking to the left hemisphere and 'appositional' thinking to the right, equating this distinction to that traditionally made in everyday speech between 'reason' and 'emotion', the 'head' and the 'heart', agreeing with Pascal's dictum that 'Le coeur a ses raisons que la raison ne connaît pas'. Neurological investigation has further indicated that the right hemisphere is paramount in the activities of dreaming, phantasizing, musical appreciation, the use of visual imagery and artistic imagination.

It seems that in all human cultures, Eastern cultures included, the left hemisphere is dominant over the right, but in some cultures it is more dominant than in others. In our own culture, ever since the Renaissance, stress has been laid increasingly on the importance of left hemispheric functions. Encouragement of these functions begins early in the life of every one of us, since all Western primary schools emphasize the need for gaining proficiency in the three Rs (writing, reading and arithmetic). Although right-sided activities such as art, music and dancing are given a place in the curriculum, much less time is allocated to them than to left-sided disciplines, and at times when money is short, it is the right-sided activities which are invariably cut back. Education reflects the ruling obsessions of society, and, as I have argued, a culture like ours which stresses the importance of rational, analytic processes rather than aesthetic, synthetic ones, and which places a higher value on material achievement that on symbolic expression, inevitably promotes what I have termed 'left hemispheric imperialism'.

This, like all forms of imperialism, is an essentially masculine concern. It took a woman of Irene's intuitive calibre to see through it and prescribe the antidote. This is not to say that she knew anything about the possible neurological aspects of the problem, because she did not: her insight came entirely from her own intuitive wisdom and from her work with Jung and with Toni Wolff. She understood that the growing trend in our society towards development of the masculine ability to use abstractions, concoct theories and exploit the material world for selfish ends had been associated with a corresponding neglect, even repression, of the feminine values of compassion and empathy and of feminine reverence for life.

Irene saw woman as more closely identified with living reality than man, more committed to nature and more involved in it. For her, 'woman in her full nature' was 'personal and concrete' and 'primarily concerned with being': she knows, feels and experiences 'as an organism'. As Stern wrote: 'the four-week cycle of ovulation, the rhythmically alternative tides of fertility and barrenness, the nine months of gestation which can be neither prolonged nor hurried – all this ties woman deeply to the life of nature, to the pulse beat of the Cosmos. What Goethe calls the law of *systole* and *diastole* enters more into her life than into man's.' (Stern's italics).

In later life, Irene was much taken by Stern's distinction between two kinds of knowledge, which he termed 'scientific knowledge' and 'poetic knowledge': 'Simple self-observation shows that there exist two modes of knowing. One might be called "externalization", in which the knowable is experienced as an *ob-ject*, a *Gegen-stand*, something which stands opposed to me; the other might be called "internalization", a form of knowledge by sympathy, a "*feeling with*" – a union with the knowable. Of this distinction there is no doubt. Whether the terms "analysis", "scientific knowledge", "discursive reason" are perfectly synonymous or refer only to phenomena with a common denominator does not concern us here. The same is true about the terms "intuition", "poetic knowledge", "knowledge by connaturality". The only thing of importance in the present context is a basic duality in the mode of knowing. (Stern's italics, *op. cit.*, pp. 42–3). Stern linked the polarity between scientific knowledge (discursive reasoning) and poetic knowledge (intuition) with the polarity of the sexes between maleness and femaleness, and argued that 'human knowledge seems to have the greatest chance to arrive at truth when the two . . . are in perfect balance.' Such a view is not only compatible with the profound truths of ancient Taoism but with the findings of modern neurology and the theories of C.G. Jung. Indeed, Jung's whole approach to psychotherapy would appear to have been designed to liberate the intuitive, symbol-forming, 'feminine' right hemisphere from the inhibitory dominance of the rational, discursive 'masculine' left, though Jung could not have known this because understanding of cerebral lateralization was still too rudimentary up to the time of his death in 1961.

Jung's emphasis on the therapeutic importance of dreams, active imagination and free expression through the arts arose from his insight that many of the psychological ills that afflicted modern men and women were due to the one-sided rationalism of our culture. He presented this diagnosis in his book, *Modern Man in Search of a Soul*. Modern man had lost his soul in the sense that he was 'all ego', his consciousness was detached from the compensatory influence of unconscious functions. Neurosis, in Jung's view, was 'self-division', 'the suffering of a soul that has lost its meaning'. The purpose of therapy must be to heal the split, to re-establish the natural dialogue between conscious and unconscious, between the ego and the Self, and thus restore the integration of the personality as a whole.

Because of this therapeutic stance, Jung has been accused of 'obsurantism' and 'anti-rationalism'. In fact, he was anti-rational only insomuch as rational consciousness was overweening. What he advocated was not the overthrow of reason or its replacement with mysticism, but the attainment of psychic equilibrium between rational and irrational functions. He believed that this balance could be achieved through mobilizing the *transcendent function* of symbols. In neurological terms, therefore, he was not proposing that left hemispheric dominance should be supplanted by dominance of the right, but that, through the transcendent function, the activities of both hemispheres should be brought into a state of more equitable and harmonious mutuality. 'Disalliance with the unconscious', he wrote, 'is synonymous with loss of instinct and rootlessnes. If we can successfully develop that function which I have called transcendent, the disharmony ceases and we can then enjoy the favourable side of the unconscious. The unconscious then gives us all the encouragement and help that a bountiful nature can shower upon a man.' (*CW* 7, paras 195–60). In his clinical work Jung found that this state of balance occurred when paralled use was made of two techniques: these he called 'the way of creative formulation' (i.e. phantasy, dreams, active imagination, symbols and art) and 'the way of understanding' (i.e. intellectual concepts, verbal formulations, conscious awareness and insight). Writing of these two approaches, Jung declared: 'One tendency seems to be the regulating principle of the other; both are bound together in a compensatory relationship . . . aesthetic formulation needs understanding of the meaning, and understanding needs aesthetic formulation. The two supplement each other to form the transcendent function.' To facilitate the transcendent function, he wrote, 'you choose a *dream*, or some other *fantasy-image*, and concentrate on it by simply catching hold of it and looking at it. You can also use a *bad mood* as a starting point, and then try to find out what sort of fantasy-image it will produce, or what image expresses this mood. You can fix the image in mind by *concentrating your attention*. Usually it will alter, as the mere fact of contemplating it animates it. The alterations must be carefully *noted down* all the time, for they reflect the psychic processes in the unconscious background, which appear in the form of *images* consisting of conscious memory material. In this way conscious and unconscious are untied.' (*CW* 14, para. 706. *My italics*). Jung's clinical intuition is in agreement with the neurological facts: dreams, phantasy-images, bad moods, all are associated with activity in the limbic system and the right cerebral hemispheres, while concentrating attention, contemplating and writing down are all left hemispheric functions. 'In this way conscious and unconscious are united'. So are the left and right hemispheres.

Dr Ernest Rossi, a Jungian analyst from Malibu, California, has suggested that the universal religious practices of mankind – prayer, ritual, the use of mantras and mandalas –

possess the same purpose as Jung's therapeutic techniques, namely the promotion of bilateral hemispheric integration. This notion is particularly persuasive in view of the finding by Dr Bernard Glueck (1975) and others that EEG records show greater synchrony between both sides of the brain in subjects practicing transcendental meditation.

Mobilization of the transcendent function is, then, the key to individuation, and it was this goal that Withymead was uniquely designed to achieve. Irene's insistence on upholding the feminine nature of the community, leaving political and economic administration to men, her provision of facilities for the practice of 'right hemispheric' activities such as painting, pottery, clay modelling, dance, music, and mime, the warm, loving acceptance with which each member of the community was treated and the honour with which his creative productions were received, meant that the whole life of the Centre was geared to heal self-division and permit self-completion. If there was one crucial principle underlying all that went on at Withymead it was respect for the individual Self and its intensely personal emanations in dreams, phantasies and art; and if deliberate efforts were made to bring masculine and feminine principles into balance both within the community and in the individual men, women and children of whom the community was composed, it was with the specific intention to promote creativity, to activate the transcendent function, and set the individuation process in motion.

Chapter VI

Therapy Through the Arts

Art therapy is not a modern invention. 'If men of worth did know what delight [art] breedeth,' wrote Nicholas Hilliard, Court painter to Queen Elizabeth I, 'how it removeth melancholy, avoideth evil occasions, putteth passions of grief or sorrow away, cureth rage and shorteneth the times, they would never leave until they had attained in some good measure or more their comfort.' Writing more than 300 years later, Jung made much the same observation: 'A patient needs only to have seen once or twice how much he is freed from a wretched state of mind by working at a symbolical picture and he will aways turn to this means of release whenever things go badly with him.' Recognition of the comfort that the practice of art can bring must go back to the Lascaux caves and earlier. What is a relatively recent phenomenon, however, is the systematic use of art in the treatment of patients in hospital.

In England it was begun in the 1930s by a painter called Adrian Hill, who had himself languished in a tuberculosis sanitorium and claimed that he had painted his way out of illness and out of hospital. After his recovery, he visited sanitoria all over the country teaching patients to paint. It was as a result of Hill's influence that Gilbert Champernowne offered his services on the outbreak of war to teach woodwork and pottery to psychiatric patients in a military hospital in North London. In developing the use of art therapy at Withymead, the Champernownes made use of these early hospital experiments, combining the experience gained from them with what Irene had learned about the therapeutic importance of the arts from her work with Jung and Godwin Baynes.

At the Champernownes' invitation, Adrian Hill visited Withymead early in its history. He brought with him a large folder of pictures painted by his tubercular patients. Irene was particularly interested by a picture painted by a young man who had lost a lung and who was very seriously ill. It was of a small sailing boat on a wide river which wound its way into the distance through orchards and fields. The boat was approaching a gigantic rock, shaped like a woman, which reared its mass above the river bank and cast a sinister shadow through which the fragile craft would have to pass in order to reach the light and freedom of the open countryside beyond. Adrian Hill viewed this picture primarily as an accomplished exercise in composition, but, needless to say, it was its symbolical implications which caught Irene's imagination. She asked about the artist's background and learned that he had a disastrous relationship with his mother and that his illness invariably took a turn for the worse when this formidable lady visited him in hospital. Irene suggested that the picture symbolized this state of affairs and that the patient needed to be free of his destructive mother complex if he was to get well and resume a normal life. Hill was interested but said that he did not consider it appropriate for him to 'interpret' his patients' pictures for fear that it would damage the artistic imagination that went into creating them.

Irene knew he was right. 'Interpretation' had to be sensitive, subtle and appropriate were it not to do more harm than good. In this regard she and her team of therapists always proceeded with great caution, though Irene's impulsive enthusiasm sometimes led her to put her foot in it, as it did, subsequently, over this very painting. The incident occurred some years later at one of the first art therapy conferences to be held in London, just after the war. In a discussion group attended by Adrian Hill, Irene mentioned the little ship sailing under the shadow of the menacing rock, explaining her feeling that in painting it the young man had externalized his conflict with is mother and given himself hope that it could be resolved. Sensing the interest of her audience, Irene turned to Hill and asked him what had become of the patient. Hill replied that he had recovered and had himself become an art therapist, and nodding towards a pale young man in the corner of the room, he said, 'He's here with us now.'

Embarrassed, Irene apologised for speaking so openly. 'But it was a gallant little ship,' she said, 'and knowing that it has come through its ordeal gladdens my heart. I've carried in my mind the memory of your picture, and it moves me to meet you at last'. The man was unperturbed. Irene was right about the picture, he said, and it had indeed represented an important moment in his life.

The difference between the approaches of Adrian Hill and Irene to patients' paintings was radical, and it was reflected in the different attitude adopted to art therapy in conventional hospitals as distinct from Withymead. The value of 'occupation' in the treatment of psychiatric patients had been recognized since the time of Pinel and the Tukes, but the Champernownes stressed in addition to this the profound importance of the symbolical dimension which, in their view, elevated art therapy above the level of a mere diversion. Not that the diversional role of such activity is to be despised: work, especially creative work, whether done in solitude or in participation with others, clearly brings its own rewards. But Irene and Gilbert considered that it failed as therapy if it did not grant due recognition to the healing power of the symbols which patients produced. The work of Adrian Hill and others in sanitoria and hospitals was admirable as far as it went, for it demonstrated clearly that creative activity was itself beneficial, but it would not do for Withymead because it neglected the transcendent function: it did not set out to activate the compensatory, homeostatic potential of the unconscious.

Withymead's studios were conceived as gymnasia for the

soul where one could develop aspects of the Self that one had never used before. Here one was encouraged in Jung's phrase 'to experiment with one's own nature', to discover new forms of perception, understanding and communication, to enter entirely new modes of experience, and thus to grow beyond one's neurotic, stereotyped ways of living. Such a conception was boldly original, it found few advocates outside Withymead except among a handful of Jungian analysts in private practice. The one art therapist outside Withymead who managed to apply a similar approach in a mental hospital setting was Edward Adamson, a sensitive and intuitive artist, who set up a studio in Netherne Hospital, Surrey, in 1946, and did remarkable work with psychiatric in-patients – many of them psychotics – until the time of his retirement in 1973. Over the years he made a collection, now housed in a medieval barn in Northamptonshire, of the extraordinary works produced by the patients under his care: most of them are rich in symbolism, and to hear Adamson lecture, as I have often been privileged to do, on the significance of these symbols for the individuals who produced them is a revelation in artistic understanding and psychological wisdom which leaves one in little doubt as to the therapeutic value of his vocation.

As is fitting for two such important figures in the history of art therapy, Irene and Edward Adamson were subsequently to become good friends. They had much in common. Both rejected the dominant psychiatric obsession with classifying people into homogeneous groups according to their sufferings and with administering mass produced remedies to them. Rather, they preferred to enter into relationship with the inner experience of each person, which they regarded as unique and filled with meaning. They made the patient see that his inner life could only become comprehensible to him if he had the courage to take it on, the determination to work at it, and the desire to release the potential latent within him so as to bring it to a birth in reality. Both recognized the contribution of the arts to this process as crucial. The essence of therapy is communication: to free the patient's need to communicate from the restrictive prison of words into the much wider vocabulary of paint, clay, music and dance, is to open up for him a new universe of possibilities within which the whole personality can extend itself in the quest for individuation. Given time and encouragement, there arise from the depths of the unconscious symbols rich in life and emotive power which, once they are made accessible to consciousness, serve to liberate the individual from his illness and lead him, like Adrian Hill's tubercular colleague, out into the sunlight of a richer, more fertile existence. Properly practiced, therefore, art therapy is the opportunity to *real*-ize what lies within: it is the act of giving form and existence to inner, psychic resources in outer, objective reality.

The inspiration for Withymead's use of the arts came directly, as we have seen, from Jung, who viewed psychotherapy as 'less a question of treatment than of developing the creative possibilities latent in the patient himself.' (*CW* 16, para. 82). Fortunately, all of us are creative in the sense that we possess in some degree the ability to bring something new into existence. Provided one can tolerate one's lack of technical supremacy, use of this ability is intrinsically satisfying. This is particularly true of the disturbed or demoralized patient, for the sense of bringing some new part of himself into existence may be accompanied by unaccustomed feelings of power and effectiveness. Moreover, when they make the effort, many people discover that they are more gifted than they ever realized, their creative talents having previously been ignored, denigrated, discouraged or repressed. Mobilizing this unsuspected potential can result in an uprush of energy which inaugurates an entirely new sense of confidence and self-affirmation.

However, it must be admitted that art therapy, as it was practiced in Withymead, did not work for everyone. Extraverted sensation types, for example, were found to be notoriously obtuse when it came to perceiving the meaning or relevence of the symbols appearing in their paintings. As with analysis, for art therapy to be productive the subject must be willing to concede that symbolical processes occurring within his psyche are at least as important as actual events proceeding in his environment. This is why introverts tend to do better in analysis than extraverts and feeling-intuitives often better than thinking or sensation types. Furthermore, a patient coming into analysis has to be prepared to abandon one of the most cherished assumptions of our culture, namely, that ego-consciousness, together with its rational functions, represents the totality of the human mind. Though they disagreed over many things, Freud and Jung were one in their view that rational consciousness constitutes only a part – and a secondary part – of the total psychic apparatus: the primary form of mental functioning was not the intellect. It was the image. When images conveyed meanings they became symbols.

Now, in order to perceive meaning in images one has to lay oneself open to areas of experience which lie beyond the realm of abstraction and logical deduction, and it is here that many modern men and women, especially educated ones, have difficulty. Indeed, it is an interesting and revealing paradox that analysis and art therapy should have developed in the twentieth century at all, so strongly does the prevailing *Zeitgeist* favour the extraverted use of the thinking and sensation functions to the detriment of introversion, feeling and intuition. To the contemporary mind, the only legitimate approach to reality lies through rational interpretation of evidence from the five senses: feeling is distrusted as an obstacle to objectivity and intuition dismissed as an unreliable and antiquated artefact.

To the art therapist and the analyst, however, symbols are indispensable because they are the raw materials of the mind: they are the bricks and mortar out of which our complexes are built. They are the concomitants of Freud's 'primary process' on which the 'secondary process' of intellectual formulation is superimposed. Moreover, because of their emotive power, symbols nourish the personality: denied them we are doomed to spiritual starvation. Thus, symbols lie at the heart of all art and all human understanding and are crucial to any therapeutic psychology that seeks to promote personal growth through insight and the comprehension of value.

Symbolism, its nature and function, was one area over which Jung took issue with Freud. He rejected the Freudian notion that symbols were mere disguises behind which forbidden wishes lurked. For him they had an altogether higher purpose. They were not a 'manifest content' concealing a latent or repressed desire; they were not distorted forms of something else. To Jung, symbols were *the natural mode of psychic expression* and there was nothing distorted or pathological about them. They were the channels through which unconscious processes became conscious, and they were as fundamental to our experience of existence as ideas and the use of sensory perception. But because their spiritual and emotional significance was so profound, enormous care was needed in one's therapeutic approach to symbols, for clumsy attempts to conceptualize their meaning in words could stultify the living impact of the symbol on the psyche. For this reason it was preferable to express symbols directly in visual or imaginal forms rather than in sentences or abstractions. The *abstraction* that thinking entails is essentially a *pulling away* from emotionally charged symbols to construct emotionally sterile concepts. It is this arid process at which Western man has become so dramatically accomplished and through which he has conquered (and polluted) the material world. And it was because of this, Jung believed, that Western man had lost his soul and become collectively sick: 'What shall it profit a man, if he shall gain the whole world, and lose his own soul?' (Mark VIII: 36). We were sick because we had lost touch with the fundamental symbols of our culture. If we were our own cure we must abandon our exclusively extraverted quest for meaning in the outer world of material objects and, instead, re-establish conscious contact with the symbol-forming capacities inherent in our own psychic nature. For Jung, the unconscious was not a Freudian repository of repressed infantile wishes but a treasury containing the most valuable assets of our species: psychotherapy and therapy through the arts were the means through which these assets could be realized. The skill of the therapist lay in providing the right circumstances for this realization to occur.

Jungians are fond of comparing the relationship between conscious and unconscious to the relationship between an island and the sea: it is not the island that sustains the ocean but the other way round. Similarly, consciousness depends for its maintenance on the continuous activity of processes occurring at levels of which we are entirely unaware. Communication and interaction between these two spheres of activity is made possible by the powerful influence of symbols. Thus, if rational consciousness 'abstracts' us too far from our imaginative or emotional capacities, allowing them to fall, as it were, into the unconscious, then it is the compensatory function of the symbol to rectify the situation. But consciousness must be sympathetic to the symbol if it is to perform its task: only then may the gap between conscious and unconscious be bridged and the neglected psychic capacities activated and made accessible to consciousness. The success of therapy, therefore, depends not only on the attitude of the therapist to the patient but on the patient's attitude to his own symbols. If he is willing to give them his serious and wholehearted attention, and if he can find the courage to follow where they lead, then he may grow out of neurosis and inner discord to achieve a richer, more harmonious existence.

The aim of Withymead was to encourage people to live the 'symbolical life', for once the conscious personality is open to the meaning of symbols it is forever opened to a source of perpetual renewal and replenishment. Every symbol has a conscious and an unconscious aspect: it is born of psychic processes which flow in a never-ending stream between unconscious and conscious and back again. Because of this continuous flux, the significance of a given symbol strikes people differently and strikes the same person differently at different stages of his life. The meaning of symbols is thus ever-changing and in this dynamism lies their fructifying and transforming power. Like all living entities, symbols have a life cycle of their own: they come into existence, they flourish, and they die. 'So long as a symbol is a living thing,' wrote Jung, 'it is an expression for something that cannot be characterized in any other or better way. The symbol is alive only so long as it is pregnant with meaning. But once its meaning has been born out of it, once that expression is found which formulates the thing sought, expected, or divined even better than the hitherto accepted symbol, then the symbol is *dead*, i.e. it possesses only an historical significance . . . It is, therefore, quite impossible to create a living symbol, i.e. one that is pregnant with meaning, from known associations. For what it is thus produced never contains more than was put into it.' (*CW6*, paras 816–7).

Much of Irene's success as a therapist was due to her delight in the living quality of symbols. She understood that their appearance in dreams, phantasies and art provided a means of renewing the life experience of every member of her community and thus of the community as a whole. She believed that 'hard work with the unconscious' and reverence for the constantly changing symbolic formulations to which the unconscious personality gave rise was the best way to overcome the resistance to change which is shown by most patients when they are encouraged to abandon outworn and neurotic patterns of existence. She knew that a successful analysis was a process of death and rebirth and that if she was to persuade her patient to exchange new ways for old she must give him the courage as well as the facilities 'to experiment with his own nature'. Lecturing on her work, she said: 'People differ in the way they create an outer expression for their inner, imaginative life, for those unlived depths of the psyche so needed to revivify the limited, mundane, almost dead fastness of ego life . . . The creator and the therapist together may be able to understand the message, not by detached, scientific analysis or interpretation, but by entering into the symbolic story or experience. This happening between two people brings into the conscious world of the creator (and, incidentally, of the therapist) a wider experience than he had before, and the ego learns and grows by virtue of the whole psyche's activities.' (*Art and therapy: an uneasy partnership*). Irene was particularly gifted in working in this way with children. For instance, a small, very distressed boy came to Withymead because his parents had separated and virtually abandoned him. It was hard to console him or contain his disturbed behaviour, born of despair. One day, Irene went into the painting studio and found him engrossed in painting a tramp steamer in the middle of a stormy sea (ships, it seems, are a favourite theme when people are free to paint what they wish). She pulled up a chair beside the boy, admired the ship, and asked where it was going.

'It's not going anywhere,' he said. 'It's sinking.' This exactly expressed his circumstances, and Irene understood at once. She drew him gently towards her, and hugged him. 'Steamers do have life boats, you know, darling,' she said.

The boy thought for a moment, then turned his large, serious eyes up to Irene. 'Do you think I should paint one in, Mrs C?' he asked.

'If you feel it's right to,' she said. And he did. Irene liked to think his clinical improvement dated from that picture, which he pinned up next to his bed.

With children, the therapeutic benefits of painting often occurred spontaneously, without any interpretation. Eve Lewis, an analyst on the Withymead staff with a special interest in the problems of childhood and adolescence, remembered a little boy of eight, who suffered from terrifying nightmares of being attacked by monstrous men. He used to come to Withymead on Saturdays and spend hours painting prolifically. One afternoon, Irene dropped in and said, 'Hello, John. What about those horrid men? Are they still bothering you?'

'No,' he replied, pointing to his pictures pinned up round the walls of the studios. 'They're all up there now.'

Eve Lewis praised the contribution of the studios in the treatment of children at Withymead. 'Exactly the right atmosphere was created there,' she said. 'Irene and Elizabeth Wills and Euanie Tippett were wonderfully skilful: they would never interfere but somehow enable things to happen. Then the patient felt free to exteriorize his problem and his symbols. The really important thing at Withymead was the total acceptance of the individual and his products. Often it doesn't matter whether one understands what is being painted, as long as it is accepted. Then the soul paints sooner or later, especially if someone is there to say, 'Yes, yes! That's what really matters.'

As Irene knew, children can enter more readily than adults into the symbolical content of a picture, and they can often express things in paint or clay that it would be impossible for them to put into words. The truth is that all children are artists, until education and life knock it out of them. Given encouragement and the necessary materials, they produce works of startling originality and power. At this stage of the life cycle, the ego and the Self are in more intimate proximity and in a state of more equal balance than later on, and this renders the functions of each more readily accessible to the other. In terms of the neurological model discussed in the previous chapter, it is as if the left hemisphere has yet to complete the establishment of its 'imperial' ascendancy over the right. So that both hemispheres are better able to pool their resources in the production of art.

Irene believed that self-expression through the arts achieved its greatest therapeutic effect when it occurred spontaneously and 'artlessly'. For this reason she encouraged her patients, whatever their age, to recover the artistic directness and the naive vision of the child within themselves. It was, therefore, the practice at Withymead to persuade especially gifted or artistically trained patients to explore the possibilities of a medium which was fresh to them. Irene considered that art therapists who allowed patients to persist in their habitual modes of artistic express-ion were no better than psychotherapists who confined themselves to counselling patients at the purely conscious level of experience: they ran the risk of merely confirming the patient in his neurosis by underpinning his one-sided, conscious view of himself and reinforcing the rigidly stereotyped circuit of values which formed the very basis of his neurotic existence. Thus, soon after his arrival at Withymead, a gifted painter would be coaxed into involve-ment with clay, or some other medium, and only at a later date would it be suggested that he might return to his painting. Usually he found his work to be informed with a new freedom and energy.

For people who came to Withymead without special talent or training in the arts, the variety of media available to them in the studios offered different degrees of structure and discipline within which to try out their abilities. To begin with, they were encouraged to be as spontaneous and childlike as they wished. Initially, this was experienced as a pleasurable release from restraint, and people often became flamboyantly productive. However, there generally came a time when they felt unduly lost in their emotions and dissatisfied with the amorphous forms which they were using to express them, and there emerged a desire for more organization and order. Painting was, perhaps, the most accessible medium to people attempting the earliest repre-sentation of their personal symbols, though the malleability of clay attracted some who were daunted by paint and enabled them to make personal statements which were often forcefully eloquent. Pottery and music, on the other hand, required the development of knowledge, skill and discipline: they offered a challenge that people could go forward to meet when they felt strong enough, thus increasing their self-respect and their sense of personal identity. But when it was a question of achieving some objective formulation of their inner experiences, most people chose painting or modelling in clay.

In their early contacts with a new patient the Withymead therapists tended to assume a recessive role, doing little more than welcome him, make him feel at home in the studio, provide him with essential materials, and quietly accept whatever he produced. Then, as his need to impose form emerged, they might begin to offer advice on technique. This was done with tact and sensitivity, the right amount of technique being made available to give some definition to the fluid colours and forms, without inhibiting the emotional power or distorting the intention of the work which the patient was creating.

The more artlessly and spontaneously one worked under these conditions, the more readily one discovered the existence of those subterrainean mental processes which flow along whether one is asleep or awake, providing a running commentry, *sotto voce*, below the surface of consciousness, burbling busily on like Schubert's brook. One came to realize that it is consciousness that interrupts or superimposes itself on the states we call reverie, phantasy or dreaming – states which artists and original thinkers know to be indispensable to creative work.

Such introspective awareness that there are always two forms of thinking that proceed concurrently has been confirmed, as we have noted in the last chapter, by modern neurological research. These two forms of thinking have been described in terms of computer technology as *digital codification* (logical, discursive and verbal processes) and *analogic codification* (eidetic, non-discursive and non-verbal processes). The abstracted, conceptual thinking which goes with left hemispheric activity is the product of consciousness, while the deeper, less coherent level of experience which finds expression in dreams, intuitions, visions religious experience, poetry and music, as well as in neurotic symptoms and psychotic delusions, is associated with the right cerebral hemisphere and deeper structures of the brain.

Robert Ornstein, the psychologist responsible for distinguishing the 'rational' functions of the left hemisphere from the 'intuitive' functions of the right, has suggested that it is as if the left hemisphere behaves like the sun and the right like the stars. Although the stars keep their station in the heavens during the hours of daylight, we are unaware of them because of the brilliance of the sun. But when the sun goes down we are no longer dazzled by its radiance, and the stars come into their own. Jung intuitively understood these phenomena long before the 'split brain' neurologists published their findings. 'In sleep,' he wrote (*CW* 16, para. 125), 'fantasy takes the form of dreams. But in waking life, too, we continue to dream beneath the threshold of consciousness'. In the alert brain, the rational, verbal brilliance of the left hemispheric system 'dazzles' (i.e. inhibits) our awareness of events occurring in the intuitive, symbol-producing right. It is usually only when the sun sets in the left hemisphere and the stars come out in the right that we become aware of our dreams, phantasies and capacities to produce symbols rich in personal significance. These right hemispheric emanations can never be precisely formulated in the language of left hemispheric consciousness and cannot, therefore, be easily communicated except symbolically in the language of the arts. Jung was convinced that those regions of the mind where dreams and phantasies originate hold the source of true individuality and guide one's steps towards self-realization. Since their purpose seems to be the promotion of psychic integration, their activities are indispensable to psychic health, and by giving them symbolical expression and serious conscious attention, we permit fulfilment of the original promise of the whole personality – a promise miraculously encoded in the Self.

Inasmuch as any one of us has been denied that original promise it is the fault of our unbringing, our educational and cultural background, our economic and social circumstances. Neurosis is the result of the compromises and distortions which personal history forces on our archetypal nature. This is where Jung's view of ontogeny (personal development) differed so radically from Freud's. Jung agreed that the origins of neurosis lay in childhood, but argued that the aim of treatment must be to discover what aspects of the archetypal programme for the individual life cycle had not been activated or experienced. The purpose of analysis was not so much to purge the patient of his infantile frustrations as to discover where his development had been blocked, to release these blocks, and give him the courage to live his unlived life. In the removal of blocks and the mobilization of unlived potential the key to successful treatment lay in *dialogue* – dialogue between analyst and patient, and, above all, dialogue between the unconscious and conscious personality, the Self and the ego. The only language in which this dialogue could proceed was, of course, the language of symbols.

The changes that came over people once they began working in the studios was a source of recurrent fascination to Irene. At the first analytic session she would often note of a newcomer that ego-consciousness seemed quite detached from the rest of the personality, that he or she appeared to be 'all ego and persona' and little else. But this would rapidly begin to alter when the first dreams had been worked on and the patient started to put his inner experience into some outer shape or form. The ego could then contemplate some previously unknown part of the Self. 'This speaks back to him,' Irene said, 'and in this way the ego comes into relation with material lying below, hidden in the person himself.' Confronting this material invariably resulted in a new balance between the ego and the Self and a sounder integration of the total personality, embracing both conscious and unconscious factors, and bringing with it a sense of enhanced personal identity.

That similar changes occur in creative artists as well as in patients practicing art therapy has been well documented by Anthony Storr in his excellent book, *The Dynamics of Creation*. For example, he quotes the American composer

Aaron Copland as stating: 'I must create in order to know myself, and since self-knowledge is a never-ending search, each new work is only a part-answer to the question "Who am I" and brings with it the need to go on to other and different part answers'. Storr comments: 'On a lowlier plane, the lady who asked "How do I know what I think until I hear what I say?" is enunciating a similar truth. For putting things into words (or music or paintings) is indeed making conscious what has hitherto not been fully so. By removing what is in our minds from within to "out there", we alter our attitude towards these contents. A phantasy which has never been spoken or written is differently apprehended by the person who harbours it from the same phantasy when it has been objectified. This is not only because, once written or spoken, it can be communicated and shared with another person; it is because it becomes an object separate from the person himself, which can be contemplated and studied by the person himself.' T.S. Eliot recognized the same truth when he wrote that 'the poet does not know what he has to say until he has said it.'

A similar view to Anthony Storr's is expressed by von Keyserling in his *South American Meditations*: 'Once a man has exteriorised an inner state the latter for him becomes a new point of departure. Thus man must again and again represent his inner reality in external form in order to progress . . . After he has created his work he is another and different man from what he was before and the same work can create a new point of departure for all who accept it as a model.' The therapist's function is to facilitate this process by quietly encouraging the patient to express what, all too frequently, he feels to be inexpressible, to give free rein to the images arising from the unconscious and put them outside himself to be seen, experienced and related to. This is what Jung himself did after his break with Freud (the results are recorded in the famous *Red Book*) and what he persuaded his patients to do, using the technique he called *active imagination*. 'The patient busying himself with the fantasy increases its effect on him,' wrote Jung (*CW*oo para. oo). 'Moreover, the concrete shaping of the image enforces the continuous study of it in all its parts so that it can develop its effects to the full. This lends it greater weight and driving power.'

Causing a patient to focus attention on his spontaneous phantasies does not mean encouraging him to flee from reality, as Freud maintained. Like attending to dreams, it can open up a royal road to the unconscious where lies the conflict making the patient ill as well as the energy capable of producing resolution and healing. And those who denigrate phantasy would do well to remember de Roberto's aphorism that among all human constructions the only ones that avoid the dissolving hands of time are castles in the air!

Jung described active imagination as *the art of letting things happen*: 'The art of letting things happen, action through non-action, letting go of oneself, as taught by Meister Eckhart, because for me the key opening the door to the way. We must be able to let things happen in the psyche. For us, this actually is an art of which few people know anything. Consciousness is forever interfering, helping, correcting, and negating, and never leaving the simple growth of the psychic process in peace. It would be simple enough, if only simplicity were not the most difficult of all things. To begin with, the task consists solely in objectively observing a fragment of fantasy in its development. Nothing could be simpler, and yet right here the difficulties begin. No fantasy-fragment seems to appear – or yes, one does – but it is too stupid – hundreds of good reasons inhibit it. One cannot concentrate on it – it is too boring – what would it amount to – it is 'nothing but', et cetera. The conscious mind raises prolific objections, in fact it often seems bent upon blotting out the spontaneous fantasy-activity in spite of real insight, even of firm determination on the part of the individual to allow the psychic process to go forward without interference. Often a veritable cramp of consciousness exists. (1962, p. 93). It seems that the left hemisphere too readily persists in its customary work of domination and inhibition, and that it requires patient practice to liberate the right hemisphere from its tyranny.

'If one is successful in overcoming the initial difficulties, criticism is still likely to start in afterwards and attempt to interpret the fantasy, to classify, to aestheticize, or to depreciate it. The temptation to do this is almost irresistable'. (*Ibid*, p. 93). But one must persevere. 'These exercises must be continued until the cramp in the conscious mind is released, or, in other words, until one can let things happen . . . In this way a new attitude is created, an attitude which accepts the non-rational and the incomprehensible, simply because it is what is happening.' (*Ibid*, p. 94).

The subjective phenomena of active imagination and its consequences may be understood in terms of the psycho-dynamics of personal maturation. In the course of childhood development, the ego, which originally grows out of the Self, becomes increasingly subject to the left hemispheric laws of time and causality. The residual Self, however, remains unconscious and exempt from these laws, and when its symbols are encountered in dreams or through the use of active imagination (the art of letting things happen), they are inevitably experienced by the ego as irrational and strange. As the American analytical psychologist, Edward Edinger, has suggested, we are each of us the two sons of Zeus – Castor, the mortal ego, and Pollux, the immortal Self. Western life and Western education alienate the two, and favour Castor at the expense of Pollux; it is the aim of analytical psychology and the goal of individuation to bring about their reconciliation. Thus, active imagination, when persisted in, has the effect of opening up the lines of communication between the ego and Self, constellating the transcendent function, undoing the inhibition of the right hemisphere by the left, and bringing both hemispheres more into balance. The subjective consequences of this would appear to be a lessening of tension and inner conflict, associated with a greater sense of personal security and healthy Self-reliance.

What went on in the studios of Withymead, therefore, was more a process of psycho-synthesis than psycho-analysis. Analysis is necessary to define the conflicts and complexes from which the individual is suffering, to discover which parts of the archetypal programme for life have been blocked or repressed; but then the vital work of synthesis begins – to activate the unlived archetypal elements, to promote the integration of previously dissociated parts of the personality, to create deeper and wider awareness of the Self in relation to the world.

By providing the facilities necessary for this work of synthesis to occur, the last thing that Withymead sought to do was to 'normalize' people. Irene enjoyed quoting Jung's aphorism that 'to be normal is the ideal aim of the unsuccessful'. At the same time, she did not conceive individuation as a mystical exercise to be performed in hermitic seclusion. Rather, it entailed, as Jung said, 'a successful adaptation to the universal conditions of existence coupled with the greatest possible freedom for self-determination'. (*CW* 17, para. 289). 'Individuation does not shut one out from the world, but gathers the world to oneself' (*CW* 8, para. 432). Self-completion requires full participation in outer life no less than commitment to the life within one's psyche. Inner and outer development, nevertheless, demand an expanded consciousness of one's living circumstances as a unique individual. 'Every advance in culture is, psychologically, an extension of consciousness, a coming to consciousness that can take place only through discrimination. Therefore an advance always begins with individuation, that is to say with the individual, conscious of his isolation, cutting a new path through hitherto untrodden territory. To do this he must first return to the fundamental facts of his own being, irrespective of all authority and tradition, and allow himself to become conscious of his distinctiveness' (*CW* 8, para. 111). This had nothing to do with self-centredness or ego-centricity, for it was necessary for each individual to be aware of his distinctiveness if he were to be authentic in his relations with other members of the community. 'Companionship thrives only when each individual remembers his individuality and does not identify with others' (*Memories*, P. 356).

In Jungian therapy, the successful application of the synthetic process is generally found to depend as much on the relationship which develops between the patient and the analyst (the so-called transference and counter-transference) as on the symbol-forming potential of the Self. This was no less true at Withymead. The classical Freudian view of the transference held it to be a neurosis caused by the patient transfering onto the analyst those neurotic feelings and distorted expectations he had developed while growing up in the care of his parents. This was all right as far as it went, because something of the sort does indeed occur, but it left out an element of great therapeutic significance, namely, the archetypal dimension. For what emerges in the transference is not just the personal parental complexes but the archetypal basis of the complexes as well. Those aspects of the parental archetype which, for one reason or another, the personal parents *failed* to actualize, together with the unfulfilled longings to which these aspects give rise, are also constellated in the relationship with the therapist, and this provides him with his most potent therapeutic instrument. It enables him to bring to birth in the psyche of his patient those attributes of the archetypal that had previously existed only as potential. As a result, the patient can complete his business with the parents, attempt some resolution of the conflicts inherent in his relations with them, and proceed on the way to individuation.

By constellating the archetype of the good, nurturing parent, individual therapists at Withymead enabled their patients to develop basic trust, use their creativity and establish personal autonomy. This, combined with their sensitive, free and intuitive approach to the arts, made it possible for people to become caught up in the creative activities they found going on round them. Inevitably, there were some patients who felt unable to make use of the studios and the media available, but then they would become involved in the kitchen, or the garden, or the mens' working party, until such time as they could risk more symbolical forms of expression. There was a refreshing lack of arty-crafty snobbery at Withymead despite the talent that abounded there, and music and painting were not regarded as more worthy than tending plants or building walls. The contribution of each individual was valued whatever form it took. Participation was what mattered, for participation in work, especially creative work, brings a personal reward which transcends the value of the work produced. The analytic understanding of all Withymead's therapists – art therapists no less than analysts – elevated such activity above the level of 'occupational therapy', for each patient's con-tribution was understood in terms of the symbolical proces-ses at work in his psyche, and these were carefully related to his total life situation. This added dimension unquestionably gave art therapists at Withymead deeper satisfaction in their work than is customary in conventional psychiatric units where personal involvement by occupational therapists in the lives of patients is not usually encouraged. At Withymead there was no exclusiveness in the doctor–patient relationship: art therapists were full participants in the therapeutic team. Just as there were no clear divisions between patients and staff, so there was considerable overlap between the roles of analyst and art therapist. That 'transference' and 'counter-transference' should develop between individual art therap-ists and patients was regarded as inevitable, and it was accepted that on occasion an art therapist would become 'special' for a patient in that the relationship would seem more important to him than that with his analyst. It was a source of surprise to outside observers that Withymead analysts did not object when this happened. Indeed, a number of individual analysts, working outside the Withy-mead context, were very critical of this phenomenon when they learned of it, arguing that the 'split transference' which resulted must militate against the successful progress of treatment. But Irene never hesitated to assure them they were wrong. 'I know that, on the face of it, the relationship with the art therapist developed *outside* the analysis,' she told me, 'but we made sure that the analysis took it into account. The patient would talk about it and dream about it, and it would provide valuable material which the analyst could handle sensitively through her rapport with the therapist concerned. At the same time it would take the analytic transference one step further out into life and reality.'

Irene's attitude was in accord with Jung's dictum that analysis is not something to be separated from life – either for the patient or the analyst. It is a process which engages the whole personality of the participants, and its success depends on the validity of the relationships which these personalities are able to create, not only with each other, but with all emtionally significant people in the environment. What prevented the split transference from actually harming patients was the regular interaction which occurred between all therapists at the staff meeting. These frequent and very frank exchanges tended to prevent conflicting views of the patient from emerging, and the insight which grew between the analyst and the art therapist in the course of these discussions was immensely helpful to the patient and helped to prevent the occurrence of demarcation disputes between those responsible for his care.

Far from impeding the analysis, work with the art therapist could greatly enhance its success. For example, highly significant material might begin to emerge in the studios some time before it had become evident in the analytic situation. This would be noted by the therapist and reported to the staff meeting, thus alerting other members of the therapeutic team to the new possibilities unfolding in the patient's life and making everyone more ready to assist in bringing these possibilities to fruition. Such regular sharing of progress reports by the team of therapists had the added advantage of heightening their interest in the patient as well as preventing biased or lopsided judgements from hampering his all round development.

The easy mutuality characterizing the dealing of the staff with each other and with their patients was largely responsible for the therapeutic success of Withymead during the high period of its fortunes in the 1950s. More readily than in conventional units, therapists at Withymead were able to commit themselves to roles which related directly to different facets of a patient's problem. For example, a male art therapist and a female analyst could between them liberate a young man from a crippling parental complex; or a therapist who was an introverted thinking type could work with an analyst who was an extraverted intuitive to help a withdrawn woman to relate to these attitudes and functions in herself. The 'split transference' could permit a severely repressed child to own hostile feelings which he would have been too terrified to acknowledge were he compelled to depend on the help of one therapist only. And so on.

Everyone who knew Withymead at this time agrees that it was an exciting place. People felt united by their participation in activities they knew to be intrinsically worthwhile. A spirit of inquiry was abroad which inspired the therapeutic and educational processes at work within the community. This was mostly due to the quality of individual members of the staff and to the harmonious relations that existed between them. 'Communication between us was wonderfully easy,' said Molly Kemp. 'There were no formalities at all, and we were so closely-knit in our work together that we understood each other and shared each other's departments to a remarkable degree.' The pay was negligible but the job satisfaction evidently great. They were one in their desire to discover more about the human psyche, and this quest conditioned their attitude to their work, their patients, and each other. What never failed to impress me whenever I visited Withymead in the '50s was the friendliness and selflessness of the staff, and the happiness with which they went about their work.

The arts were crucial to this felicitous atmosphere: nearly everyone was consumed by artistic activity of one sort or another. Since the staff was mainly composed of artists and art teachers this was not altogether surprising, but their commitment to the arts infected the patients and carried them beyond considerations of unconscious symbolism and personal psychology. This brought people, often for the first time in their lives, into direct contact with the mainstream of artistic life, which opened up a new world of beauty and excitement whose existence they had never previously suspected. By creating a cultural atmosphere in which the arts could flourish, Withymead invariably stimulated latent talent, and it was not unusual for people who had been there to continue to paint and use clay long after their period of treatment was over. This was one of the many legacies which Withymead offered to its alumni. Moreover, the therapists were themselves eager to acquire the skills and techniques of their colleagues, so that the art therapist would improve her dexterity with clay under the guidance of the potter, while both would enjoy singing under the direction of the music therapist, and so on. They delighted in being teachers and pupils to each other.

Irene and Gilbert were justifiably proud of all this. 'The give and take between the Centre and the staff was pretty equal,' said Irene. 'And what I feel proudest about is that no matter what the staff had to put up with in the way of poor pay, hard work, and little spare time, I don't think a single one of them failed to grow by virtue of being at Withymead. It gave them a chance to round off their bad corners and live creatively, and they took it. They all used the studios as much as the patients, if not more, and the all round participation was marvellous.'

The growth of the therapists, no less than that of the patients, depended on the symbol-producing capacity of the Self as much as on the transference or the warm, personal relationships they established with each other. The intense interest shown in expressive representations of phantasies and dreams derived from a general awareness that these phenomena were 'personification' of previously unlived archetypal components. As people worked in the studios, they became increasingly conscious of these components as 'inner objects' or 'part personalities' within themselves. For what often started as detached images would gradually coalesce into a human figure with a life and a personality of its own. Following the example of Jung himself, some patients developed the knack of holding imaginery conversations with these characters – a practice which existentialist and gestalt therapists have subsequently developed without recognizing its archetypal foundation and with no acknowledgment to Withymead or to Jung. The more attention given to these figures the more tangible they became, so that both patient and therapist could treat them as real people.

As time went by, an interesting development would occur in the transference relationship: the patient became less dependent on the therapist as he found increasing security in his inner relationship to the archetypal components being activated in his life, and as he began to recognize the immense creative potential of the Self. He was then, almost without knowing it, well embarked on the individuation quest.

This was an important discovery. It meant that art therapy, when sensitively used, could promote 'resolution of the transference' – that it encouraged the development of personal autonomy and healthy Self-reliance rather than passive dependence on, or anxious attachment to, the person of the therapist. But the process had to occur in its own time and in a manner appropriate to each individual: it could not be forced, mass produced, or legislated for. Originally, in the transference, attachment is the means of archetypal actualization; it is the constellator of the transcendent function. But once the individuation process is initiated, the attachment loses its anxious quality, and the transference is superseded.

At Withymead, these things usually happened quietly and inwardly, but occasionally they took bizarre, public forms. When this happened, the staff accepted it and did their best to cope. For example, the analyst Eve Lewis had vivid memories of a girl who came to Withymead with a diagnosis of schizophrenia. 'Whether or not the diagnosis was accurate, it was plain to all of us that she needed to regress to a state of total dependence if she was to discover her own reality. In fact, she regressed to the point where she announced that she had to go back to the womb and be born again as a baby. She ceased to speak and lay in bed.

'Withymead was marvellous with that girl, as it was in many similar cases where patients *had* to act everything out. With some people talking, phantasizing, painting and modelling achieve nothing. They have to relive things. So she lay in bed, and Withymead looked after her.

'Then the baby was born, and she was the baby. Everyone knew about it, and she knew everyone knew, for just a fragment of ego remained intact. She was given baby food, and she was given a bottle and people called in and asked, "How's the baby?" And she would tell them how the baby was and at the same time *be* the baby. They brought her toys and played with her.

'Gradually she began to emerge from all that, and she became herself *with* a baby to look after. You'd see her walking down the lane from the Barton where she was living, or standing by the mill stream, leaning down and holding the baby by the hand, showing it the ducks and flowers, and so on. Eventually the baby was integrated and disappeared. I can't remember how long it took, but it was quite some time.

'When she was well enough she left Withymead and I continued to see her. She got a secretarial post at a university, where she was very successful and exceedingly well liked. She became one of the wholest people you could imagine, and there was no recurrence of her "schizophrenia"'. Withymead may have been unconventional, but it was precisely because of its unconventional willingness to go more than half way to meeting peoples' needs that it achieved remarkable things.

Chapter VII

Family Matters

The archetype active at the heart of Withymead's existence was that of the family: its influence permeated every aspect of daily life, determining the way in which the community conducted its affairs. Wherever people gathered together – in the studios, kitchen, dining room, gardens or their rooms – the family archetype was constellated, guaranteeing a sense of shared intimacy, security and 'belongingness'. Irene and Gilbert believed that continued activation of this archetype was fundamental to the community's survival, and history was to prove how right they were.

Remembering Withymead as it was in the 1950s, Molly Kemp told me, 'We were all basically aiming at the same things, and there was a sense of unity in the place: that made a sort of magic circle that held people.

'But then, later on in the 1960s, the circle got broken and awful things began to happen, like open breaches between members of the staff, and suicides among the patients. New people in authority who didn't understand our ways, began to make us work within the letter of the law; but our strength had been that we *never* worked within the letter of the law. Duty lists were drawn up stating who should be responsible at breakfast-time and who should lock-up at night, instead of allowing such things to occur in the sort of family way they always had done. Then our times became more definite, and as soon as you begin that sort of thing a different spirit creeps in. When free time becomes official, you jolly well see that you get it! But when Withymead was really successful we never thought like that. If you saw that somebody was in trouble and in need of help you gave it, even if it was your time off. Later, when things got more regimented, Withymead became less human.'

However, throughout the 1950s, the family life of the community persisted with its casual informality and over-riding sense of shared life and purpose. As with any large family there was lots of fun as well as hard work, with treats and celebrations, outings to the seaside at Exmouth and Dawlish Warren, expeditions onto Dartmoor, often ending up at Postbridge, where Gilbert and Irene leased a house overlooking the clapper bridge, and later, when they gave this up, visits to their snug little cottage in Kenn, still an unspoilt village in those days, just a few miles from Withymead, where Father John Hooper, an old friend of Irene's was vicar of the parish.

Father John was loved by many at Withymead and, although he seldom went there, they often came to him. He received them in his vicarage with warm hospitality, listened to their difficulties, and gave wise advice, for like all good priests he was a natural psychotherapist.

On Sundays, everyone who wanted to go to church piled into 'Duxie', Withymead's elastic old Austin, and Mary Pye drove them to Kenn. 'I used to take the children too,' she said, 'and we'd walk through the lanes and meadows looking for wild life while the grown-ups were in church. Then, on the way back, we'd stop Duxie and all get out in the fields to pick mushrooms or blackberries.'

Over the years, several festivities became regular events. These gradually assumed the character of community rituals which had the dual function of holding the residential community together by stressing everyone's membership of it and of providing occasions when old Withymeadians, no longer in residence, could reaffirm their identity with the community by returning specially to take part. The most important of these family get-togethers were the carol party, which Molly Kemp organized every Christmas, and the great breakfast held in the River Room on Easter Sundays.

At the carol party, the Withymead choir led everyone in singing carols, most of which were old favourites, but some were unknown ones which Molly had collected for their beauty and included to add variety. Between carols there were poems and stories read by Irene and Gilbert and other members of the community.

On Christmas Eve many went over to Buckfast Abbey to attend midnight mass, returning to Withymead in the early hours of the morning for mince tarts and hot chocolate before going to bed. Then on Christmas Day there would be a grand Christmas dinner with presents in the dining room, which was decked with holly and bright decorations, and there was a large Christmas tree in 'Introverts' Corner' – the secluded alcove where people who felt unable to cope with large gatherings could eat in peace.

Easter was no less of an occasion. One person who was at Withymead in its heyday remembers it well: 'On Easter Friday lots of us would go to church at Kenn. Then on Saturday we'd sit round painting Easter Eggs and preparing little posies of flowers for everyone. Then we used to lay it all out in the River Room ready for breakfast on Easter Sunday. People who weren't in residence would often join us on that day: it was a lovely sort of Spring Festival. And the preparations were always such fun. There was something for everyone to do, and so much care went into it all – each egg not only had someone's name on it, but an appropriate illustration as well.' Thus, Sylvie, who was as devoted to her hives as to her patients, would receive an egg resplendent with an enormous bee.

'These events were a vital symbol for many of us,' said Mary Pye. 'And for people who had never had a secure home of their own they had special significance. Only last Christmas one of them who spent her childhood in an orphanage sent me a card with a picture of the fields near Kenn, because our outings to Rene's cottage, our walks there, picking primroses for Easter, and so on, have stayed with her as fond memories ever since.' 'To have missed a carol party at Withymead,' wrote one ex-patient, 'would have been a real loss to me. Nowhere have I been to an event that so deepened my sense of having roots.'

In addition to these regular festivals, Withymead was not slow to seize other occasions as an opportunity to go *en fête*. When Elizabeth Colyer married David Wills, the writer and educationalist, and when Michael Edwards married Ngareta, an art teacher, and took her to live in Primrose Cottage, no effort was spared to make both weddings joyous occasions. When Martin Lambourne, the Centre's horticulturalist, married Jill Stevenson, the housekeeper, Father John refused to allow Martin's earlier divorce to deter him from blessing their union in Kenn Church, where, after the ceremony, Withymeadians formed a triumphal arch with an impressive variety of garden impedimenta. For the potter, Jo Guy, her marriage to the artist Desmond Sawyer was an unforgettable event: 'Everyone was absolutely marvellous. Gilbert had a new suit made specially. I never expected my wedding to be really special, because I'm not at all a sentimental person, but it *was* special. Withymead saw to that. I couldn't have been better wed.'

The River Room, the inevitable venue on these happy occasions, gave ample return for the money and effort that had been put into converting the old garage, for its usefulness was by no means confined to high days and holidays. Molly had the Bluthner grand piano in virtually constant use, accompanying people as they sang or played on different musical instruments. Veronica Sherbourne and, later, Carol Paul-Jones ran regular music and movement groups there, using the techniques of Rudolf Laban, who had himself made a number of visits to Withymead in the late 1960s. Lectures took place there, with people like Barbara Hannah coming from Zurich to talk, for example, about the archetypal symbolism in Mary Webb's *Precious Bane*, which all Withymead read beforehand. And gramophone recitals, impromptu concerts, square dances and reels were prone to happen there, usually quite spontaneoulsy, in the evenings. When Guida Swann was at Withymead for a while in the mid-1950s her passion for drama spread throughout the community and some extraordinary productions were mounted, at negligible cost and for one performance only, in the River Room.

One year, Barbara Hannah lectured on 'Tobias and the Angel' after which Guida gathered everyone together to act it out, a performance which Irene Champernowne never got over: 'Guida was a genius at turning a story into a kind of grand charade, full of possibilities for everyone, so that we were all drawn in. Many of our people were incapable of learning whole plays, so we never attempted straight drama. But Guida got us to improvise, and the most touching, wonderful things came out of it. She achieved the same thing with *Pilgrim's Progress*, which was half improvised drama and half movement. There were moments when I was frankly terrified. During the Slough of Despond I thought the unconscious was going to break out into something violent and destructive, there was such suction and gloom. It was a dangerous thing to do, but somehow we got through. Gilbert was the Giant Despair, and I was his wife. Bill Elmhirst played Christian. It was all very extraordinary, but only because we had the right person to create it. After Guida had gone it all died away again.

Amongst residential institutions for the mentally ill, Withymead was not of course unique in having customs, rituals and special occasions, for these are important aspects of every human community. What was different about such events at Withymead, however, was the spirit with which they were organized and conducted. For example, Dr David H. Clark comments in his book *Social Therapy in Psychiatry*: 'The main English midwinter festival, Christmas, is still a very important family occasion in the general community, but has unfortunate institutional overtones, many pithily summarized in the folk ballad, " 'Twas Christmas Day in the Workhouse". In many traditional English mental hospitals Christmas became a curious and unpleasant Saturnalia where

the decorations and congratulations were merely the preliminary to prolonged drunkeness and licence among the
staff.' At Withymead, drunkeness and licence were unknown, not because there existed any Puritanical rules for its
suppression, but because such behaviour was alien to the
family culture which Gilbert and Irene had created. The
maintenance of this culture was naturally dependant on all
members of the staff, but they were as much in the grip of the
family archetype as Withymead's founders. This was the
fundamental attribute which made Withymead different
from all the other therapeutic communities and on which its
survival and integrity depended – as was to become sadly
apparent when, later in the Centre's history, the family
archetype lost its all-pervasive influence.

David Kennard, a clinical psychologist who has done
valuable research into the structure and function of therapeutic communities, had noted that the most important determi-
nants of a community's culture are (1) the number and
relative permanence of the staff, (2) their attitudes to
treatment, (3) the skills available between them, and (4) the
characteristics of the leader(s). His analysis makes clear the
degree to which therapeutic communities diverge from the
family model on which Withymead was based. Kennard's
conclusions may be summarized as follows:

(1) *Numbers and permanence*: 'A larger staff group is likely to
produce both a wider range of attitudes to treatment and
greater possibilities for the formation of splits and subgroups
or cliques. The larger the staff, therefore, the more time,
effort and skill will be needed if the resulting tensions are to
be explored and resolved. In all likelihood the process will
always remain far from complete.'

In contrast to Withymead, where staff permanence was
regarded as great virute, Kennard finds that in therapeutic
communities it is invariably relative and best kept to
'between one and four years'. He argues that old-established
staff tend to routinize things and inhibit innovation. Staff

who stay only a few weeks, on the other hand, give rise to other problems: 'a pervasive atmosphere of uncertainty, each person watching the other for cues and sometimes following inappropriate leads' (i.e. the blind leading the blind) and 'the continuation of procerdures handed on by earlier generations of staff without understanding the reason for them, so that they assume the quality of rituals'.

(2) *Attitudes to treatment*: 'In any treatment situation one is likely to meet a range of attitudes, philosophies or idealogies about treatment. The growth of a therapeutic community culture will be limited where there is a wide divergence of attitudes which may exist where the community is not in control of who comes on to the staff.' In therapeutic communities generally, the preferred attitude seems to combine 'radicalism' with 'willingness to self-disclose' in the group situation.

(3) *Skills*: opinions vary about what skills and training are necessary. While a few therapeutic communities have a staff of highly trained personnel like Withymead, many eschew any kind of professional training because 'members of the community are seen as being sufficiently able to help one another by virtue of their experience as human beings.'

(4) *Leadership*: here Kennard notes a paradox: 'when a treatment setting becomes more democratic, the role of the leader appears to become more, not less, significant.' The reason he gives for this is as follows: 'To the extent that hierarchies, rules and regimentation protect staff from feelings of doubt and anxiety, the removal or relaxation of these devices may be manageable only where there is someone to absorb or contain these feelings when they threaten to become overwhelming . . . The necessary element seems to be that the leader should appear to be in control of himself and the situation, thereby inspiring some confidence in others that they too can be in control. This ability in a leader probably is a component of "charisma".

At Withymead none of these four factors was an issue.

Each was determined by the nature of the family which Gilbert and Irene had founded. Family circumstances limited the number of staff the Centre could accommodate and feed. Their relative permanence was dependent upon the usual family exigencies of marriage and death. As far as Irene and Gilbert were personally concerned, they were there for life – a conviction which most of their colleagues shared. Questions of therapeutic attitude, skill and leadership were settled by the training, experience and personal qualities of the 'father' and 'mother' of the community, and, as a consequence, there was little discussion or dissention about them.

Thus, the family archetype solved the problem of structure for Withymead – a problem which has beset all other therapeutic communities, and was to afflict Withymead itself when the family configuration was later abandoned. But, in its heyday, the structure of the Withymead community was intact and stable precisely because it was founded in the archetypal reality of the collective unconscious. This single factor gave Withymead an immense advantage, for the entire therapeutic community movement has often come close to disaster over the fundamental issues of structure and organization, many community therapists wanting to dispense with such concepts altogether. Two authorities, Bob Hinshelwood and Sheena Grunberg, for example, report that 'The main debate at every conference of the Association of Therapeutic Communities that we have attended has centred around the issue of structure and organization. It has been the flashpoint of many heated exchanges; and at a previous conference such division was reached over the simple structuring involved in the appointing of a secretariat that many members abandoned the conference.' Grunberg finds it necessary to plead that 'the study of structure' should actually be permitted, bravely complaining that 'the tenacity of the anti-authority belief systems' has led to the erroneous notion that 'structuring undermines the ideology behind the therapeutic community system'.

The sort of anti-structure, anti-authority Utopianism of

which Grunberg complains, the belief that you can have a lovely, spontaneous time without any structure or authority, responsibility or order, is characteristic of an other-directed 'puer' society, with its bondage to the mother archetype, untempered by the father. It goes hand in glove with the naive view espoused by a large group of therapeutic community writers that the development of structure is purely a defensive operation, designed explicitly to reduce the anxiety of the staff.

The more mature attitude prevailing at Withymead took the family structure and organization of the community largely for granted, and few aspects of its administration were subject to debate – except those relating to finance. Over financial matters there was indeed a debate, and it was to continue with increasing bitterness throughout the rest of the Centre's history.

The facts were these. The foundation of the Withymead Trust in 1950 relieved Gilbert and Irene of immediate financial worries. But they were concerned, nevertheless, to do all they could to make the Centre pay its way. Initially they hoped that the modest expansion of the community made possible by Elmgrant support would, through the admission of more patients, generate more income. But in practice this did not happen. Instead, the Centre persisted in making a steady loss of between £3,000 and £4,000 a year, which had to be met by the Elmgrant Trust. It was a worrying situation, for although the Elmgrant Trustees showed benevolent understanding of Withymead's problems, it was by no means certain that they would continue to do so indefinitely. Indeed, the declared purpose of the Elmgrant Trustees when they originally agreed to back the Centre had been to 'put Withymead on its feet' in the sense of making it economically viable.

As the 1950s wore on, a clear relationship emerged between income and the size of the community, and it was of little comfort to the Champernownes. The trouble was that every time the Withymead Trust created more facilities for more patients to generate more income, so it became committed to greater capital expenditure and increased running costs. More patients needed more staff to look after them. More staff needed more accommodation, which meant more capital investment and more money for salaries. This in turn required more income to be raised from patients, either by increasing their fees or by increasing their numbers. Since few patients could afford to pay more, it became necessary to increase their number. And that gave another spin to the vicious spiral.

No one saw the situation more clearly than Gilbert, and at a Management Committee Meeting held at the beginning of 1954, he made an earnest plea that a strict limit be imposed on the size of the community. The family intimacy of the small community, he said, was a crucial factor governing its therapeutic success, and it must never be sacrificed. As a result it was unanimously agreed that the upper limit for the residential community should be set at 47, the full complement of the new dining room that Ben Belton had planned. This at any rate would prevent another turn of the cost spiral, but it remained to be seen whether other means could be found to balance the books.

Leonard Elmhirst was also concerned about Withymead's financial problems, which is not surprising in view of his responsibility for covering the annual deficit. It is much to his credit that he recognized that the Centre's ills were susceptible to no simple remedy, and his sympathetic understanding of the principle issues involved is demonstrated by his letters, his minuted comments, and the private notes he kept in his own hand (which have been preserved in the archives at Dartington). For example, after a Management Committee meeting held in September, 1954, he noted his personal assessment of the situation confronting Withymead. While he agreed with Gilbert that the community must not be permitted to get too big, 'or the spirit needed will be spread out too thin and may, at bad moments, give out', Leonard believed that it should, nevertheless, be of sufficient size to employ a staff large enough to allow adequate holidays and rest periods and be able to pay them a reasonable salary.

In the long term, Leonard appreciated that Withymead would have to meet in its own way the destiny awaiting all self-perpetuating bodies, of which he citied Oxford and Cambridge colleges as familiar examples. Although such institutions are undoubtedly able to survive and retain their peculiar identity for long periods of time, they dwell in constant danger of losing touch with their original sense of mission, subsisting as a shell merely, resting aimlessly on faded laurels and paying no more than lip service to their founders' intentions. While it was true that communities choosing their officers in perpetuity from among their own fellows have managed to maintain their original functions for as long as any known human institutions, they too are subject to lapses under their self-denying ordinances, and can fall into debased policies of self-promotion sustained by complacency. Loss of idealism, if it persists, inevitably ends in the failure and ultimate liquidation of the community. It follows, Leonard concluded, that the survival of institutions of this type depends on their ability to find time and space in which to evolve organically, admitting new members to positions of responsibility and leadership only when they have demonstrated to all other members of the community that they have grasped with full understanding the ethos on which the community is based.

Leonard's analysis was both perceptive and, as it turned out, prophetic. Within a decade, the community was indeed to lose touch with its original sense of mission, it did fall into debased policies and become guilty of self-promotion and complacency. And this was precisely because the community did admit new members to positions of responsibility and leadership before they had grasped the ethos on which the community was based and before they had become 'members of the family.'

But these disasters lay in the future. For the time being, thanks to the continued support of Elmgrant, the life and work of Withymead continued to thrive. However, several members of the Management Committee were already expressing some anxiety when they thought about what lay ahead from the community. Gilbert was beginning to show his age, and there was no knowing how long Elmgrant money would continue to flow in to meet the annual deficit. If Withymead was ever to enjoy a sense of permanence, the succession to the Champernownes would have to be assured and some way would have to be found of putting the Centre's finances on a more secure basis.

Attempts to take some of the load off Elmgrant by making applications to other charitable Trusts resulted in a few hundred pounds here and there, but no organization showed the slightest interest in guaranteeing the kind of sum Withymead needed if it was to keep going indefinitely. Various fund raising experts in London were consulted who gave conflicting advice, though most agreed that unless a Trust could be found whose Trustees were as deeply interested in the Centre and as personally committed to its welfare as Leonard and Dorothy Elmhirst applications for large sums were likely to prove fruitless.

Fears that private resources might one day be unavailable to meet Withymead's needs inevitably caused some people to consider the possibility of applying to the government for help. The vast majority of hospitals and residential units for the treatment of mental illness had been under state control since the inauguration of the National Health Service in 1948. But there were, nevertheless, a few private mental hospitals and nursing homes left, and some of these had made successful applications to the Ministry of Health for state aid, in return for an undertaking to place themselves at the service of patients referred to them by the N.H.S. Examples were the Tavistock Clinic, which at that time was thought to receive a government grant of £44,000 a year, the Cassel Hospital, and the Lady Chichester Hospital, all of which had been entirely private and now, despite their change in status, still enjoyed a considerable measure of autonomy.

The prospect of state aid for Withymead was in many ways attractive. The N.H.S. had at its disposal vast sums of money, and those responsible for its administration had completly abandoned the notion that psychiatric services should be expected to pay their way, accepting without question the principle that such services were in the social interest and should, consequently, be supported by the nation as a whole. To such a huge organization as the N.H.S. Withymead's financial needs would represent a minute fraction of total annual expenditure, in return for which the Service would obtain access to a unique therapeutic environment and would enjoy the kudos of supporting an advanced experiment which was already becoming internationally respected.

However, the disadvantages would be very great. And Gilbert was not slow to point them out when the question of opening negotiations with the N.H.S. was discussed by the Management Committee at Withymead in April, 1956. Gilbert was convinced that Withymead and the National Health Service just would not mix, and that any attempt to amalgamate them would be a disaster for the community. The N.H.S. was a highly organized, bureaucratic administration accustomed to dealing with large, impersonal units which increasingly tended to become standardized. Withymead, on the other hand, was a family community concerned exclusively with individuals. The contradiction in aims and attitudes between the two organizations was fundamental and irreconcilable: if they came together one would have to change out of all recognition and it would not be the National Health Service. Maurice Ash, the Elmhirsts' son-in-law, was in complete agreement with Gilbert. Once Withymead become subject to inspection and outside interference it would lose its unique intimacy as well as its autonomy. In addition to the radical administrative changes that would be imposed, the availability of patients' records to other eyes would damage the therapeutic power of the staff meeting, the confessional aspect would be lost, and the spiritual quality of Withymead devalued. Moreover, the delicate balance which had so far been maintained between the age groups and different diagnostic categories would be destroyed because the Centre would be unable to refuse anyone and could at any time be inundated by unsuitable patients.

There seemed to be no way out of the predicament. All the committee could do was reaffirm the Centre's gratitude to the Elmgrant Trust and go forward in the earnest hope that subsidies from that source would continue to be forthcoming. Leonard did his best to reassure them at the next Management Committee meeting held in May, 1956, saying that the Elmgrant Trustees had underwritten a sum of up to £3,600 a year until 1960 against possible loss on the general expenses of the Centre. This came as a great relief to everybody, but the more percipient recognized that Withymead's financial problems had been postponed rather than solved.

Meanwhile, undaunted by the traumas that lay ahead, the community went cheerfully about its business. As in all families, an essential part of it concerned children, who were particularly well catered for at Withymead. Being childless themselves, Irene and Gilbert took a special interest in them, and few visitors came away unimpressed by the love, sensitivity and above all the tolerance with which all children were treated, even the most disturbed of them. The two members of staff with particular responsibility for their welfare were the analyst, Eve Lewis, and the ex-teacher, Mary Pye.

Children in residence lived with Mary Pye in Red Wing, the modern pavilion built by Ben Belten on the Barton lawn. Mary thought Ben's design was a complete success: 'Mind you, he was terribly good about discussing it and we spent hours talking over the details, so I suppose I had some little share in it all. I asked if we could have a fireplace in the sitting room, but Ben said it would cost too much to put in a chimney. But he did manage to provide us with a closed-in stove, which the children loved because it have us a nice live fire to sit by when I read them their bed-time story'. In addition to the sitting room there were three bedrooms, and when these were not all needed for children, Richard Fitzsche, who ran the pottery, lived in one of them. 'In his quiet way he gave them just what they needed. He was a male figure whom they could easily relate to because he naturally honoured whatever they were doing. And because of his practical skill with materials and mechanical things the boys absolutely loved him.'

The sitting room in Red Wing also served as Mary's bedroom. 'One's private life was very much at the mercy of Withymead, but that was what made it a home and not an institution. Just as Gilbert and Irene made their personal home-life in Withymead and shared it with everyone, so the rest of us did the same. Nobody was time-conscious. Even if you'd had a heavy day, you might still have to sit up all night because someone was very disturbed or had run off somewhere and you'd have to drive into the wilds looking for them. But in those days I don't think it ever really got too much for us. One felt so much part of it all that events took hold of you and carried you through.'

'Mary Pye had a wonderful way with children,' said Eve Lewis. 'A lot of the successes I had with child patients at Withymead was due to her. The children were also helped by the wide distribution of the age groups which made up what was essentially a complete community – like a medieval village. Every stage of life was represented from very young to very old, and one generation supported another. The adolscents were helped by seeing the younger children act out their feelings and conflicts in a way that they had been unable to. They often experienced their own regression through the younger ones, and that was very important because it meant they were freer to experience the regression creatively.

'But it was the exceptional tolerance of the adults at Withymead that made it possible to treat children successfully there. You see, very often a sick child is not tolerated by a whole community. It may sometimes be tolerated at home, or occasionally at school, but not by society at large. But the ready understanding of everybody at Withymead that a child was sick made him feel supported and helped, particularly in the middle-childhood years when containment by a group is of fundamental importance. I am utterly convinced that the most effective way to treat people – children particularly – is within the "medieval village" group, where all ages are intimately contained within one community.'

Most of the Centre's therapists agreed that the relative numerical balance between members of different generations was a factor of great significance for the continuing stability of the community. In this, as in other matters, history was to prove them right. For when, in the 1960s, much larger numbers of adolescents were admitted, they tended to gang up together and disrupt the easy reciprocity which had hitherto governed relations between the generations at Withymead.

During the 1950s, however, only a handful of children were usually in residence, though these numbers could be swollen temporarily by day patients, many of whom used to come on Saturdays, or by children who came to stay because their parents were being treated as residents, it being not unknown for Withymead to accommodate whole families. Children were never separated from their parents if it could be avoided, and many were admitted not because of any obvious signs of disturbance in themselves, but because their mother had broken down and the staff had encouraged her to bring her child with her when she came for admission. The community would automatically assume the responsibility for the child that the mother could not carry herself, until such time as she could. When a mother was initially so sick as to be incapable of looking after her child in any way, Mary Pye would deputise for her, letting the child know that his mother was there, but that she was poorly and in need of a rest. Mary would point out the mother's bedroom window, and if she appeared they would wave and blow kisses: 'That was reassuring to the child and to the mother,' said Mary. 'It avoided the awful break that so often happens. At Withymead we did all we could to keep the link between mother and child alive and help it to grow stronger. Mother wasn't "gone", she was "there", and that made all the difference. Then, gradually, we would bring them together again, as the mother could bear to take it on. In this way we were usually able to avoid the crisis which occurs when a mother comes out of hospital and returns abruptly to the demands of her home and her children, who, all too frequently, have themselves been seriously disturbed by her absence.'

So, in a manner of speaking, 'family therapy' was practiced at Withymead, but in a living, natural way and not through any formalized procedures. At the same time, there was little that was haphazard about what was done, for the threads were always picked up from all sides at the staff meeting and everyone was made aware of what was going on, so that the overall situation could be appreciated. The wider consciousness generated at the staff meeting was then fed back to the parents in the course of analytic sessions and, more indirectly, to the children during their daily activities. My own correspondence and interviews with ex-patients have left me in no doubt that by using this approach Withymead was able to salvage an impressive number of families.

Lack of formality was very evident in the relations which therapists established with the children in the community. Frequent, easy-going contacts were preferred to scheduled analytic sessions. 'Rene would just encounter them during the day,' said Mary Pye, 'in the studios, or in the dining room at meal-times, or she'd go for a walk with them round the garden. We tried to weave insight and healing into the daily life of the child.

Emotional security was enhanced in children by the personal interest taken in them by all members of the community, not least by 'Mr and Mrs C.', for in a very real sense they were the community's children, the youngest members of the family. 'The men's working party was particularly good to them,' said Mary. 'Once they built a great raft for them, and a house at the top of a tree. Then they made them an underground den, with a chimney that stuck up through the earth with a fireplace underneath, and, oh, they did love it so!'

Though a gifted teacher of long experience, Mary Pye did not attempt any formal education of the children entrusted to her care at Withymead: 'I just followed their lead, encouraging their own explorations. We used to go a lot into Exeter, to shop, to the Cathedral, looking at the misericords and carvings under the seats, and the other lovely bits of Exeter like the Miller's Clock and the old Customs' House on the Quay.

Mary particularly remembered a little boy of four, who was greatly excited one morning by witnessing the birth of a calf at a nearby farm. 'Afterwards, we went to the Cathedral together,' Mary recalled, 'and he happened to notice that medieval wood carving of the shepherds singing about the birth of Jesus. This excited him even more – on top of the experience of seeing the calf born – and when we got back to Withymead, he got out all the toy farm animals, spread them all over the floor, and said "Play me the piano." So I played for him, and he sang and sang for three-quarters of an hour, his own song of birth which he made up as he went along. All the time he was singing he built a circle of fences and animals around himself, totally absorbed in what he was doing. All I had to do was go on playing his favourite tunes and rhymes. Afterwards he wouldn't allow anything to be moved. We had to leave it all as it was on the floor.

'I was thankful that that particular morning I had only one child to be with. It couldn't have happened if I'd had a group of them. It was a marvellous experience for both of us – a celebration of birth.'

While Gilbert and Irene knew that preservation of the community's family configuration was essential to its success and survival, they did not betray any facile optimism about the ease with which this could be achieved. As we have seen, the cost to themselves, materially and emotionally, was immense, and both recognized that a crucial part of the archetypal reality of family life meant tolerating its shadow as well as celebrating its joys. Withymead could not hope to escape the crises, tensions and tragedies that all families suffer: these had to be confronted and lived through if people were also to share in the benefits which family intimacy can bring.

For this reason, neither Gilbert nor Irene was in the habit of putting a gloss on things 'for the sake of the children'. If they were upset they showed it – just as readily as when they were pleased. If they were worried about money or somebody's behaviour, for example, they made no effort to conceal the fact, but shared their feelings openly with whoever happened to be about at the time.

Irene was particulary free with her feelings in this way. The truth of the matter was that for her, Withymead was a theatre in which she, her staff, and her patients lived out the central dramas of their lives. Many people have testified to the dramatic quality of life at Withymead, attributing it in large measure to the ease with which Irene gave vent to her emotions. 'Irene was always larger than life,' said Mary Pye, who had known her since they were at College together. 'Everything in her seemed to go so much further than with ordinary people, and often in opposite directions. At Withymead her warm-hearted mothering was always generous and far-reaching; but so too was her negative side. She was so loving that she'd never hesitate to sit up all night if somebody needed her, however weary she might be. And yet she could be just as hard and ruthless in anger, and there were sometimes really terrible rows. For years I lived in terror of having to face one of Irene's negative outbursts. But it was this freedom of living in her own reality that gave people who came to Withymead the freedom to begin living in themselves.'

Mary went on: 'I remember watching Rene driving her car up a hill. It was an old car and wouldn't climb very well. She just grasped the steering wheel and rocked determinedly back and forth, as if urging it over the brow of the hill. That was typical of Rene – so *in* everything she did. She was always a creature of impulse. She plunged in without reflection, regardless of the situation of the person. Her love saved lives, but her rage could be devastating. But, after all, you can't have one without the other. If you're going to have that great, generous, mothering warmth, which she was full of, then you've got to put up with the other side as well, or it wouldn't really be balanced.'

Practically everyone who ever worked with Irene express-ed a similar view of her duality. 'She is both creative and destructive,' her old colleague, Florida Scott-Maxwell, told me. 'She can be wonderfully loving and bitterly hating as well. She has always been, and always will be, a maker of drama. She is the archetype of the powerful mother: she either mothers or destroys. At Withymead I saw wonderful things and I saw terrible things. Rene's passionate maternal-ism sometimes made people punch-drunk: she would kiss them on one cheek and then slap them on the other!'

Mrs Scott-Maxwell was a very different person from Irene – introverted, highly cultivated and self-controlled – and she found life at Withymead more than she could take. 'For me, the good of Withymead was offset by the never-ending internal dramas. Part of the problem was the hot emotional intensity that Withymead seemed to breed. Rene had such a charge of energy that she needed a group of people round her to pour it into, but it overcharged them too. I got weighed down by the strain of having my patients living on top of me, and, eventually, I just had to pull out, coming in a few times a week. But Rene could have carried on to the grave. She couldn't move even without four or five of them in her car! But it was her force and passion that made Withymead last as long as it did.'

Eve Lewis entirely concurred: 'Irene is an extremely

emotional person who could be most difficult to work with. But against the casualties one must set the new insights, the mended lives, the great positive contribution that she made. So closely identified was she with the place that Withymead was inconceivable without her, as history subsequently proved.'

That Irene could be 'most difficult to work with' cannot be denied by anyone who has tried it. She could be wilful, headstrong, and ruthless in getting her own way. Usually, her colleagues tolerated this out of admiration for her genius as a therapist and their affection for her as a person. But every so often she would go too far: there would be a major row, and the colleague, feeling that enough was enough, would resign. This pattern was repeated several times in the 1940s and 50s but was to occur a good deal more often in the 1960s, as more professional personnel – particularly doctors – came in from outside and, through their insensitivity to Withymead's ways, incurred the full impact of Irene's wrath.

This wastage of staff through emotional wear-and-tear was not always easy to make good, despite Irene's gift for attracting able and talented people to the community. Not only was it difficult to find analysts and psychiatrists of the right callibre who would be willing to adjust their lives to the exigent demands placed on them by Withymead, but the financial constraints under which the Management Committee operated made it impossible for them to offer salaries anywhere near those paid to consultants by the National Health Service. As a result of this dilemma, members of the Committee began to argue that the problem of appropriate staffing could only be solved if Withymead promoted a policy of breeding its own therapists within the community.

One idea, received with some enthusiasm, was that Withymead might plan its own training programme in collaboration with the Society of Analytical Psychology (then the only Jungian Society in London) and the C.G. Jung Institute in Zurich. Since the early '50s, the Centre had been organizing regular courses which social workers, teachers and psychiatric workers from outside Withymead were invited to attend. The increased dining room capacity and the completion of the River Room achieved soon after the arrival of Ben Belton, had meant that a fair number of participants could be catered for. The courses were usually conducted by the combined psychotherapeutic staff and were designed to illustrate the uses to which the arts could be put in the treatment of mental illness. Some notable speakers from Zurich and London contributed to these courses and seminars, and they proved increasingly popular and successful. It did not seem too far-fetched to imagine that, with the cooperation and supervision of professional bodies in London and Zurich, these intermittent educational initiatives could be welded into a more consistent and extended programme.

Everyone agreed that an obvious candidate for further training was Joanna Hogg. Her therapeutic gifts were widely recognized, and more and more of her secretarial and social work had been taken over by others so as to give Joanna more time to be with patients and thus help Irene with the large case load she was carrying. Irene, who had the highest regard for the quality of her work, was wholeheartedly in favour of the idea that Joanna should undergo formal training as an analyst. A modest start was made in 1956 when, with assistance from a bequest from Dr Joyce Partridge, a psychiatrist with whom Irene had been associated since her arrival in Exeter during the war, Joanna began going to London one or two days a fortnight to attend lectures and have sessions with a training analyst. However, Joanna found this sporadic training to be of limited usefulness, and began to feel that the only proper course would be for her to take three years' leave of absence from Withymead in order to go away to Zurich and do the full Jungian analytic training there – if only a way could be found to cope with the considerable financial burden that such a course would entail, both for Joanna and for Withymead.

Although Withymead was continuing to perform its

functions very admirably, the anxieties experienced by the Trustees and members of the Management Committee when they contemplated what might be in store for the Centre were by no means confined to the annual deficit which persisted at approximately £4,000. Even if they succeeded somehow in making the community solvent and its financial future secure, there was still the problem of how to guarantee Withymead's professional and spiritual survival when Gilbert and Irene decided to retire. Gilbert was aging rapidly: his arthritis was so bad that he could walk only very slowly and painfully with the aid of two stout walking sticks; he was getting very deaf, and was subject to bouts of depression, when he could hardly bring himself to grapple with the routine administrative affairs of the Centre. As for Irene, she was still vigorously in her prime, but it was nevertheless realized that she could not be expected to bear indefinitely the full clinical weight of the community.

For the time being Withymead was able to manage. But its success was due, in no small measure, to the dedication, hard work, and rare personal qualities of Joanna and her brother Ben. Indeed, as everyone said, it was hard to imagine what Irene and Gilbert would do without them – an opinion which Irene and Gilbert shared and which they were not slow to acknowledge. This invaluable pair had, in fact, become like a son and daughter to them, and the evident affection and intellectual sympathy which existed between the older and younger couple formed an inner circle at the heart of the community which seemed to guarantee its security.

It was scarcely surprising, therefore, that the thought began to grow in the minds of those responsible for the future of the Centre – particularly John Trevelyan and Leonard and Dorothy Elmhirst – that the solution to the problem of Gilbert and Irene's succession might reside in the persons of Joanna and Ben. Indeed, the thought must have occurred quite early on to Irene herself, for in a paper she prepared in 1955 she wrote: 'I see the conscious community as small and dependent on woman's consciousness . . . as if the libido has to return to the mother in order to find the basic image of the community – the "family" archetype, which lies in woman's unconscious. And the daughter is the only one who can carry this on in continuity from woman to woman, giving man a chance to relate to it, for it cannot be actualized except by his relation to it . . . The devotion of the daughter is the activity which gives it body.' It is hard to see that Irene could have had anyone else in mind that Joanna to play Kore to her Demeter.

Among the Trustees, John Trevelyan was especially enthusiastic in support of the idea that Joanna should receive adequate training to secure Withymead's future. Her long experience of Withymead linked with her filial devotion to Irene and Gilbert would ensure that when the time came for her to assume responsibility for the Centre's life the essential traditions of the community would be respected and perpetuated through her.

Since no one seemed to know where money could be found to finance Joanna's training as an analyst, John Trevelyan took it upon himself to see what he could do on her behalf. He was at that time married to Joan Scott, sister of Irene's friend, Peter Scott, Chairman of the Provincial Insurance Company. Since Joan and Peter were both interested in Withymead's work, John Trevelyan felt encouraged to approach the Scott family Trust with a request for a grant to cover the cost of Joanna's training. The application was successful, but Trevelyan did not at once transmit the glad tidings to Withymead: 'Some cautious instinct prompted me to act through Leonard Elmhirst,' he told me. 'So I wrote to him, saying "I leave it up to you as to what you do about it."'

Sadly, when news of Trevelyan' successful initiative eventually reached Withymead it was not received with unqalified joy. The trouble was that the sum involved – £1,500 a year – was a considerable one at that time in Withymead's history, and Irene and Gilbert felt very strongly that if Trevelyan wished to make so much money available he should have proceeded differently: he should not have made up his own mind as to how it should be spent without reference to the Management Committee or the Directors of the Centre (i.e. Gilbert and Irene) and he should not have declared his intentions behind the scenes, as it were, in a private letter to the Chairman of the Trustees. Gilbert and Irene discussed the matter at length, and the more they thought about it the more convinced they became, rightly or wrongly, that they must take a stand over the issue.

The result was a row of the kind that can only occur in families. The parties who had previously been bound together by love, loyalty and shared identity, suddenly felt themselves to have been betrayed, and the acrimony which followed was so intense as to imperil the whole future of Withymead. In every way it was a tragedy. Not only did it lead to deep estrangement between the older couple and Joanna and Ben which, in Gilbert's case was never to be resolved, but also to a confrontation with the Trustees which was to place an almost intolerable strain on the Champernownes' friendship with the Elmhirsts, eventually causing the latter to cut off all financial supplies to Withymead, with consequences which were ultimately linked with the disintegration of the community and the closure of the Centre.

In retrospect it all seems tragically unnecessary. In view of the understanding which had united all parties hitherto, it is extraordinary that such fierce differences should suddenly erupt to the surface, so that the sensitive lines of communication once shared by everyone should be cut at a stroke, and harmonious unity replaced by bitter dissent. But from the moment Irene and Gilbert decided to take their stand over what they regarded as an important matter of principle, they appeared to Joanna and Ben as ungenerous parents determined to thwart the legitimate ambition of their offspring, while Irene interpeted the resentful rebelliousness of Joanna and Ben as evidence of a desire on their part to take advantage of Gilbert's declining health to organize a palace revolution with the objective of taking over Withymead for themselves.

It was a terrible time for everyone, not least the Champer-nownes, for it was now apparent that Gilbert was very ill indeed and had not much longer to live. His illness, together with the bitterness of the quarrel with Joanna and Ben, combined to drive him into a despair from which Irene, for all her love and skill, was powerless to rescue him. Then, in September 1959, a specialist whom he had consulted saw Irene and told her that Gilbert had cancer of the pancreas.

'Have you told him?' she asked.

'No,' replied the doctor. 'You shouldn't tell him. He could live for nine months or a year.'

'I shall tell him,' said Irene. 'We've always shared everything.'

She collected him from the hospital where the diagnostic tests had been done and drove him to Kenn. There she stopped the car in a meadow near their cottage and told him what the doctor had said.

'You mean I'm dying, Rene,' he said.

'Yes, darling,' she said. 'I'm afraid it's true.'

He sat silent for a while, staring at the beech trees turning red in the autumn sunlight. Then he said, 'I wonder what it will be like.'

Later she asked him whether he wanted to die at Kenn or at Withymead. 'I want to die at Withymead,' he said.

And so he did. Not nine months, but nine weeks later.

Chapter VIII

A House Divided

Like so many things about Withymead, Gilbert's decision to die, as he had lived, a committed member of the community, represented the reversal of a contemporary trend: not for him the anonymous, curtained cubicle of a hospital ward, leaving the family to get on with its life undisturbed and insulated from its grief.

'He died at seven o'clock in the morning after a very difficult night,' said Irene. 'Molly, Mary, Sylvie, my neice and I were all there. Everyone in Withymead knew he was dying, and over the last few days they'd all looked in to say goodbye to him. So I put up a little notice to say he'd died and went into my room to rest while Sylvie did all the necessary things.

'About an hour later I heard a lot of bustling going on in the next room, so I opened the door, and there was all Withymead, it seemed, arranging flowers and candles – a "lying in state" was in progress! Afterwards, many of them said that it was their first experience of death, but now they'd seen it they wouldn't fear it any more.

'We buried Gilbert at Dartington in the family grave after a service in the Church at Kenn. Dorothy gave us lunch afterwards up at the Hall. And then I went to Oxford to be near John Hooper.'

Father John Hooper had been moved from Kenn to Oxford in the summer of 1959 to become Vicar of St Mary Magdalen, and his translation could not have come at a worse time. Now, in her grief, Irene had great need of him, feeling that only near him would she be able to come to terms with the enormity of her loss. As several people have testified, Irene's grief was quite terrible to behold: she was annihilated by it.

Between them Father John and Doris Layard, who also lived in Oxford, helped her through the three weeks after the funeral, at the end of which she returned to Withymead. 'I was dazed but I managed to work. No matter what happened to me I've always seemed to be able to cope with patients. Of course, they would talk about Gilbert, or dream about him, and then I'd be tearful, and I used to worry about that, but, you know, it didn't do any harm. They'd entered into it all, anyway, and so they could sorrow with me, and that made it real, and it didn't matter. The work wasn't affected at all.'

But however little it affected her work with her patients, there can be no doubt that in the months following Gilbert's death Irene's anguish affected her judgement in dealing with her colleagues and friends. Her state had not been helped by the joint departure from Withymead of Joanna and Ben before Gilbert died – Joanna to study at Zurich, and Ben to return to architectural practice in London. In the unhappy climate accompanying their departure, Gilbert and Irene had decided to oppose John Trevelyan's continued Trusteeship, since they had convinced themselves that his interference was responsible for the tragic row that had poisoned the last months of Gilbert's life.

On learning of the Champernownes' attitude, Trevelyan had written to Leonard Elmhirst offering to resign. But Leonard was reluctant to let him do so and preferred to allow his letter to 'lie on the table'. The situation was still unresolved when Gilbert died, and it was not long after Irene's return from Oxford that it came up for consideration. Unfortunately, Irene now felt impelled to adopt a totally inflexible attitude over the matter. Together she and Gilbert had decided they must insist that Trevelyan should go. 'Either he resigns or we do,' they had told Leonard. In Irene's mind this ultimatum now assumed the sacred force of a death-bed injunction, and she stood by it, unreservedly.

Feeling that Irene was being unreasonable about this, Leonard proposed to her that she meet with the Trustees other than John Trevelyan (these now included Lord Chaplin as well as Maurice Ash and Leonard) to put her point of view and see if they could reach an agreement. But Irene replied that she could not face a formal meeting with the Trustees. Instead she asked to see Leonard and Dorothy alone to discuss the matter with them personally. This request Leonard reluctantly refused, pointing out that it was an important issue affecting the whole Trustee body, and that each of the Trustees must be fully appraised of the situation so that they might decide what was to be done, since none of them could see any reason why so valuable a Trustee as John Trevelyan should be forced to resign.

To Leonard's consternation Irene remained adamant. Under no circumstances could she meet the Trustees. 'I dug my heels right in. Leonard wanted the Trustees to come over and see me, but I just wasn't in a fit state to receive them. I was too tearful. I'm a tearful person anyway, but at that time I could not have faced those Trustees. So I wrote to Leonard saying, "I just cannot meet you all, and I *won't* meet you all. I've told you my decision: I'll see you alone, but I will *not* see all the Trustees together."'

Faced with this total intransigence, the Trustees came to the conclusion that there was only one course open to them. They resigned. All of them.

Thus was the goose well and truly cooked. And it was no ordinary goose. For ten years it had, regularly and without complaint, laid large golden eggs. But now the situation was desperate, and when the news reached Withymead it was received with utter bewilderment. People shook their heads and muttered that had Gilbert been alive things would never have reached this pass. But he was not alive, and with some alarm Irene and the community realized that they were now really on their own.

This was the turning point in Withymead's history. The double catastrophe of Gilbert's death and the loss of the Elmhirsts' support dealt a blow to the Centre which was ultimately to prove fatal. Although Leonard's termination of his association with Withymead was characteristically generous – he agreed to continue making an annual grant, on a declining scale, over the next three years – in fact no new source of income was ever found to make good the loss of Elmgrant subsidies. And while it was true that the community was essentially feminine in nature – a womb, a vessel, a temenos which took people into itself until they were healed – Irene's conviction that the feminine community needed a masculine figure at its head and in its heart was to prove absolutely justified. Try as she did, she could never find a male figure capable of taking over Gilbert's role: administrators and medical directors came and went but none of them succeeded in relating sensitively to the community or in becoming its spokesman as Gilbert had done. As a result, the masculine and feminine poles of the community drifted steadily apart until, eventually, they became implacably opposed to one another, and the family group was shattered. The sad truth is that from the moment of Gilbert's death, Withymead followed an erratic downhill course which resisted all attempts to reverse it, the whole community becoming the victim of a messy struggle for pre-eminence between the patrist and matrist components on whose hormonious relationship the health and security of the Centre was based.

The story of Withymead's decline is worth telling because it is both dramatic and instructive. It not only demonstrates how crucial is the masculine/feminine balance for community survival but also how vulnerable are such original experiments as Withymead to the dead hand of bureaucracy in our increasingly syndicalized society. Withymead was a casualty of that form of 'social progress' which resulted in institutions becoming more impersonal as they surrender to legislative interference from outside. As this stultifying affliction attacks institutions for the care of the mentally sick, so the inner meaning of an individual patient's distress dwindles into insignificance and is smothered by a barren idealism which preaches Adaptation To The Norm – at the minimum of cost. The disintegration of Withymead is also a cautionary illustration of what happens when in defence of sectional interests people lose sight of the whole, when to advance what they see as their cause they strike political attitudes, form opposing factions and begin collectively to project their shadows on one another.

The political battles which accompanied the decline and fall of Withymead were faught unequivocally along gender lines. The female party (known to the males as 'The Old Gang') consisted of Irene, as undisputed leader, and her close colleagues Molly Kemp, Mary Pye, Euanie Tippett (art therapist), Sylvie Wiess, Eve Lewis, Doris Layard, and other women therapists who served at various times on the staff. The male party was made up of whoever happened to be medical director at the time ('Monsieur de Maintenant' as some wags called him), the male Trustees (when they were appointed) and male members of the Management Committee, and, despite all his noble efforts to remain impartial and the friend of both parties, Douglas Crosse (Withymead's very able legal adviser).

The policy of the female party was uncomplicated and uncompromising: it was simply to preserve Withymead as it had been in its heyday. To achieve this they had to find a director capable of replacing Gilbert and a benefactor willing to replace Leonard Elmhirst. When these two indispensible figures were found it was imperative that they understood and respected Withymead's ways and did nothing to change them.

The male party, on the other hand, saw its primary objectives as financial and operational. The books must balance. If no private source of money could be found to cover the Centre's losses then there were three possible courses of action: (1) closure; (2) reorganization along commercial lines; (3) association with the National Health Service. Avoidance of the first possibility could only be achieved if Withymead 'put its house in order', cut out uneconomic practices, and adapted more readily to the standards and expectations of the medical and psychiatric establishment, which constituted the main source of patient referrals from outside. In the absence of a private backer, Withymead would *have* to change its ways and, whether they liked it or not, the female party would just have to face up to the fact.

Hostilities began almost as soon as Irene had recovered sufficiently from the loss of Gilbert to take an interest in Withymead's affairs. As time went on and the gap between the two parties widened, so exchanges between them became more charged with personal animosity and less inclined to appreciate each other's point of view. The wear and tear on the nerves of protagonists on both sides was considerable.

The position following the mass resignation of the Trustees was that the property of the Withymead Trust became vested in Irene, Douglas Crosse and Michael Loup (Irene's solicitor in London). Together this 'interregnum triumvirate' formed a governing body responsible for Withymead until new permanent Trustees could be found and a New Management Committee appointed.

Being conscientious men the two lawyers wasted no time in subjecting the Centre's financial affairs to careful examination and they were not satisfied with what they found. 'It is quite clear that Withymead cannot continue to run its finances as hitherto,' wrote Loup to Crosse. 'The system of subsidising patients from a budgeting point of view must end and the budget must be based on the patients paying the full charge of 20 guineas [per week].' For his part, Crosse looked into the staffing arrangements and what he found struck him as 'quite fantastic'. 'For an average number of residents of 16 and an absolute maximum of 20, it seems almost incredible that there are 16 professional staff (of whom 10 have board in addition to their salaries), 7 household and office staff (of whom 4 have board in addition to their wages); there are 3 garden staff and no less than 12 domestics.' In round figures, annual expenditure on wages and salaries was running at the rate of £9,300 a year. The breakdown was as follows:

medical and nursing staff	£3,400
teaching and remedial staff	£2,800
domestic staff	£ 500
office and secretarial staff	£1,260
outside and maintenance staff	£1,400

Both men agreed that some belt tightening was indicated, a procedure they knew Irene would not take to kindly. Crosse confided to Loup that he had recently been consulted by a lady who was a patient at Withymead. In the course of obtaining his instructions, he had inquired of this lady how long she could afford to continue paying 16 guineas a week in respect of fees at Withymead. He was flabbergasted when she replied that she certainly couldn't pay such fees but that Withymead was 'being very good to her and had taken her onto the staff at £4 a week plus board,' and that she merely had to pay the Centre for each analytic session she had with Mrs Champernowne. 'If we were to enquire into this,' opined Crosse, 'we should probably find that this lady is paying about 2 guineas a week for her sessions, and the result is that Withymead is losing 14 guineas a week in respect of fees (754 p.a.), plus wages of £208, making a total of £962 p.a. One hesitates to think what would float to the surface if one really stirred this administration.'

In addition to shaking up the administration, both Loup and Crosse considered it important in the interests of Withymead's legal and professional status that the Centre should eventually become registered as a mental nursing home under the provisions of the new Mental Health Act of 1959. As a first step in that direction it was essential that Withymead should be placed under the clinical direction of a medically qualified consultant. They hunted for a suitable candidate and believed they had found their man in the shape of one Dr Kimber, a retired physician superintendent of a large mental hospital. Crosse had a talk with him and was impressed: 'He put forward some really excellent suggestions and it was a real treat to deal with a psychiatrist who has both feet firmly on the ground.'

Though far from enthusiastic at the prospect of Dr Kimber's appointment, Irene acknowledged that the Centre would have to be registered under the Act and that as a necessary preliminary to registration a medical director would have to be installed. In Dr Kimber's favour it could be said that he was an enlightened psychiatrist who had fostered the use of psychotherapy in the hospital where he had worked, and if Withymead must have a medical director it could do worse than appoint him.

Unfortunately, Dr Kimber was now an old man, and he had spent a life-time in the hierarchically structured world of conventional medical and psychiatric practice. When he took up his duties at Withymead he found much to shock him: clinical records were sparse and far from complete, clinical meetings were a general free-for-all where scant respect was shown for medical authority, and admission procedures struck him as hopelessly haphazard. Moreover, he considered that the Centre's therapists were insufficiently aware of the need for full medical cover and that they failed to appreciate the grave legal and professional responsibility that was carried by Withymead's doctors. As the Centre's new director, Dr Kimber saw it as his duty to remedy these deficiencies as rapidly and as effectively as possible.

His efforts, of course, brought him into a head-on collision with Irene. Instead of appreciating the need for his good intentions, he was hurt and dismayed to discover that she roundly rejected them as subversive and as an attack on the fabric of the community. She acquainted the Management Committee with her views in a letter to the Chairman (Douglas Crosse) and she did not pull her punches: 'The community life rests on an inner authority vested in a weekly staff meeting at which *all* differences are *openly* discussed and a working compromise arrived at. This method is probably too democratic for a man of Dr Kimber's standing but it is essential for the *inner life* of the Centre which, by means of this strong team unity, makes possible the treatment of the difficult, despairing and sometimes destructive people who come.' Rapid, easy communication and absolute trust between staff members on an informal basis was the essence of the Withymead approach and attempts to disrupt this pattern of staff relationships by the introduction of a hierarchical medical organization would be a disaster. Patients, maintained Irene, relate to the group 'as one': 'the transference is shared by the community'. The staff must never allow itself to become stratified along divisions of rank and medical responsibility. Medical authority has always been respected at Withymead. Dr Geoffrey Willcock, the Centre's G.P., has given Withymead his close attention and skill for years, and he had been perfectly happy that the medical cover he provided was adequate until Dr Kimber began to sew doubts in his mind. 'The core of the life of the Centre will break up if Dr Kimber's medical, authoritative blueprints are forcibly superimposed on its life . . . We cannot alter our methods very much without making life untenable, nor can we consent to Withymead becoming a psychiatric unit. The whole meaning and purpose of its existence would be lost.'

Before he knew what had hit him Crosse found that he had a first class row on his hands. It was particularly sad that in the polarization of attitudes which ensued, Dr Geoffrey Willcock, who was a much loved member of the Withymead family circle, felt himself compelled to back Dr Kimber's position. Indeed, they both felt so strongly about the matter that they wrote a joint letter to Crosse tendering their resignations 'unless the medical direction and the treatment of patients is definitely placed in medical hands.' They went on, 'We both feel that we have a moral, professional and, we believe, a legal responsibility for securing this position, on which we cannot compromise.'

Though concerned about the situation, Crosse felt competent to deal with it because he now had the backing of two recently appointed permanent Trustees (the Bishop of Exeter and Sir George Hayter Haymes) and a strong, reconstituted Management Committee. In addition to Dr Kimber and old familiars like Doris Eyles (an old college chum of Irene's), Molly Kemp, Dr Willcock and Irene herself, Crosse had also persuaded to serve under his chairmanship Mr M. Holland-Hibbert, the local director of Barclays Bank, Mr Bob Taylor, local secretary of the National Union of Teachers, Dr David Sime, a local psychiatrist, later destined to be a medical director of Withymead, Mr J.L. Smeall, the Principal of St Luke's College, Exeter, Mrs Pillippa Clark, the wife of a local barrister, Mary Willcock, Geoffrey's wife, and a nominee of the Bishop of Exeter, the Rev. W.H. Dormer. That Crosse was able to recruit people of this calibre says much for his powers of persuasion and for the reputation enjoyed locally by Withymead and its work.

Crosse decided to make use of this backing in seeking a solution to the present crisis. Accordingly, he set up a clincial advisory subcommittee of the Management Committee charged with solving the problem of medical responsibility. Dr David Sime's presence of this subcommittee was of great assistance to Crosse and they were able to draft sensible proposals which were sent to Irene, Dr Kimber and Dr Willcock for their comments. The committee confirmed Irene's position as senior psychotherapist 'in complete charge of the residential side of Withymead', while stressing Dr Kimber's reponsibility 'for overall psychiatric supervision and guidance'. As far as admissions were concerned, all new patients should be seen by one doctor and one psychotherapist, final acceptance being decided by the staff meeting. These conciliatory proposals had the effect of cooling passions for the time being and, to everyone's relief, all three potagonists wrote saying they accepted them, while Kimber and Willcock withdrew their resignations.

The truce was brief, however. Within a few weeks Dr

Kimber began to express concern that the good name of Withymead could be tarnished as a result of delinquencies or suicides on the part of patients and to argue that special rules should be introduced to protect the administration and deal with these eventualities should they occur. This idea of introducing rules, regulations and official guidelines to deal with emotionally charged situations was so counter to Withymead's traditional way of doing things that Irene was incensed. She fired off another of her letters to Crosse: 'The community has always tried to meet these difficulties and live them down by virtue of the work. We are indentified with the so-called failures of life, and we accept the consequences because we do not share the same assessment of the word "failure".' To become anxious about the reputation of the Centre, she argued, would be to produce the very thing they feared, 'out of the hundreds of patients with whom I have dealt in the last 25 years, the larger portion have at some time wanted to take their lives, and many have confessed to delinquent tendencies, or to delinquency itself. If we do not grow fearful, we can usually carry this, whether it is known by the whole community or not. We hope that the good name of the Centre will be maintained without our having to keep too conscious an eye on what the world will think of us. This takes away the simplicity of our approach which, I believe, is a stronger preventive than an active, *direct* attempt to protect out position.'

This was wise, true and well argued, but her message went unheeded because Kimber was not in touch with the spirit of the traditional community, and the rows continued. 'The present troubles', wrote Irene in another letter to Crosse, 'are because the real aim and purpose of the Centre as a psychotherapeutic community are not understood by those in authority. A house divided against itself cannot stand.' This quotation was to find increasing use over the next few years as its truth became ever more relevant.

Further attempts were made to define and regulate the differences between Irene's role as senior psychotherapist and

Kimber's role as medical director, but to little avail. To Irene and her close friends and allies on the staff, all attempts to impose formal structure on the procedures of the community and to categorize the residents in their care constituted a violation of the values of the very heart of Withymead's life, and they would have no part of them. Irene's skirmish with her elderly medical director was but the first round of a what was to be a protracted contest between the medical establishment on the one hand and those who saw themselves as the guardians of Withymead's integrity on the other.

Irene found all this irksome enough, but by the autumn of 1962, Dr Kimber was nearing the end of his tether: 'I am in an utterly false position which is affecting my health, and I would like to resign my post.' Geoffrey Willcock had also had enough and his resignation took effect, together with that of Dr Kimber, on November 17th. With their departure, it looked as if Irene's side had won the day. But their triumph was short lived. The decisive battles still lay ahead.

Dr Kimber was not the only one to feel that Withymead got him down, Douglas Crosse also found the pressure hard to take. His belief in Withymead caused him to work indefatigably on its behalf in return for a purely nominal fee. In addition to serving as a transitional Trustee and as chairman of the Management Committee, he committed himself to a huge correspondence, frequent journeys to London for discussions with Michael Loup, and an unending series of interviews with members of staff and of the Management Committee. Moreover, as he confessed in a letter to Leonard Elmhirst, he had increasingly felt the weight of Irene's personality bearing down on him, 'her telephone conversations often driving me to the very limits of nervous exhaustion!' His plaint struck a sympathetic cord in Leonard: 'You have exactly expressed the difficulty under which the previous board of Trustees operated,' he replied. 'What they found most difficult was the determination of

Mrs Champernowne to have her own way regardless of any constitutional machinery devised, and in the face of a deteriorating economic position. I doubt whether Mrs Champerowne will ever realise what a burden she lays on her best friends and business associates until she sees, in the form of an itemised account, the real cost of the way she operates.' Leonard ended his letter on an intimate note, warning Crosse to look out for himself: 'My last six months of effort as a Trustee helped to induce six further months of internal discomfort and, finally, the development of a sizable peptic ulcer. I would not wish you either experience.'

Crosse's anxieties were not made any easier by the continued deterioration of Withymead's financial position. All efforts to find a private benefactor proved fruitless, and Irene remained implacably opposed to any accommodation with the National Health Service. Crosse began to despair of saving the situation, unless he could use his good relations with Leonard Elmhirst to persuade him to forget the past and encourage the Elmgrant Trustees to return to Withymead's support. He made a number of determined efforts to achieve this, but Leonard remained obdurate. Irene's behaviour after the death of Gilbert evidently still rankled: 'When a woman like Mrs Champernowne decides to part company from a body of Trustees who supported her to the limit and financed her, she cannot expect the Elmgrant Trustees to go on indefinitely rescuing an enterprise which refuses to face financial realities.'

Crosse felt obliged to agree that Irene had 'only herself to blame' for Elmhirst's attitude, but he refused to lose faith: 'a great deal of good work has been done by Withymead and, provided a firm control is taken, will continue to be done. I have felt all along that our ultimate aim should be to obtain medical control, and by that I mean control by a doctor to whom Mrs Champernowne is from the start both administratively and medically subordinate.' But even as he wrote these words it is doubtful that Crosse imagined that Irene could ever be persuaded to 'subordinate' herself to anyone.

The trouble was that to men of affairs, even those like Leonard Elmhirst with a touch of the visionary about them, Irene often seemed cussedly irrational, if not downright impossible. Seriously preoccupied as they were with the vexed issues of Withymead's economic survival, Irene's male advisers were driven distracted by her apparent indifference to practical realities. With Irene, the 'priestly role' came first: her deeply intuitive grasp of the community's needs – which she seemed incapable of mediating to laymen in language they could understand – caused her to adopt attitudes which not infrequently struck her advisers as intransigent and unreasonable. Financial discussions made her impatient, especially when they led their participants away from the burning psychological issues as she saw them. The loving compassion that flowed abundantly from her great, warm heart drove her ever further into comtemplation of the suffering of the human soul and possessed her with visions of how she and Withymead could heal it. 'The work' was of such importance that the necessary cash *must* be found and, as she saw it, it was the responsibility of the Trustees and the rest to find it, and not to encumber her with constraints and administrative interference. She had the vision. She 'knew' *as a woman* what was needed if the community was to survive in psychological terms. It was for the Trustees and the Management Committee to find ways of making Withymead viable in the practical sense: not for them to obstruct, but to listen and provide. Her valiant optimism and mystical belief in the rightness of 'Life' convinced her that the necessary money could always be found somewhere; and when people at meetings – usually 'men' – were tirsome enough to 'go on' about it, she tended to switch off and think about other things, while performing flamboyant doodles on her agenda.

After the departure of Dr Kimber and Dr Willcock, the problems of Withymead's medical cover and administration were temporarily solved by the presence of Dr Dalziel, an amiable psychiatrist with a special interest in the arts, but everyone recognized the need for a permanent solution. The loss of Geoffrey Willcock's support was a severe personal blow to Irene, but it was not long before she met, and wooed, a possible replacement in the form of Dr Murray Cox, a young G.P., married with children, who was interested in psychotherapy, and was working hard to obtain his Diploma of Psychological Medicine so as to qualify himself for full-time psychiatric practice. A kindly, sensitive and attractive person, everyone who met him took an instant liking to Murray Cox, and it was not long before all Withymead began to look on him as the hero/saviour who would lift them out of their plight. Douglas Crosse was no less hopeful of him, and discussed with other members of the Management Committee the possibility of selling the Coxes a plot of Withymead land on which to build a house so that Murray might live and work within the community as medical and administrative director. 'I was impressed that although he was a young man of 32, he was clear thinking, forthright and appeared to have the necessary strength of character of such an office,' Crosse noted. He discussed the possibility of appointing Cox with Geoffrey Willcock, with whom he remained on good terms. Willcock was encouraging: he said he felt Cox was the only person who could save Withymead and considered that his appointment would mollify the local psychiatric fraternity which had viewed with evident concern the recent debacle over Dr Kimber.

While he agreed with everyone else that Murray Cox was the man Withymead needed, Crosse worried, inevitably, about where money could be found to pay his salary. Now that the last of the Elmhirst money had been received, Withymead was just managing to survive on its income, subsidized by small grants from the Rowntree Trust and more substantial sums from an 'anonymous donor' (who was, in fact, Molly Kemp). But it was a close run thing, and a visit from Murray Cox's accountant did little to reassure Douglas Crosse. He could not advise Dr Cox to give up his practice in London and move into Withymead, the accountant said, unless the Centre guaranteed him a salary of not less than £2,500 a year. 'I passed a remark,' says Crosse in his notes of their conversation, 'that in the present circumstances I could not see how Withymead could afford to pay Dr Cox a salary of £2,500, bearing in mind that the highest salary paid now was £900.'

Nevertheless, Douglas Crosse was nothing if not a tryer and, conscious of his gall, he again approached Leonard Elmhirst: 'It seems to me that unless you support us suffiently so that we are in a position to appoint Dr Cox, the closing of Withymead within the next two or three years is inevitable.' He cannot have been surprised when he received another firm refusal: the Elmgrant Trustees had entertained serious doubts about the management of Withymead, Leonard said, ever since Gilbert's death, and these new plans in no way mitigated their scepticism.

Clearly, the prospect of the Elmgrant Trustees ever again committing themselves to Withymead had now become so implausible that even Douglas Crosse must have given up hope. On the advice of Miss Appleby, Secretary of the National Association For Mental Health, to which Withymead was now affiliated, an adviser from the Nuffield Foundation was called in to review the overall situation at Withymead. His report was uncompromisingly pessimistic. Not only did he consider that Withymead had no hope of obtaining from charitable sources the kind of money needed, but he felt the Management Committee was hopelessly unrealistic about fees. They had just brought out a new brochure in which they described Withymead as 'a non-profit making Trust': this he thought 'a masterpiece of understatement!' He went on, 'They state that the weekly cost of keeping a patient at Withymead is £25, and at no stage have they ever attempted to get more that 18 guineas for this, and are apparently willing to consider reducing this amount in one way or another should they consider it to be necessary (in the patient's interests).' On the whole he thought the Centre was in a totally impossible position unless the

Management was prepared to contemplate a very substantial increase in fees. The only alternative to such a course was for Withymead to become a registered nursing home under the Mental health Act and to receive patients who would be paid for at a realistic rate by the Regional Hospital Board.

A no less forceful adviser was Miss Amy Buller, a remarkable woman and an old friend of Irene's, who, with assistance from H.M. Queen Elizabeth, the Queen Mother, had founded a residential centre at Cumberland Lodge in Windsor Great Park where students, lecturers and professors of differing nationalities and disciplines could mix freely together for long weekends in an effort to close intellectual and international divisions created by educational specialization and power politics. Miss Buller considered that her experience of running Cumberland Lodge gave her considerable insight into Withymead's problems and she persuaded Irene that, in addition to the appointment of Murray Cox, whom she liked and amired, Withymead needed a full-time bursar or administrator whose sole function it would be to put the Centre's finances in order and liaise with outside sources of private and public money. With the assistance of such an administrator Miss Buller had managed to keep Cumberland Lodge afloat and she could not see why someone like him would not do the same for Withymead.

There was little enough reason to believe that she was right. Withymead was, after all, a very different institution from Cumberland Lodge and lacked all the advantages that can come from Royal support. Moreover, it was difficult to see how the cost of appointing an extra administrator could be justified in the circumstances, for there had been no shortage of attempts to liaise with outside sources of money and they had invariably proved unsuccessful. But Amy Buller was a woman for whom Irene had the greatest respect and, after some reflection, she decided to take her advice. As it turned out, it was a decision that she was later to regret.

Oddly enough, the Management Committee was persuaded to agree, and an advertisement for a resident administrator was put in the *New Statesman*. Irene, who had made herself ill with overwork, was staying for a few days with Doris Eyles in her country cottage when a reply to the advertisement came from a retired Army Officer, Major Kenneth Folkes. Irene got in touch with him at once and, taking Doris with her, went over to Taunton to meet him in the Country Hotel. She thought him able, energetic and determined, and arranged for him to meet the Bishop who 'thought he really might be our man.'

Kenneth Folkes' appointment came as a relief to everyone. It was as if the problem of Withymead's impending bankrupcy was in some measure solved by the mere act of appointing someone to deal with it. 'The Major', as everybody called him, spent several days testing the weight of the burden he was to bear before agreeing to take it up, apparently having concluded that his shoulders were equal to the strain. But his was an unenviable position, and one has to admire his courage in taking it on. From now on, the community's struggle for survival would be vested in him, and he must have realized from the outset that unless he could by a miracle reverse as no one else had done the economic forces at work, then he would be made to take much more than his fair share of the blame when these forces resulted, as it seemed they must, in the Centre's ultimate liquidation.

The Major's arrival was as much a comfort to Irene as to anyone. The strain of recent events has begun to tell on her too, and, with some anguish, she made a firm decision to withdraw herself permanently from the centre of Withymead's life. After talking it over with Douglas Crosse and Michael Loup she arranged to sell Withymead House and the adjoining house to the Withymead Trust and, in turn, to buy a plot of land from the Trust in the orchard above School Lane on which to build what was called her 'dower house'. The valiant Sylvie, who was now getting on in years, would retire as the Centre's nurse, and go to live with Irene as cook/housekeeper in the new house. There Irene would continue to see patients but would gradually hand over her administrative functions to the Major and her therapeutic functions as parent of the community to Murray Cox and his wife. As luck would have it, the Major's wife was a state registered nurse and would take over Sylvie's job when she retired. Since the Coxes would be building their own house, it was agreed that Irene should give up her rooms in Withymead and hand them over to Major and Mrs Folkes, whose presence, it was hoped, would fill to some extent the vacuum created by Irene's departure. It would be some months before Irene's new house was ready and, until then, she decided it would be more agreeable to live in her cottage at Kenn.

Not one to sit about twiddling his thumbs, the Major at once got down to work. The first priority, as he saw it, was to get Withymead registered under the Mental Health Act. Discussions with members of the Management Committee convinced him that the most sensible way to achieve this would be to convert the Barton into a nursing home unit in accordance with the standards laid down for such an establishment by the Ministry of Health. In order to provide the facilities required, an extension would have to be built joining the Barton to Red Wing to provide an additional bathroom, toilet and kitchen.

The trouble with this scheme was that, even the values of 1964, such an undertaking would have cost somewhere in the region of £25,000. For an organization already heavily in debt, with a bank overdraft growing daily, it says much for the Major's enthusiasm and for the Management's commitment that they were willing to give serious consideration to such a step. However, when one reads the letters and memoranda which circulated between responsible members of the community at this time, and when one contemplates their content in the light of Withymead's overall position, one cannot shake off feelings of unreality, or an uneasy intuition that, at this juncture, personal devotion to the ideal of Withymead's survival at all costs had begun to prevail over considerations of practical economies. It is an impression which, as the months passed, the Major's activities were to augment rather than diminish.

Unquestionably, a factor which kept hope alive was the prospect of Murray Cox coming with his wife to live and work in the community. Everyone agreed that this course, provided it could be funded, and provided Irene could be encouraged to withdraw from her commanding position leaving the community in their hands and under their leadership, might well enable the essential spirit of Withymead to survive for several more decades.

That Murrary Cox, almost completely inexperienced in psychiatry and without any analytic training, could be considered ideal for the post of medical director is, at first sight, rather curious, but it demonstrates the community's fundamental concern that the man destined to be its father figure should have what were considered to be the right attitudes and personality characteristics: there was no member of the Withymead community who did not feel that these considerations outweighed all others. If the Mental Health Act insisted that they must have a medical director then they would find one, and, provided they felt certain that he was the right man for the job, it mattered little to them whether he had on paper the necessary qualifications.

But it mattered to Murray Cox. He sat the first part of the D.P.M. examination in the summer of 1964. To the despair of everyone, not least himself, he failed. It was an agonizing situation for him and for Withymead. He thought about it for days, and then he wrote to Irene and to Crosse saying that with deep regret he must decline the post of medical director.

It was a mortal blow. With hindsight one can see that Murray's decision put the seal on Withymead's doom. If he and his wife had come, it is just possible that the community might have held together through all the painful changes necessary to make it economically secure. For it was the prospect of their arrival which prompted Crosse and Folkes to keep working towards solvency; it caused the 'anonymous donor' to give £2,000 towards Murray's salary (she had already given £4,000 to keep the community going); it inspired applications to the Rowntree Trust, which yielded a further £1,000; and it was a persuasive factor in enlisting the help of the local Medical Officer of Health to get the Centre registered as a nursing home and to encourage local authorities to contribute to the cost of sending patients to Withymead from their respected areas.

But now, for many Withymeadians, the loss of Murray Cox meant loss of faith in the future; and the realistic course at this point would undoubtedly have been to close before the Centre's debts, already huge, got any bigger.

However, closure was not a question that anyone discussed. For those who held Withymead's destiny in their hands were now beyond realism. It was unthinkable that the life of the community should be brought to an end: there was far too much at stake for too many people. If Murray Cox could not be medical director then somebody else must be found in his stead. Who could it be? Someone suggested that the choice was clear: since the responsibility should be given to a psychiatrist who as well acquainted with Withymead and its problems, and obvious candidate for the job was Dr David Sime, who had served on the Management Committee for the last two years. What better choice could there be? Everyone agreed that there was no better choice, and so David Sime was appointed.

It is not difficult to appreciate why many viewed David Sime as a good substitute for Murray Cox. Possessing personal charm and evident intelligence, he was friendly and urbane in his dealings with patients and colleagues. Patients particularly liked him. His kindness was immediately apparent, and he had that capacity for intelligent listening which is the hallmark of a good psychiatrist. As the father of a large family, he was especially good with children and young people, who found him warm, approachable and a mine of kindly advice.

Unfortunately, there was one important drawback to his

appointment, and this, as it turned out, was of crucial significance: *he lived out*. Fundamental to the family feeling of Withymead was the principle that parental figures lived in, sharing totally in the entire 24-hour cycle of the Centre's day. But in Dr Sime's life his own family and home came first; Withymead, his place of work, came second. This might not have damaged the cohesiveness of the Withymead family as much as it did had Sime been unusually gifted at forming close relationships with numbers of people at a time, but unfortunately this capacity was no more than normally developed in him, and it meant that, from the moment of his appointment, Withymead had a 'nine-to-five' father whose primary affections and emotional commitments were lodged elsewhere. In any conventional psychiatric unit David Sime's right to a private family life would have been taken for granted, but Withymead was not a conventional psychiatric unit, and the appointment of a conventional psychiatrist with a conventional home of his own was yet another blow to the community.

To be fair to Irene and the staff, they were not unaware of this drawback when David Sime was appointed, but they hoped that they would find adequate compensation in the presence of Major and Mrs Folkes living in the rooms which Irene had vacated. But this arrangement did not sufficiently take into account the emotional significance for a community whose raison d'etre was psychotherapy of splitting 'the father' in two, separating his administrative power (i.e. his 'instrumental' function) from his therapeutic role. Important though an administrator was, it must be acknowledged that as far as a community of sick people was concerned it was the father as healer, as guide, philosopher and friend whose presence was most immediately needed. Major Folkes and Dr Sime were both in their different ways capable of carrying the paternal imago for the community, but it was a sad stroke that the wrong father 'lived in'.

Withymead, its problems, and its way of life were, of course, by no means unknown to David Sime. But although he realized he was in for a hard time he took up his post as the new medical director with the enthusiasm of one who felt equal to the challenge. It seems likely, however, that if he had really known what he was letting himself in for, he would have settled for the comfort and security of his job at the Starcross Institution and left Withymead severly alone.

With the insight into Withymead's problems which his service on the Management Committee had given him, Sime decided to leave legal and financial questions to Crosse and Folkes respectively while he devoted his attention to clinical matters. Painfully aware of the fate that had befallen Dr Kimber, he was determined that he should not go the same way. He decided that he must establish his medical authority beyond doubt from the outset so that there could be no misunderstanding of arguement about it. He therefore insisted that the extent of his authority should be clearly defined in his service agreement, and, acting on behalf of the Management Committee, Douglas Crosse agreed. By the terms of this agreement, the new medical director was granted direct medical responsibility for 'all patients and non-staff residents', and it would be his duty to see all new patients and to allocate them to a therapist. A firm touch of the mental hospital creeps in with the requirement that 'all correspondence concerning patients on medical or adminis-trative matters shall be addressed to Dr Sime as medical director', and that all requests for admissions should be addressed to him: 'No admission shall be accepted except on his authority or that of another doctor delegated by him to do so.' Thus, the loose informality and shared responsibility of the traditional Withymead admission procedure, designed tactfully to weave the newcomer into the fabric of the community, was to be replaced by the stereotyped doctor/patient model of the conventional hospital or clinic.

However, Sime's tactic in persuading Crosse to draw up such an agreement turned out to be a serious miscalculation. Far from pre-empting strife by demanding compliance with the letter of the law, it succeeded only in mobilizing the opposition. When Irene and her friends learned of the agreement they took it as an outright attack on their position and prepared for war: they had prevailed in the past when Kimber sought to impose a similar régime and, God willing, they would succeed again.

The best available account of the unhappy weeks that followed is given in a letter which Kenneth Folkes wrote to Douglas Crosse. He began by saying that from the moment David Sime took up his new appointment there developed between him and Mrs Champernowne 'a mutual mistrust that militated against the smooth and efficient working of the Centre.' He continued, 'It has become abundantly plain to me that Mrs Champerowne has felt unable to work to anything like the maximum of her capacity while she is under medical constraint, and she has attempted to persuade Dr Sime to allow her to work with her patients on her own lines without any interference from him, yet on the understanding that *if* she deemed it right *in her opinion* to consult Dr Sime about her patients then she would co-operate with him in doing so. This Dr Sime has persistently refused to permit on the ground that it would undermine his total authority over the patients and staff and lay him open to criticism and blame if something untoward happened to one of Mrs Champerowne's patients. As I understand Mrs Champerowne's view, she cannot agree with medical interference with her patients, with whom she is in analytic relationship, nor does she concede that a medically qualified person is (necessarily) qualified to interpret psychotherapeutic material.

'The whole matter was brought to a head-on clash when Dr Sime criticised Mrs Champernowne concerning her conduct over a patient at a recent weekend, when Mrs Champernowne told Dr Sime in my presence that she could no longer work under him unless she was given freedom of action, and that, therefore, she would be forced to exercise her option to terminate her service agreement.

'As I understand Dr Sime's attitude, it is this: non-medical psychotherapists *must* work under the medical umbrella of a doctor. In out-patient work the problem would appear to be less difficult, but in the case of in-patients at a Centre such as this where the Medical Director is closely involved at a psychotherapeutic level as well as a medico-legal level, he must be in a position to maintain a close control or liaison over the therapist which involves a full feedback of psychotherapeutic material by the therapist to the doctor. Dr Sime takes the further point that the clinical and medico-legal responsibility falls solely upon him as Medical Director, and so, if he concedes to Mrs Champernowne, he could, in certain circumstances, find himself placed in a intolerable situation. A case in point could be one where a therapist is in relationship with a patient who, in the opinion of the Medical Director, should be hospitalized, and, in the opinion of the therapist, should not be.

'As you well know, this is not the first occasion in which differences of opinion have occurred at the Centre between the psychotherapeutic view and the medical responsibility, but on those occasions there was never a Medical Director in total control, as is now the case, and so the present position is, to my mind, both different and infinitely more accute than on any other occasion.

'There is no doubt in my mind that the cleavage between the two parties is both fundamental and deep – neither is there any doubt that harm is being caused to the Centre in more ways than one: and as I conceive that my duty is primarily towards the Centre as an entity, I venture to suggest that the present impasse should be resolved with the minimum of delay . . . Whoever is to resolve this very unfortunate dispute must be clear in their understanding of the essential differences between analysis, psychotherapy, and psychiatry, and they must also be completely cognisant of whatever variances there may be in the minds of Dr Sime and Mrs Champernowne as to what these differences are.' He concludes, 'for my part, knowing perhaps better than anyone how Mrs Champernowne works, I accept totally the sincerity of her views.'

For a layman, the Major had, as this letter shows, a good grasp of the issues involved, and he presents them trenchantly, yet with a refreshing lack of partisan spirit. Crosse, possibly because he felt that he had been here before, must have been slow to reply to the Major's alert, for a week later Folkes was writing to him again: 'The atmosphere here can be cut with a knife and makes life intolerable. I could put up with it for a little time longer, were it not for my fear for the patients. Everyone is at loggerheads or sixes and sevens. I am the only one in relationship with all and the strain is great: I have to keep so many balls in the air at the same time – but, never mind that, we must think of the patients. This afternoon a patient has been rescued from taking aspirin – she is in relationship with three therapists who do not relate to each other as they should do, basically because medical control is not acknowledged.' He apologised for burdening Crosse with this additional letter, but, he said, 'Rome is burning'.

Folkes was particularly irritated by the clinical squabbles going on round him because he felt confident that he was making progress on the economic front. By a series of ingenious manoeuvres, some of which brought him into conflict with Irene and Co. on account of their unorthodoxy, he managed to persuade the Ministry of Health to circularize all Regional Hospital Boards authorizing them to pay Withymead fees in respect of patients referred there by N.H.S. psychiatrists, once Withymead had become registered under the Mental Health Act. Although he was as far as ever from obtaining £25,000 for the necessary conversion of the Barton, he, nevertheless, put in hand the minor structural alterations required by the Exeter Fire Officer (paid for by the Scott Trust, which had financed Joanna's analytic training in Zurich) as a preliminary to registration and, together with Crosse, was able to convince the Medical Officer of Health and the Physician Superintendent of Exe Vale Mental Hospital that Withymead was now under medical control and being run on the 'proper lines' (i.e. like a conventional clinic). Folkes was optimistic that having achieved these strategic advantages, the assurance of a steady flow of income from the National Health Service would enable him to raise the money for the Barton conversion.

The Major's optimism might have had some justification had those responsible for the therapeutic work of the Centre been able to settle their differences. But despite the joint efforts of Douglas Crosse and himself to reconcile the medical and lay personnel, relations between the two sides continued to deteriorate.

A new and bitter row broke out over the staff meeting. In line with his policy of establishing 'total medical control', Dr Sime had decided that now he was medical director, he would in future chair all staff meetings. This decision, together with Sime's manner of implementing it, infuriated the old guard. Molly Kemp wrote about it to Douglas Crosse: 'When I first came to Withymead, the meeting consisted of only about seven people. It was completely informal. It has always been a "free for all" in what was said, and is often long-winded. As the years went on, outside doctors and therapists came to it and their time was limited, so there came a point when we thought it might expedite matters if we had a chairman.' Nobody seemed to think that Irene or a doctor should do it, and so Micheal Edwards was the first chairman, and, when he left in 1960, Molly herself was elected and she had chaired the meeting ever since.

Just before the first staff meeting held after David Sime took up his appointment as medical director, he informed Molly that he would be taking the chair. She replied that she thought this a mistake and that he would do well to wait and see how things worked out before he started making radical changes. But Sime explained that he had made chairmanship of the staff meeting one of the conditions of his appointment when he first discussed it with Douglas Crosse. 'If this was so,' commented Molly, 'he had weeks in which to do me the courtesy of telling me of his intention, by letter if necessary. I told him I took a poor view of being told five minutes before the meeting.'

Aware that he had got off on the wrong foot, Sime decided not, after all, to chair his first meeting, and sat tactfully by, 'seeing how things were done.' He chaired all subsequent meetings, however, though out of consideration for Molly's feelings invariably asked her to deputise for him if he were called away to the telephone or to see a patient. Though resenting what they regarded as the medical director's high-handedness, the staff accepted his action as a *fait accompli*, and meetings proceeded regularly, if somewhat uneasily, under the new régime. Then, a few weeks later, the balloon really went up.

Sime had taken a patient to Nottingham, even though it was staff meeting day, and, with what seems to have been a serious lack of tact, left a note for Kenneth Folkes asking him to deputise for him as chairman of the meeting. Predictably, when Irene got to hear of it, she hit the roof and told the Major roundly that since he was not a clinical member of staff he had no right to chair the meeting and that if he did she would refuse to attend.

'Then', continued Molly, 'I went in to the Major prepared for war, to find an unexpected situation.' He handed Molly a letter addressed to herself, saying that he would not be attending the staff meeting because Irene objected to him chairing it and he wished to avoid an embarrassing situation.

The absurd formalities of exchanging letters in so small and, formerly, so intimate a community is illustrative of the ludcirous pitch to which the events were progressing. Folkes, confronted with the storm that Sime's ill-considered note had provoked, realized that a tactical withdrawal was the only course open to him, and as this would mean flouting David Sime's wishes, he preferred to put the reason for his action in writing.

That David Sime should go off in this way, making his depositions by note, suggests that the absence of an harmonious working relationship with his staff was compelling him to retreat into his formal position as medical director and to impose his decisions through use of his 'power' rather than personal influence as Irene and Gilbert had done. In some ways, Irene was more of an autocrat than Sime, but as mother and founder of the community, she could more easily persuade its members that her decisions were right and taken in the Centre's best interests.

David Sime's was a most unenviable situation: increasingly he found himself cast in the role of an unenlightened despot who, failing to win the confidence of his subjects, felt forced to rule by decree. His choice of the Major as his deputy demonstrates that he was becoming preoccupied with political rather than clinical considerations, and suggests that the medical director's sense of alienation from his colleagues was so complete that he now saw Folkes as the only influential ally he had left within the community who might be trusted to make statements with which he could agree.

As if there were not trouble enough, this latest rumpus also resulted in the revelation to Irene that the Major enjoyed access to clinical files. She at once sent a letter to Crosse expressing her sense of outrage at this state of affairs and threatening to write to her professional society and any doctors she knew who wanted to refer patients 'that the confidence factor at Withymead is not strong any longer.'

Thus the cheerful informality of the old Withymead gave place to the mutual antagonism of the new. The Major thought it was high time someone knocked a spot of discipline into the ranks, and wrote to Crosse to tell him so: 'The matter of the deputy chairman of Staff Meetings is quite a thorn in some peoples' flesh here – as is the question of access to clinical files. You may decide that both such matters are for the Medical Director to decide. If so, or indeed, if not, the dissidents should be told.' So, poor Douglas Crosse, who invariably seemed to get cast in the role of peacemaker in these disputes now found himself set up as disciplinarian as well.

After thinking it over, Crosse decided the best plan would be to call a meeting of the staff and go to Withymead specially to address them. His awareness of the profound dissentions which had opened up within the community made him believe that a conciliatory talk from him as chairman was the only hope of pulling things together.

The notes which he used on this occasion show that he prepared his talk very thoroughly. He began by reviewing the history of Withymead's financial decline since the final subsidy from Elmgrant was received in 1963, and praised Kenneth Folkes' efforts to halt this decline. Having gained official recognition for Withymead for the Ministry of Health, the Major was on the point of launching a National Appeal in the Spring of 1966 for money to convert the Barton, pay off the bank overdraft (now standing at £20,000), and create an endowment fund for the future. While the Appeal was under way, it was essential that all hands pulled together and refrained from rocking the boat.

In dealing with the explosive issue of medical responsibility, he used all the tact at his disposal. He pointed out that by no means all patients at Withymead were treated by psychotherapy alone: many of them were on drugs; and since 'medical treatment must be under medical supervision', they were bound by law to have a medical director. Furthermore, the Mental Health Act of 1959 required that all private mental nursing homes must be under medical control, otherwise they were not permitted to register; and those which were not registered exposed their directors to the danger of being charged, in certain circumstances, with criminal offences. Moreover, the prospect of finding adequate financial support was very slim unless the Centre could be seen to be under strict medical control and could satisfy N.H.S. psychiatrists that it was the sort of efficiently run psychiatric unit to which they could confidently refer patients.

Next, he spoke warmly of Irene Champernowne's 'genius, skill, courage and persistence in building up this unique Centre.' While things could never be the same as they were, she could still do as much for Withymead as she had in the past. In the name of Withymead and the future, he begged that she and David Sime would resolve their differences and work together in close co-operation and harmony.

Speaking of the future, he tried to reassure those who feared that in adapting to the requirements of the law and to the standards of the National Health Service the traditional ethos of the Withymead community would be betrayed. Personally, he said, he had not spent five years struggling to keep Withymead open 'only to destroy the very thing we have been preserving.' It was precisely because Withymead was 'unique and precious' that it commended itself to the generosity of Trusts and indidvidual benefactors. There was, therefore, no need for doubt and suspicion and every reason for hope. But 'please understand', he concluded, 'that the future of Withymead lies in *your* hands – not *mine*.'

It was a brave effort. If anyone could have saved the situation it was Douglas Crosse, whose skill and integrity had kept him from taking sides, with the result that he was still liked and respected by everyone. But, alas, the time was out of joint, and his carefully chosen words fell on deaf ears, ears that now heard only the inner rumblings of their owners' resentment and hostility.

Only six days after Crosse's conciliatory address a new row broke and Irene was once more on the warpath: 'So often when one is not taken into the confidence of one's senior colleagues, and yet has to work in close contact, situations become *worse* . . .' She was put out because big events were happening about which she was kept in the dark. Weeks could have elapsed before she discovered what was afoot, had it not been for her uncanny intuition. Working on some casual remarks dropped by the Major and David Sime in her hearing, Irene came up with the dead accurate assumption that someone had approached the Trustees with a significant proposal and that surreptitious negotiations were going on with him behind her back.

The proposal came, in fact, from a Jungian lay analyst who had recently qualified in Zurich. A member of a ship-owning family, he was well-heeled, and had caused a minor sensation in Withymead's ruling oligarchy by offering to put up a considerable sum of money. His name was David Holt.

Holt had visited Withymead in the summer of 1965, after which he wrote to David Sime announcing that he would be willing to make £20,000 available to the Trustees 'provided I can be actively associated with the administrative and therapeutic work of the clinic.' His original intention, on qualifying, had been to start a residential clinic on a much smaller scale than Withymead, running it as a two-man show in association with a medical psychiatrist. He was diverted from this course when he discovered that Withymead was at a critical point in its life and that he could be of assistance to it. He liked David Sime and felt that he could work well with him, and he also thought it important that he had trained in the same tradition as Irene Champernowne.

News of Holt's offer was kept a carefully guarded secret between Sime, Crosse, Folkes and Holland-Hibbert, the local director of Barclays Bank. They evidently feared that if Irene and her friends heard about it they would start making conditions that could frighten Holt away. Soon after Irene did get to hear about it, however, her annoyance at not being consulted was further inflamed when the Management granted Holt's wish to become involved in the therapeutic work of Withymead by appointing him, together with two other new-comers, Dr Hinton and Dr Bartlet, as a visiting psychotherapist. Irene knew this to be a disastrous decision, not because she had any doubts about Holt's professional ability, but because experience had taught her that therapists at Withymead must be *permanent* and not 'visiting'. She wrote to Crosse complaining bitterly about 'the most inadequate, expensive and unsuitable arrangement of appointing three people acting as psychotherapists for one (3 hour) session a week each. This means that the patients cannot responsibly be *held* in treatment by any of these three.' She argued that it was false economy to pay so much in salaries to visiting therapists who confused the therapeutic situation rather than reinforcing it – especially 'considering how shockingly the hard working resident members of staff are paid (in comparison with senior non-resident members) upon whom the brunt of the work falls.' She was extremely angry about the way she was ignored. 'Dr Sime never consults me – I am merely told . . . It seems such a pity that my long experience of work in the Centre and knowledge of the snags and difficulties and needs arising in this community is seldom if ever appealed to. Major decisions need to be viewed in the light of experience and by discussion . . .'

The sad truth was that the very thing that Douglas Crosse feared had already come to pass, and David Holt had arrived on the scene too late to save the situation. The attempt to impose on Withymead the structure demanded by the psychiatric establishment as a precondition for their recognition and support had, in fact, resulted in the destruction of the old community with its informal communications, mutual trust and reverence for the individual. This, combined with the warfare that persisted between the male authorities and the female staff now began to have a catastrophic effect on the patient population, and the delinquencies, suicides and general mayhem that Dr Kimber had tried to legislate against were henceforth to become frequent occurrences.

The trouble was made worse by Folkes' policy, endorsed by Crosse, of trying to keep the Centre's bedrooms filled to capacity with patients paying full fees: 'every room means over £1,000 a year.' This could only be achieved by the Centre becoming much less selective about the people it admitted, and the result was that the proportion of young patients, many of them disturbed or suffering from severe personality disorders was increasing. There were serious lapses of discipline which, Irene maintained, were not the fault of the resident staff whose hands were tied, and these had led to 'havoc, violence, running away (five residents missing at one time), people leaving, causing loss of revenue and a steady decline in Withymead's reputation.

'In trying to keep everything in his own hands,' Irene went

on, 'Dr Sime fails to grip the *total* situation. While believing so profoundly in status for himself, he allows no status or authority or freedom of action for his colleagues. It has become abundantly clear that a Medical Director who seeks really to serve a resident community must himself be part of the resident community itself, and feel and carry the true weight of the residential life . . . Commuting each day, often being absent evenings, weekends, public holidays and other times unstated, is impossible for a community. Almost any but the most unusual Medical Director under these conditions could not be anything other than an irrelevant authority. The lack of discipline in time and commitment leaves the community unable to rely on an authority, whilst being refused its own.'

When Irene wrote this letter, David Sime was on holiday and the inevitable problem of chairing the staff meeting had again arisen. This time Dr Sime did not repeat the gaffe of directing the Major to take the chair, but he did not appoint Molly either. Instead he asked Dr Rosalind Hinton to deputise for him. This was an unfortunate choice as Dr Hinton, newly arrived and not analytically trained, had herself just returned from holiday and was rather out of touch. Repeatedly she fell back on Molly, asking her what she should do and whom they should discuss, so that Molly became *de facto* chairman while Dr Hinton remained *de jure*. The farcical aspect of the situation did not, of course, go unnoticed by the staff, who had begun to get a certain *schadenfreude* from the medical director's political bloomers.

A week later, David Sime was back and things had deteriorated further. 'I am exceedingly anxious about the state of the Centre,' Irene wrote to him. 'The resident staff are at breaking point, and some beyond it. *But the patients are not held.* The evil, fear, madness, violence are flowing around, much of it unchecked. The atmosphere of the place overwhelms me to the point of despair. Our reputation decreases rapidly.

'Yesterday, Maggie twice ran up to me, just as I was

leaving, begging me to take her away, anywhere, with me. Maggie is not my responsibility but she was running about mad, really mad, poor child, unchecked, unheld. The thin staffing made it impossible to deal with her. I went back and tried to calm her, found Michael and told him to take her to you.

'The night before at the same time of day – after 6 p.m. – I was detained by the violent assault of Lee on Ruth. Both days I had yet another hour's session waiting for me to do at Kenn, and I was already very late. The summer holidays for members of staff have begun and this leaves us outrageously understaffed and ill-equipped to carry such a load . . . *The place is in a very dangerous condition.* I judged this from experience . . . It is *absolutely essential* to appoint *more resident staff* . . . We are heading for a complete breakdown, David, and something must be done quickly. Coming daily, even non-resident, the atmosphere in the Centre hits me as terrifyingly chaotic and so full of undealt-with sickness as to make *me* feel really ill, and I am used to carrying a heavy load as you know.

'I feel much for you but cannot help more than I do under present conditions. The *final* stronghold in the struggle – a tightly knit staff group confident in their power and authority – has been broken up, and one by one they have fallen into great despair, and feel utterly and personally depotentiated. The loss of this inner authority is the last undoing of the Centre, and introducing three one-day visiting therapists will disintegrate the whole place further.'

Squandering the Centre's dwindling resources on outside staff, while neglecting the welfare of the resident staff who carried most of the emotional load, was clearly a short-sighted policy which could only further poison relations between the old guard and the new. When taxed on this issue, David Sime explained that he had tried to find qualified people willing to live and work in Withymead, but without success. Irene retorted that she was not surprised: 'No one could want to come and work at the Centre now for little money, no recognition, no honour, no sharing in the life or policy of the place . . . There has always been little money, there has always been too much work, but [in the past] the members of staff have been *in on* the life of the place, sharing in its development. They have not been mere pawns in the game of the two senior members in charge.'

By the mid-Summer of 1966, Irene's new house, 'Up-withy', built in the old orchard at Withymead, was practically ready for her to move into, but the prospect of leaving the tranquility of 'Thatched Cottage' at Kenn provoked in her an agony of indecision. With events running as they were, should she commit herself to a move which would throw her once more into the maelstrom of Withymead, or should she give up the struggle altogether, resign her post as senior psychotherapist, sell 'Upwithy' before she had entered it, and go right away to start life again elsewhere at the age of 64?

'I have wandered through the unfinished house,' she wrote to the Bishop of Exeter, 'and looked down on Withymead and prayed to make the right decision.' Sitting on a plank in the empty house, surrounded by workmen's paraphernalia and assailed by the smell of concrete and new paint, she decided to give it a year's trial. 'It might possibly prove easier from my new house, for I need not go into the Centre so much, but work here in my own home and do all I can to support people from there.'

But if Irene planned to work peacefully in her 'own home', David Sime intended otherwise. He wrote informing her that he would not grant her medical cover if she practiced from 'Upwithy'. Instead he would make a consulting room available for her in Withymead house and she would be required to see patients there. Irene promptly wrote to Crosse: 'I have been building my house with the firm knowledge of everyone that I shall be working from it. I have built my study to take all my books, files, desk, phones, etc. At my age I need the peace of this and the opportunity for working with my books around me. Analysis needs this (as *I* do it); my books are valuable. A woman living alone can keep a little house going, can plan much more easily – meals and household things – in between, if she is not working outside. This makes such sense at my age.'

She telephoned Michael Loup and asked what she should do. He advised her to assume she would work at 'Upwithy' as originally planned, and he wrote to Crosse that he: 'would ask the Management Committee to endeavour to bring home to Dr Sime that "total medical direction" means that in matters pertaining to the health of the patients at Withymead the Medical Director has the final word. On other matters it has always been my understanding that the Management Committee is in charge.'

This neat barb had the desired effect, for when the dispute was put to the Management Committee they agreed unanimously, much to Sime's displeasure, that Irene should practise from her house.

The medical director accepted the decision with bad grace: he persisted in his view that it was important from the medico-legal point of view that Irene should practice under the same roof as himself. Since the Management had declined to concede this, he felt obliged to clamp down on Irene in other ways. He wrote a curt letter informing her that 'every inpatient and outpatient you receive . . . must be brought to me immediately', and that she must 'within the next fortnight' give him 'a complete list of all outpatients you have been seeing . . . At the same time I shall require from you a brief clinical note in writing on these patients with the diagnosis.'

Such tight supervision was intolerably humiliating to Irene, for not only was she a therapist of considerable experience, but Sime was demanding of her a way of working which he knew she had never used. Possessing an encyclopaedic memory for patients' personal details, she did not take notes because she found they got between her and the patient, interfering with the intimate contact which, to her, was the crux of successful treatment. Nor did she think in diagnostic categories. For her patients were people with problems, and it did not occur to attach labels to them like 'neurotic', 'manic-depressive', 'psychopath', and so on.

In despair she sent Sime's letter on to Michael Loup who, in turn, wrote to Crosse, referring to the medico-legal problem as 'this "bogey" which crops up in all our dealings with Dr Sime . . . I really cannot see what all the fuss is about, particularly when I am told by Dr Sime's solicitors that he has a high regard for Mrs Champernowne's ability. In my view there is clearly no technical ground for the point he has made, and there is certainly no technical ground for the fear which he keeps expressing, in the light of Mrs Champernowne's and the Centre's records. Why cannot we put an end to what has become an issue of importance out of all proportion to the reality of the problem?'

It was not an unreasonable question. As Loup pointed out, Withymead had functioned for years without a single action for negligence being brought against the Management Committee or members of the staff, and it is hard to escape the impression that Sime had either allowed himself to become obsessed with the issue, or that he had embarked on a policy of deliberate harrassment to get Irene out. Certainly, if he had been more flexible in his attitude much of the heat might have been taken out of this particular conflict; but it is only fair to acknowledge that even if the medico-legal 'bogey' were dispatched, then equally profound differences would probably have emerged over some other issue. This was merely one of the possible battlefields on which the old guard and the new drew up their forces.

If David Sime really had made up his mind that Irene must be removed from Withymead, he was not alone in his opinion. By August, 1966, a majority of the Management Committee had reached the same conclusion. As Crosse wrote to her: 'It is with considerable regret that we feel that it is impossible for you and Dr Sime to work together jointly in the interests of the Centre.' She was given a year's notice.

Now that it began to look as if the war of attrition between Sime and Irene might eventually end with Sime's victory

David Holt wrote to Douglas Crosse saying that he had studied the situation at Withymead and had reached the conclusion that the Centre could be made financially viable. He proposed that a committee be set up, consisting of himself, Crosse and the Major, to report to the Trustees on the reconstruction of the Centre. Then, provided the Trustees accepted the report, he would make available a sum of not more that £30,000 on the security of the deeds of the freehold assets of Withymead.

However, it was not to be an easy or straight forward operation: Irene's friends saw to that. Alarmed with the way things were going, Molly Kemp and five other members of the resident staff assembled their grievances and expressed them in a document which they circulated among the Trustees and all members of the Management Committee. This was highly inflammatory stuff: not only was it bitterly critical of the policies being followed but often scathing in its comments on the personal qualities of those who were carrying them out.

'The Document', as it came to be known, was not altogether a surprise to Douglas Crosse: 'Experience has shown me,' he later wrote to Leonard Elmhirst, 'that they are very forthright in expressing their views at all times, frequently causing me some embarrassment, but I am bound to say, I was extremely unhappy when I concluded reading this report as it not only showed (and committed to paper) a much more serious situation than I believed existed, but it was full of very serious inaccuracies both as to facts and inferences.'

The timing of the Document's circulation was most unfortunate from the Trustees' point of view, as they were naturally anxious to obtain David Holt's full commitment to the Centre and were afraid that the staff's militancy might put him off. Their worst fears were realized when Holt called on Crosse in his office and declared, as Crosse reported in a letter to the Bishop, that in his opinion the Document 'revealed a most unhealthy situation which would have to be resolved before he completed negotiations with the Centre.'

In an effort to repair the damage, the Management Committee decreed that a 'big four summit' meeting should take place between Dr Sime, Major Folkes, Mrs Champernowne and Miss Kemp to consider whether it was possible for the Centre to continue and whether the problems exposed by the Document were capable of solution.

But the summit never took place. The differences between the two parties were now so great as to preclude them from sitting down together in the same room. 'I think that even if such a meeting had taken place,' observed Crosse with delicate irony, 'we should have been singularly fortunate if we had had any unanimous joint report.' Instead, each of the four submitted a minority report, which Crosse had stencilled, sending copies to each member of the Management Committee.

Irene's report reiterated her usual charges of high-handedness and lack of consultation on the part of the administrator and the medical director, both of whom, she said, had proved a disaster to Withymead by their failure to understand 'the true nature of the therapeutic community.'

Molly's report laid the blame for the failure of the summit to be held squarely on the shoulders of David Sime and Kenneth Folkes: 'The events of this week highlight once again the unwillingness of one side to enter upon the kind of group meeting which, until this year, had been taken for granted as part of life here. Indeed, it has been one of the mainsprings of the Centre's vitality.'

David Sime's report showed him to be nearing the end of his patience. He clearly believed that Withymead was hell-bent on self-destruction. 'It does seem such a tragedy,' he wrote, 'that the concept of a psychotherapeutic Centre based on an analytic approach, and which is quite unique in this respect, is brought to a standstill by the responsibility of a handful of staff . . . Unless we obtain the financial support required we cannot survive, and I cannot see how any responsible group of people would be willing to finance [our] situation after the shocking revelation of unreality that is expressed in this document.'

The Major was of like mind: 'I am forced to the irresistible conclusion that as the [Document] clearly shows that some members of the crew (but not all of them by any means) are unhappy in their service to the centre, they should be permitted to leave the ship, but not to scuttle it . . . One has high regard for the qualities and integrity of each of the signatories *individually*, yet I find that when they conspire together as a whole they become a destructive unit which is inimical to the life and success of the Centre.'

The failure of the summit, and the content of the minority reports, now convinced most people, not least Crosse and Holt, that the differences between Irene and Molly on one side and Folkes and Sime on the other were profound and irreconcilable. Even as fair-minded a man as Douglas Crosse had to face the fact that the time had come for taking sides. Since David Holt held the financial key to Withymead's survival and was more in sympathy with David Sime than Irene, Crosse felt, albeit reluctantly, that he must go along with the new order.

It was not that Holt was unsympathetic to Irene or to Withymead's traditional mode of functioning, but he felt that both had failed to come to terms with economic reality and that they were reluctant to face the inevitability of change. Moreover, from the beginning, his discussions had been almost exclusively with Crosse, Folkes and Sime and he had had little real contact with the 'rank and file of the community' as Irene called the resident staff. Thus, he had come to see things more and more through the eyes of the male administration, which had already established some-what shaky control by the time that Holt made his first overtures to Withymead.

Although disconcerted by the antics of the female staff, Holt, to the relief of the Trustees, was not scared off by them. He reaffirmed his intention to proceed, but, privately, he was resolved to get rid of Irene and her friends as quickly as possible. He wrote to Crosse saying that 'the clinic', as he now referred to Withymead, 'must develop along lines which will cut across the family loyalties of the old centre.' He went on: 'we must recognize that the present split must be resolved once and for all in favour of financial solvency and medical responsibility. This is going to be painful for those to whom Withymead had been as much a home as a profession.'

The Trustees having agreed to Holt's plans for a new and reconstructed centre, Crosse called a meeting of the staff at Withymead on November 9th, 1966, to explain what was happening. He was not given an easy ride. Holt, who also attended the meeting, wrote to Crosse the next day: 'I found the meeting with staff yesterday extraordinary. Mrs Champernowne's friends seem unable to regard the place as anything except their own home, in which they have a right to expect the world to maintain them at the expense of others!' This sentiment evidently struck a cord in Crosse for he pencilled 'How true!' against it in the margin.

But Irene and her old friends and colleagues were deeply saddened by the turn events were taking. Towards the end of November, Irene sent out a circular letter to all 'Friends of Withymead', announcing that the Centre was being taken over by a new Management who planned to turn it into a clinic 'with an entirely different ethos from the one which drew a number of us together in the work from 1942 onwards for 25 years.' Withymead, she explained, had 'failed financially', and the Trustees had been obliged 'to sell us or go bankrupt. Gilbert and I were never able to make it pay from the very beginning. Perhaps it is true we were not competent in this direction.' But she had always had 'great doubts' that the Centre could ever be made to pay its way.

The main purpose of her letter, Irene said, was to let everyone know that she had been asked to resign by the middle of 1967. 'My feelings are very mixed as I sit in my newly built house, for I have loved Withymead and everyone who has passed through it during a quarter of a century of its life, but I do not think I could be happy in working with a newly run clinic, even if I were wanted.' Neither did she know whether her colleagues, with whom she had 'worked in such spiritual harmony', would be wanted or whether they would want to continue. The Carol Party this year would be 'our last Christmas effort together . . . I can only add that Gilbert and I could never regret what happened to us when Withymead grew around us – but I am sad, and I know he would be if he had lived, that the ethos of Withymead, its name, and its life, will not be carried on into the future.'

Irene's reference to her 'great doubts' that Withymead could ever be turned into a paying concern are characteristic and reveal her essentially different view of a psychotherapeutic centre from that embraced by the men who had, since the withdrawal of Elmgrant, been in charge of Withymead's fortunes. As Crosse noted in a letter to the Bishop, the Centre could only be made solvent if 'the old system carried on by Mrs Champernowne (who has said on innumerable occasions that psychotherapy cannot pay its way) is finally abandoned.' Irene, he said, had always considered that Withymead should be run upon lines which were acknowledged from the start to be uneconomic and that she accepted that the Centre was bound to make a loss.

David Holt, on the other hand, held a very different view of the matter, and was determined that the new clinic would balance its books without subsidies from outside. Holt felt, therefore, that it was now important to establish publicly that 'the Centre has a life of its own apart from Mrs Champernowne, and that the Trustees intend to develop the Centre independently of Mrs Champernowne.'

Unfortunately, Holt's plans for a brave new Withymead did not sufficiently take into account the fact that Irene Champernowne's identification with the Centre was the main reason why large numbers of the people wanted to go there, and that Irene's circular announcing her withdrawal, and her lack of sympathy with the new order, would result in a dramatic decline in the admission rate. But for the time being, Holt persevered. On December 21st, he interviewed Molly Kemp, Euanie Tippet, and Mary Pye individually and told them that their services were no longer required. The following day, Crosse wrote to each of them confirming that the Reconstruction Committee had unanimously agreed that 'it was best for all concerned' to ask them to resign with three month's salary in lieu of notice.

That Christmas they had their last carol party together and they were determined to make it a good one. Douglas Crosse must have got wind of their defiant enthusiasm, and fearing some kind of demonstration, he decided to put a damper on. Among his papers there is a note in his own hand which reads: '1. No presentation at the Carol Party: it may be made at Upwithy at any time but not on Withymead's premises. 2. No remarks about the Centre, past, present or future. Unless I have a firm undertaking, I cancel the party.'

However, when the carols, the turkeys and the Christmas pudding were finished, the people who had known and loved Withymead since it began found they had little to rejoice about. On December 28th, Doris Layard resigned: 'I've come to the conclusion,' she wrote, 'that I could not contribute much to the new régime.' Two days later, Irene wrote a bitter letter to the Bishop: 'had I known that this onslaught onto the community was being planned I would never have sold my property to the Trust. I know that the financial state of affairs was such that something had to be done, and in my innocence I believed it would be something honourable.'

Irene took the dismissal of her good friends and colleagues very ill, not least because the power to do something to ameliorate their circumstances no longer lay in her hands. In the past when there had been financial difficulties, 'Gilbert and I always used to say the staff "even if Withymead fails, there will still be this house, and you can stay here until you find somewhere else to go."' Now she couldn't even say that.

The Bishop replied with a courteous, well-reasoned résumé of the masculine position on Withymead. He deeply regretted that as a conseqence of the Trustees' acceptance of Mr Holt's offer, Irene felt as she said in her letter that 'the heart and life of the Centre' had been destroyed, but he hoped that in the course of time she would come to see that a great deal of value had been preserved. 'A therapeutic Centre will continue,' he concluded bravely, 'and will provide a form of therapy which is not obtainable within the National Health Service.' In fact, it was not to continue for much longer, and what therapy the Centre did provide was to a rapidly dwindling number of patients.

The departure of Irene and her friends might have been expected to coincide with a period of relative tranquility in Withymead's affairs, allowing the men to implement their plans and proceed quietly about the business of reconstruction. But it was not to be. For, having ejected the women, the men now began to quarrel among themselves. The chief protagonists were the Major and David Holt.

The point at issue between them was the question of Withymead's size. Holt favoured a small clinic run along commercial lines, whereas Folkes persisted in advocating the old policy of expansion funded by private Trusts and by the state. This division of opinion spread to the Board of Trustees, which had been joined by two new members – James Smeall, Principal of St Luke's College and John Trevelyan, now chairman of the Board of Film Censors and attracted back to Withymead by the news that Joanna Hogg, recently qualified, would be joining the staff of the reconstructed Centre.

The split came dramatically into the open when the Trustees met at the end of May, 1967. John Trevelyan could not be present but he made his views plain in a letter to Crosse before the meeting took place: they were in complete agreement with Holt's ideas, being in favour of contraction and a reversal of the fund raising policies of recent years. The Bishop and Smeall, on the other hand, infected by Folkes' unflagging optimism, were in favour of carrying on as before and 'would in no way accept that it was unrealistic to attempt to raise as much as £100,000 at this present juncture,' as Crosse told an incredulous Trevelyan after the meeting. 'They both felt that if we were to go out for a small sum, such as a few hundred pounds, or even say £5,000, we might as well do this by way of T.V. or wireless appeals coupled with personal approaches, but that once we got up to a figure of £25,000, even if we related it strictly to a building project, we would be approaching the same persons as we would if we wanted to raise £100,000.' Intoxicated with the vision of so much pie in the sky, the Trustees called in Kenneth Folkes and instructed him to bring some of it down to earth by formulating an Appeal.

It was a disastrous and quite unrealistic decision. For years Withymead had been making appeals for large sums of money, but Charitable Trusts had clearly indicated that they were not interested in salvaging an organization in such an advanced state of decay and insolvency. Now that things had deteriorated even further, it is hard to conceive how Folkes and the two Trustees could believe that yet another Appeal would prove successful. What in fact they did succeed in doing was to alienate the one man who, since the end of the Elmgrant era, had shown himself willing to back the Centre with the sort of money it needed. It is possible that if the sound advice given by Holt and Trevelyan had been heeded, useful work might have continued at Withymead, within a much smaller organization involving Joanna Hogg, at least until the occasion of her sad and untimely death from cancer three years later. Instead, the Trustees' decision to go along the Major rather than David Holt meant that the last opportunity to save Withymead was thrown away.

Events now followed a predictable course. Trevelyan, believing that Folkes and two of his fellow Trustees were following a hopelessly misguided couse, resigned; and Holt, similarly disillusioned, withdrew from all administrative and therapeutic work at Withymead and indicated his unwillingness to proceed with any financial commitment to the Trustees.

Folkes was indefatigable in his efforts to keep things going, but by the end of 1967 the financial position was calamitous. After the Bank had debited its charges, the overdraft stood at £27,000, on which the Centre was paying interest at the rate of £32 a week. Income had fallen off drastically because ever since the departure of Irene only a trickle of patients were referred. Folkes estimated that by mid-January, 1968, there would be about four inpatients and, at most, seven outpatients. As if this were not bad enough, Folkes' Appeal was an almost complete flop. Of the forty-five Trusts applied to, only half bothered to reply, and the overall result was a slap in the eye for the quixotic Major and his credulous Trustees: in terms of hard cash the total response amounted, as Folkes confessed, to 'something less than £500' – a somewhat smaller sum than the £100,000 originally envisaged.

The Major attempted to blame the failure of his Appeal on the Wilson Government's devaluation of the pound (in anticipation of which, he said, many Trusts had transferred their liquid assets into equities), but he had now to recognize that the game was up. He could no longer ignore the depressing truth that, even if his Appeal had met with a resounding response, and all his cherished building projects achieved, it would have been of little avail, for the Centre was emptying itself, the supply of new patients having almost completely dried up. At last, both Management Committee and Trustees realized that they could bury their heads in the sand no longer: whichever way they looked there was no glimmer of hope. There was nothing else to do but close the place down.

This was a bitter blow for Joanna Hogg, who, all unknown, was rapidly approaching the end of her life. Although she had left Withymead for Zurich feeling resentful and misunderstood, her devotion to the ideals on which the community was founded never deserted her, and when she returned after Irene's departure, she was full of hope that she might, through he own intervention, prevent those ideals from being lost. She had been convinced from the start that Holt's policy of contraction was right, and she had no doubt that the final break up of the Centre was due to the unrealistic policies adopted by Folkes and the Trustees. She wrote to tell them her views. It was, she said, a tragic culmination to so many years of creative and devoted work.

When Leonard Elmhirst heard that the Withymead Trustees were on the point of selling up, he and Dorothy discussed what should be done with £10,000 (which Elmgrant had provided as a loan in 1960 on the resignation of the Trustees) should it be repaid. They decided to offer it to Joanna Hogg and Dr Hardy Gaussen (a good, kindly psychiatrist who had worked at Withymead happily and without political rancour during its heyday) to set up a psychiatric health centre for the students of Exeter University.

But, as he explained in a letter to John Trevelyan, he was not over-optimistic about the sum he would eventually receive. 'There is,' he wrote, 'a tendency on these occasions for banks to take everything that is due and for lawyers to see that their labours are well covered, so that there can be precious little left to cover gentlemen's agreements.' This remark, though it did less than justice to Douglas Crosse, who, as far as Withymead was concerned was unmercinary to a fault, showed great prescience, for when the sale was eventually completed and all the costs met, Leonard received as repayment of his loan, a cheque for £200. It was a small return for the £70,000 which the Elmgrant had poured into Withymead over the years. But when I asked him what he thought about it shortly before he died, he said, 'Dorothy and I never regretted a penny of it. It was money well spent.'

Epilogue

The two most striking features of the story of Withymead are, first, the sad loss of a fine achievement, and, second, the heroic struggle of those who fought to keep the achievement alive. The ironic paradox at the heart of the story, however, is that the struggle ultimately destroyed what everyone was fighting to preserve. What was it about the place that inspired such blind, such passionate loyalty? How was it that, long after it was realistic or politic to do so, women like Irene Champernowne and Molly Kemp, and men like Douglas Crosse and Kenneth Folkes faught so bitterly – and so valiantly – to keep Withymead, as they conceived it, going?

There is no simple answer to these questions. Withymead represented such a rich and turbulent field of human activity that the factors contributing to its success and durability as a therapeutic community are too complex to permit any neat analysis. For this reason I have thought it best to present the facts of the community's rise and fall in some detail so that the reader may form his own opinions. I have not hesitated to drag personalities into the tale because Withymead was fundamentally about people, and to attempt to recount its history entirely in general terms would be to betray the very nature of the organism one is attempting to describe.

Douglas Crosse's contribution to the story is a case in point. Though he had never wished to become permanently involved in the Centre's affairs, and had frequently expressed a desire to be released from his obligations, it would be hard to imagine a more conscientious, patient and conciliatory chairman. Since no one would ever allow him to resign, he could easily have obtained his release by advising his Management Committee to close the Centre – advice which, if well timed, they would almost certainly have acted upon. However, it never seems to have occurred to him to do so, and his determination to keep Withymead going, which sometimes appears quixotic to the point of folly, was unquestionably based on his deep appreciation of its value and on the conviction that closure of the Centre would mean the destruction of a remarkable human experiment. Certainly, no one could accuse him of continuing for mercenary reasons. Although Withymead took up much of his – and his office's – time, as well as imposing great strain on his nerves, his fees for professional services to the Centre were tiny. Throughout the troubled years of Withymead's decline, Crosse's behaviour showed consistently a remarkable degree of altruism for one occupying a position not his own seeking. On the practical, financial and administrative side, Douglas Crosse was the most faithful servant that Withymead ever had, and it would have been nice to think that he received more appreciation than he did.

That Withymead survived so long was due very largely to Crosse's exceptional powers as a conciliator, which enabled him to remain on good terms with all parties virtually to the end. His ability to sympathise with both sides in a dispute contrasted starkly with the outspoken patisanship displayed by Irene once she became convinced that her concept of the community was under attack. Irene's passionate loyalty to her friends and to the principles she believed in often caused her to react explosively to proposals coming from the male opposition. Instead of reflecting carefully and adopting a balanced approach to an issue, her feelings readily drove her onto the offensive, so that she laid vigorously about her, smiting her enemies with a zest that owed more to the lust of battle than the championship of light and sweet reason. Warm, emotional creature that she was, Irene Champernowne was a fighter all her life, and as Dr Sime and the

Major discovered, she could be as ruthless an enemy as she was devoted a friend. Deep in her heart there burned the spirit of a Crusader and, when her blood was up, she waged Holy War.

Frankly, what people – particularly men – found hard to stomach about Irene was her pigheadedness: she always 'knew best' and it seldom occurred to her in any situation that she might conceivably be wrong. That she often did know best is not open to dispute, but the belligerence with which she asserted her position did little to advance her cause, for it merely served to intensify opposition to her and to fracture the consensus on which the life of the community was based. Her handling of the question of Joanna's analytic training, for example, her row with John Trevelyan over the money involved, her tactless behaviour towards Leonard Elmhirst and his fellow Trustees after Gilbert's death, as well as her war of attrition with Dr Kimber, Dr Sime and Major Folkes, all contributed their measure to the destruction of the family group that she and Gilbert had so lovingly created.

To be sure, conflict can never be eliminated from communal life, but no community can survive unless it strives ceaselessly to achieve consensus in the midst of a never-ending flux of agreement and disagreement between its members. It is never a satisfactory policy to sit on dissention or pretend it does not exist: in the long run it has to be recognized and dealt with, while at the same time prevented from getting out of hand. Irene knew this as well as anyone and it was one reason why she initiated and championed one of Withymead's few formal institutions – the staff meeting. She frequently repeated Jung's plea, 'In God's name make a vessel to contain your evil,' believing that at Withymead such a vessel existed in the analytic situation, in the staff meeting, and in the studios. The trouble was that when thwarted she was, in her own case, prepared to smash the vessel. And the daemonic energy released was in need of greater constraint that could be provided by a wise and conciliatory chairman.

The commonest techniques used by human communities to discharge negative emotions which build up among their members are catharsis and scapegoating. Catharsis, the process of purging oneself of negative feeling, is achieved as Aristotle taught, by examining the cause of the trouble, giving it full expression, and exploring its implications. In the scapegoat ritual, on the other hand, all the evil potential of the group is attributed to one being or group of beings, which may be inanimate, animal or human, which is then sacrificed or driven away, in the belief that all the nastiness will disappear with it. Of the two methods scapegoating is, unfortunately, the more usual, since it permits a partial, but never lasting, solution of the problem because it spares those who use it from the painful necessity of acknowledging the evil in their own hearts while absolving them of any guilt feelings they might share. But it is not a technique that any therapeutic community should espouse, and it was in order to promote catharsis that all Withymead's dirty washing was given a weekly airing at the staff meeting.

In fact, the staff meeting was Withymead's one indispensable institution. In a very real sense it functioned as 'the ego of the community' as Irene insisted: for in addition to 'containing the Shadow' and promoting catharsis, the meeting was also responsible for decisions which could profoundly influence the life and welfare of all community members. In this respect Withymead resembled other intentional communities, all of which, according to Benjamin Zablocki who has studied them, hold regular meetings for the ventilation of personal feelings and for making community decisions. In his book, *The Joyful Community*, Zablocki reports: 'An extremely important latent function of such meetings was the fostering of communal solidarity. It was often noted and reported that the more difficult the decision was to make, the closer together the decision brought the community members.' Interestingly enough, Zablocki found only one community where the meeting apparently had the opposite effect, and that, he concluded, 'demonstrated that there was not any real underlying consensus among the members, and that, therefore, the community was doomed to failure.' Thus, it would seem that the regular occurrence of such meetings is crucial to the survival of small communities, and this is a conclusion that the history of Withymead does nothing to contradict. Until the arrival of Dr Sime and Major Folkes, dissentions within the Withymead staff were never so great that the meeting was unable to thrash out common ground on which the dissidents could reconcile their differences, because until then in all important matters the staff members had respected and trusted one another. The later polarization of the community into two irreconcilable factions followed swiftly upon the departure of trust from the staff meeting.

Doris Layard joined the staff late in the Centre's life: 'I saw Withymead at a time when it was struggling to maintain an image of itself which was no longer true. The unity of the staff was so damaged. We used to have the most awful staff meetings. People used to curse and swear at each other. They were a free-for-all. Once I remember a row going on between Euanie Tippett and the Major, and one of the residents said to me in the corridor outside, "The people who need analysis in this place are the staff, not the patients."'

Eve Lewis, who worked as an analyst at Withymead over a longer period than Doris Layard, said: 'At the staff meeting not only the collective Shadow of Withymead, but our own individual Shadows, got an airing, and we were all helped. But later on, in rather a cowardly fashion, I ceased to go.' Instead of coming away refreshed and more aware of her Shadow side as she had at first, Eve Lewis began to feel that her experience of staff meetings was getting increasingly destructive. She blamed this on David Sime's insistence on his medical authority and on the admission of Kenneth Folkes: 'The Major had never been analysed. He had no experience of the Jungian attitude to life, and I opposed his being brought in from the start. You need analysts, not administrators, in a group like that. If you are going deep into the unconscious then you need to be able to dissociate yourself from it as well. And unless you are constantly disinfecting yourself then, over the years, the group Shadow gets into you below the belt.'

When distrust and resentment prevail, when 'the group Shadow gets into you below the belt', people lose their sense of proportion and become too jealously concerned with defending their own interests to risk searching for what Zablocki calls 'the higher unity that always lies beyond apparent discord'. Factionalism at Withymead meant the end of catharsis and the inauguration of the ritual of the scapegoat. Each faction projected its Shadow onto the other to an accompanying barrage of accusations and counteraccusations of treachery and bad faith. More than any other single factor, the staff meeting held Withymead together, and there can be no doubt that when David Sime eventually abandoned it, its demise led directly to the disintegration of the community.

An important characteristic of any stable group is its propensity to foster a shared system of beliefs, values and percepts which individual members use to validate their attitudes and conduct towards others and towards themselves. Withymead was no exception to this rule. The view of life and human nature which predominated was, as we have seen, uncompromisingly Jungian; but in addition to the influence of Jung, any new arrival who was absorbed into the community encountered a commonly shared stock of opinions and received wisdom, some, but by no means all, stemming from Irene herself, and expressed in what one might describe as the 'Withymead voice'. These views found their most forthright exponents in the more animus-dominated member's of Irene's devoted female staff, and if the newcomer had the misfortune to dissent from an accepted Withymead opinion, one of these good ladies could be relied upon to put him right. A trivial example will serve to illustrate this.

On my first visit to Withymead in 1956 I developed a cold. Everyone was sympathetic and I was put to bed in my room at the Barton with a hot lemon drink. A few hours later I was visited by Sylvie, who pumped up my pillows and asked if there was anything I would like. My head had begun to ache and my temperature was raised, so I asked if I might have some aspirin. Her refusal was polite but emphatic: it was wrong to take aspirin in my condition, I was told, because one never knew what one might be covering up. Aspirin suppressed symptoms instead of letting them out. Argument was useless. She gave my pillows a final thump, wished me good night, and left me sadly to my fever and my headache.

Several hours later, these symptoms had become worse, I got out of bed, put on my dressing gown, and went in search of other Barton residents who might possess the forbidden drug. I found two – both Withymeadians of some years' standing. Each gave me the same kind but firm reply: one should not take aspirin for a cold because one never knew what one was covering up.

After that I seldom went to Withymead without taking with me a small cache of aspirins. But the interesting thing about this was that every time I did so I experienced a twinge of guilt. It was as if, having been accepted into full membership of the community, I was bound in some measure by its beliefs, be they rational or irrational, trivial or profound.

I have recounted this unimportant incident because it gave me the first of many insights into the striking homogeneity of attitudes shared by the heterogeneous collection of individuals who made up the Withymead community. I began to understand how the sense of security which the community provided depended to a critical degree on solidarity between members of the community and on their willing conformity to community values. Just as Withymeadians accepted that is was bad to take aspirins for a cold, or that 'organic' gardening was preferable to the chemical alternative, so they tended to accept without question the assumptions on which Jungian psychology is based, to believe that the inner life of the individual is his most precious asset, and that the practice of creative activities is one of the most desirable means by which a human being can spend his time. These *idées reçues* were the links which held the community together and, understandably, the community put pressure on individual members to leave them undisturbed, so as not to weaken them. Thus, on one occasion in the pottery studio I began, in a very undergraduate way, to question Jung's concept of the collective unconscious. I was interrupted by Ben Belton in the middle of my first sentence: 'I'm here to stop that kind of talk', he said firmly.

What did more than anything else to disrupt the stability and cohesion of the Withymead community in the 1960s, therefore, was the arrival of powerful newcomers to the staff who did not share the *idées reçues* which had prevailed since the Centre was established in 1942. Furthermore, none of them shared the same model of the community they were entering: David Sime's model was that of a progressive mental hospital which he superintended every day from nine to five, the Major's was of a loosely disciplined military unit where he mucked in with the men, David Holt's that of a para-medical clinic in need of an administrative shake up, while Douglas Crosse thought of Withymead as a valuable experiment whose existence he was fighting to preserve without any clear understanding of what it could be.

When the inevitable polarization into factions occurred, it was of more than coincidental significance that the division took place along gender lines, the innovators being men and the guardians of tradition, women. As hostility between the two groups increased, so the women began to accuse the men of ganging up together in a cowardly fashion and of organizing a 'masculine conspiracy' to destroy the essentially feminine nature of the community, while the men blamed the women for allowing irrational prejudices to blind them to economic reality and the need for change. As we have seen, both groups eventually become incapable of understanding the positive intentions of the other, so possessed were they by their perceptions of each others' negativity.

Some years after the final closure of the Centre, Irene summed up for me her feelings about this masculine invasion: 'They could not see that the community as they found it was autonomous, an organism with a life of its own, with its own Ego and Shadow, carrying on its own self-determining struggle against economic difficulties and later against outer man's destructiveness which called itself "reconstruction". As the men increasingly took us over, imposing full medical cover, Whitley scale nurses, administrators, hospital routines, and so on, the worse everything became, and the spiritual core of the community, which carried the despair and the sickness of the patients, was destroyed. Of course, I can see that David Sime felt he must chair the staff meeting, but he didn't appreciate how democratic we had always been, and it was never a free meeting after that. I think he feared its power, but it was only power capable of dealing with the sickness. Then when the meeting – the heart of the spiritual struggle – was disbanded, we lost the very weapon we had always used to fight the powers of spiritual disintegration, and we were all of us in real trouble.

'I know I was thought to be stubborn, headstrong, unsubmissive,' Irene continued, 'but the truth of the matter was that the organism to which I was mediumistically joined and committed was fighting for its life, and through my understanding of its inner nature, I had to act as its spokesman. The more desperate things got, the more disturbed the patients, the more suicides began to happen, the more determined my stand became.'

But Irene was, of course, much more than a mere 'spokesman': she was the mother of the community, a position which carried great unconscious authority and power; for as many with intimate knowledge of Withymead have affirmed, the community was not just a family: it was what one is tempted to term a matriarchy. Modern anthropology teaches that true matriarchies (where political supremacy, as well as economic and religious supremacy, is possessed by women over men) have probably never existed as stable or enduring cultural norms, but even so, much of what J.J. Bachofen had to say about matriarchal cultures in his classic work *Myth Religion and Mother Right* can be directly applied to Withymead: he describes such cultures as essentially free from formal restrictions and hierarchical structures, as given to delight in festivals and the arts, and to celebration of the blessings of brotherhood, sisterhood and love. 'Whereas the paternal principle is inherently restrictive, the maternal principle is universal; the paternal principle implies limitation to definite groups, but the maternal principle, like the life of nature, knows no barriers. The idea of motherhood produces a sense of universal fraternity among men, which dies with the development of paternity . . . Every woman's womb, the mortal image of the earth mother Demeter, will give brothers and sisters to the children of every other woman; the homeland will know only brothers and sisters until the day when the paternal system dissolves the undifferentiated unity of the mass and introduces a principle of articulation.'

At Withymead, the succession of medical directors and administrators who followed on from Gilbert Champernowne attempted to introduce 'a principle of articulation', to replace the matriarchal unity of the community with the differentiated order of paternity. But the mother, and through her the community, resisted them with increasing ferocity until the moment when they ejected her, thereby destroying the fabric of the culture.

Like Irene, Bachofen believed community to be a fundamentally feminine achievement: historically, the 'transition from nomadism to domestic settlement is a necessary part of human development, but it is particularly in keeping with the feminine nature and occurs most quickly where the influence of women is paramount. The observation of still-living peoples has shown that human societies are impelled towards agriculture chiefly by the efforts of women, while the men tend to resist this change. Countless ancient traditions support this same historical fact: women put an end to the nomadic life by burning the ships; women gave most cities their names, and, as in Rome or in Elis, woman inaugurated the first apportionment of the land. In bringing about fixed settlement, womanhood fulfills its natural vocation . . . All civilization and culture are essentially grounded in the establishment and adornment of the hearth . . .'

It seems probable that the ancient cultures described by Bachofen were in reality matrist or matrilineal rather than matriarchal – i.e., their pantheon was ruled by a mother goddess but their political affairs were conducted in her name by a dominant oligarchy of men. Be that as it may, the parallels between the story of Withymead and Bachofen's account are clear. Certainly, the impetus for the foundation of Withymead was primarily Irene's (Gilbert took a lot of persuading) and the matriarchal spirit which suffused its life was hers. Gilbert never constituted a threat to the matriarchy, because his quiet, introverted nature lacked the "Dionysian", phallic qualities needed if the matriarchal structure of the community was to be overthrown: rather, he preferred to go along with it, lending it the stability of his presence, only occasionally modifying the course of the community took, without attempting revolutionary changes in direction. Indeed, the tack and integrity with which Gilbert filled his role as consort was crucial, as the success of Withymead depended on the very fact that it was a matriarchy, a vessel, a womb, a sanctum, ruled by a loving mother; and that the differentiating, objectifying paternal principle, with its rational concepts of order administrative efficiency and clinical authority, was relatively unobstrusive. At Withymead one was not processed or classified: one was received, nourished, healed. And although it is true that Withymead, at its best, represented but one possible environment for the treatment of the mentally sick, the unanimously glowing testimony of those who were patients there, in contrast to those treated in other institutions, does raise the challenging, but as yet unanswerable, question whether the ideal model for all residential psychiatric units might be a matriarchy, with a recessive father figure working quietly at the mother's side, using his masculine understanding in the service of the essentially feminine ethos of the community.

The opportunity for Withymead to discover an alternative mode of functioning occurred on Gilbert's death, but all attempts to float a new model of the community foundered on the failure of the masculine and feminine authorities to achieve a new synthesis. It is interesting to speculate what might have become of Withymead if, instead of the unrelated succession of male administrators who followed Gilbert, Irene had become possessed in her private life by a man who was Gilbert's opposite, a Dionysian man capable of carrying through the administrative and financial reorganization which the community needed while, through Irene, remaining emotionally in tune with it. But instead, Irene found herself drawn to spiritual men outside the community, like Father John, who were able to support the widowed mother but could not regenerate the Centre. Thus Withymead continued on its downward path, the hapless victim of warring parents engaged in a messy divorce.

The dominant features of this conflict, chronicled in the last chapter, are summarized in the schema on the next page.

The men, unconsciously motivated by the archetypal influence of the paternal principle, were primarily concerned to meet the demands which society made on Withymead to set its financial, administrative and clinical house in order. Their actions were governed by what they considered to be rational deductions based on a realistic appraisal of social and economic facts: their attitudes were essentially pragmatic. When they encountered opposition to their policies they would justify them with appeals to logic and principle, and, when such appeals went unheeded, they would either persevere inflexibly or threaten to resign.

The women, on the other hand, unconsciously prompted by the mother archetype, were primarily concerned to protect the ethos of the community and to ensure that those of its members who were most in need of succour should continue to receive it in the traditional Withymead way. Their actions were determined by intuition and 'inner knowledge' (i.e. *woman's* knowledge); and when attacked they responded with a passion essentially maternal and protective, though occasionally its belligerence assumed Amozonian proportions.

In short, schism rent Withymead because the protagonists worshipped different gods; and the more fervently they asserted their faith, the more widely were the gods forced apart. And when two groups of people were thus affected, each possessed by a different archetype, it is futile to attempt to apportion blame between them for the acrimonious destruction that ensues. 'As psychologists,' wrote James Hillman, 'we are not taken in by the relative value of the arguments, on which side truth lies, or deviation, or evil; nor are we taken in by the strength or weakness of the people, their merits, their personalities. Our interest lies, as psychologists, in the phenomenon itself – schism – the extraordinary passion with which it is charged, and the specific quality of this passion, so tearing and so intellectual.'

In his celebrated analysis of the nature of tragedy Bradley wrote: 'The *dramatis personae* fall into antagonistic groups and the conflict ends with the defeat of the hero. The calamities of tradedy proceed from actions, and those the actions of men. These actions beget others, and these beget others again, until this series of interconnected deeds leads by an apparently inevitable sequence to a catastrophe. These actions and the consequent catastrophe are not only phenomena which happen to the person concerned but equally they are phenomena which are engendered by themselves. The hero always contributes to the disaster in which he perishes. The leading characters are themselves the authors of their proper

Schema summarizing the main features of the masculine-feminine conflict that split the Withymead community.

	THE MEN	THE WOMEN
unconscious archetypes	the father the wise man	the mother the priestess/healer
aims:	establishment of medical authority and efficient administration	maintenance of the authority of the community and the staff meeting
priorities:	solvency first, provision of psychotherapy second	therapy first, financial considerations second
main pre-occupations:	'outer reality' and the demands of society	'inner knowledge' and the needs of the patients
predominant functions	sensation, thinking, rational consciousness	intuition, feeling, relation to the unconscious
predominant principles:	the reality principle	the Eros of relationship
predominant attitudes:	pragmatic	'religious'
response to opposition	appeals to logic, principle and reason; threats to resign	passionate maternal protectiveness; Amazonian attack

woe.' 'The principle of evil,' wrote T.R. Henn in *The Harvest of Tragedy*, 'when once it is loosed, is self-generative.'

The tragedy of Withymead, like the evil which was loosed in its declining years, was not attributable to inherent villainy in the men and women who became so implacably opposed to one another. Individually they were good people struggling to preserve what they believed to be of great human value. The evil and the tragedy lay in their inability to bridge the gap of misapprehension that opened up between them and the sad loss that this inability produced.

Though much went wrong during the final years, the concepts on which Withymead was based were essentially right: the intimacy of the small 'archetypal' community, the sympathetic acceptance of personal suffering, the emphasis on the value of the individual, on the meaning of his illness and on the mobilization of his own resources to find a cure, the beautiful surroundings, the ease of access and egress, the anti-bureaucratic informality and family configuration of the group, the provision of sanctuary for as long as it was needed, the satisfaction of peoples' attachment needs with no attempt to force them into 'compulsive self-reliance', the facilities for creative self-expression and the collective 'honouring' of whatever was expressed, the collaborative enthusiasm and shared idealism of the staff – all these features combined to create an evironment and an atmosphere which people who went there experienced as genuinely therapeutic.

For all its shortcomings, then, is the Withymead experiment one that should be repeated? Personally, I am convinced that it should. There is nothing obsolete about the care that Withymead provided: indeed, such care is needed more now than ever before, and the need for it will persist well into the future. Developments in brain chemistry and psychiatric pharmacology will doubtless lead to the discovery of new drugs capable of relieving more efficiently the symptoms of mental distress; but drugs can do nothing to treat the social or ontogentic *causes* of mental distress, nor can they provide an understanding of its *meaning* in the life of an afflicted individual. Whatever scientific or social progress may be made in the next few decades, people will continue to become mentally ill, and however many drugs they are given, they will still seek sanctuary from the social and economic stresses that impinge on them and request professional help to deal with what has gone wrong with their lives. In its heyday, Withymead provided an admirable model of just how well these needs can be met, and, since it closed, no other residential centre has succeeded, to my knowledge, in filling the vacuum created. In my professional life I am confronted time and again by patients on the point of breakdown who ask, 'Isn't there somewhere peaceful I could go to get away from everything and have time to sort myself out?' Whenever this happens I lament the demise of Withymead and wish that somewhere like it existed.

If some reader, therefore, knowing the hazards, feels tempted to risk such an undertaking, I shall feel that my labours in writing this account have not been in vain. Since it is just possible that such reckless souls may actually exist, I will attempt to summarize for their benefit the main elements which, in the light of Withymead's history, may contribute to the success of so brave a venture:

Site and surroundings: these need to be quiet, beautiful and accessible. The accommodation provided must be homely and absolutely non-institutional; it should be large enough to house the whole community and its facilities in one place, and should be surrounded by enough land to permit the cultivation of flowers, vegetables and fruit, provide room for domestic animals and attract indigenous forms of wild life.

The community: this should be limited to between 40 and 50 members including permanent staff, who should live in. Turnover among staff members must be discouraged so as to sustain bonds of attachment and a sense of living continuity. The community must be balanced between age groups and between the sexes. Ideally, patrist and matrist elements should be in a state of harmonious equilibrium, but if one is to predominate over the other then it is preferable that the matrist component should prevail with its natural propensity to nurture, cherish and contain. Regular meetings must be held between all leaders of the community so as to maintain a consensus view of policy and to permit the resolution of conflict. In its routine functions the community should avoid bureaucratic procedures; and the introduction of rules and regulations should be looked upon as a sign of failure. The later history of Withymead is an illustration of the Taost aphorism, 'When the way is lost, then come laws.' Without doubt, the most stable and emotionally satisfying configuration for the community to adopt is that of an extended family.

The directors: there can be no evasion of the fact that these have to be exceptional people: on them depends the whole success or failure of the venture. They should be a man and a woman, preferably a married couple, whose relationship with one another is strong and abiding, based on love, trust and mutual understanding. They should both possess the attributes necessary for charismatic leadership, while at the same time, being gifted with sensitivity, insight and compassion. They should be trained and experienced in one of the schools of depth psychology, and they need to be clear in there own minds about the ideals and therapeutic principles on which their community is based, so that these ideals and principles may be readily passed on to new members as they arrive. Above all, the directors must be dedicated to their work. Only then can they hope to bear the lack of privacy, and emotional strain, the endless trials and tribulations attendant upon sharing their home with a community of sick people. Running a therapeutic community along Withymead lines is not a nine to five job for well-meaning 'helpers' but a daunting labour requiring the kind of selfless devotion traditionally displayed by those entering a Holy order. No one intending to give less should attempt it.

The staff: members of staff need to be chosen with great care: in addition to being intuitive, intelligent and kind, they must understand and share the ideals on which the community is based. They should be tolerant of human frailty and should possess a facility for making warm relationships with each other and with their patients. Ideally they should have had some analytic experience and some training in the therapeutic use of the arts. Like the directors, they should be dedicated to the work of the community, they should be prepared to work long and irregular hours, and they should not be particularly interested in financial rewards.

Attitude to patients: true respect for the individual patient is fundamental to the success of the whole undertaking. The last thing wanted by people close to breakdown is to be treated like a commodity, to be subjected to administrative routines, or be condescended to on account of their plight: on the contrary, they desperately need their anxieties to be shared; they want loving kindness, gentle reassurance, genuine sympathy and real understanding. They need time to tell their story, to express the full extent of their unhappiness, and to make sense of the circumstances which have laid them low. Then they need help to see that the capacity to repair the situation lies within themselves, and they should be given support, comfort and encouragement as they seek to put this capacity to good use. Essentially, the attitude to patients which prevailed at Withymead may be summed up as loving acceptance combined with willingness to help. If these are consistently present then the community will be therapeutic.

Therapy: this should be individual, analytically orientated, designed to elucidate the meaning of the patient's suffering, and conducted in such a way as to mobilize his own creative potential for healing. The therapeutic use of the arts can be of critical importance. For this approach to succeed it is essential to avoid the pitfalls of the 'therapeutic community move-ment' – i.e. the politicking, the emphasis on symptomatic behaviour and role playing, the compulsion to extraversion, the public exposure of intimate personal material, anti-authoritarianism for its own sake, viewing the patient as a unit within a system, and so on. In other words, ultimate value needs to be seen in terms of the individual and not in terms of the group. The theoretical orientation does not have to be Jungian, but some kind of orientation is needed if the patient's illness is to be understood in terms of the chronological stage he has reached in the human life cycle. Without such an orientation there is a danger that treatment will not involve personal illumination and development but a series of profitless excursions into unknown territories with the blind leading the blind.

Finance: funds need not be limitless but they must be adequate to minimize financial anxiety. The history of Withymead demonstrates the impracticability of running such a community for profit, even when members of staff are willing to work hard for small salaries. It is important that patients contribute what they can afford to the communal exchequer for that strengthens their sense of commitment and their right to belong, but it is unrealistic to expect that fees alone will provide the resources necessary to keep the Centre functioning. Some additional source of private or public money will be required if the survival of the community is to be assured. However, care must be taken to preserve the community's ideological independence, and this is particularly true if the source of subsidies is some bureaucratic institution of the State. Anyone attempting to set up a psychotherapeutic community on the Withymead model would, therefore, be well advised to avoid becoming emeshed in the tentacles of the National Health Service: he should remember that when it comes to providing residential care for the mentally ill 'small is beautiful.'

The incompatibility between the Withymead approach and that of the N.H.S., so clearly recognized by Gilbert Champernowne in the 1950s, is even more fundamental today. For the march towards syndicalization, which has characterized our society since the second world war and which determined the structure that the N.H.S. was to adopt, has continued its inexorable progress, with the result that reverence for the individual of the quality displayed by Withymead has become increasingly anachronistic. As our organizations grow in size, the more impersonal they become, the more subject to legislative interference, to rules, regulations and directives, so the inner meaning of an individual's experience dwindles into insignificance. So, in the name of a liberal humanitarianism which advocates free care for all, we sustain a bureaucratic monster capable of truly caring for none, a social instrument based fundamentally upon the archetype of order, whose projection at the collective level Jung saw, ultimately, as underlying all totalitarian systems: it is the archetype of the ant hill.

Should the socialist attack on what remains of private medicine in Britain succeed, then the complete triumph of the bureaucratic system will effectively rule out the possibility that therapeutic communities possessing the originality and seminal value of Withymead could ever come into existence again. The only hope for the future would then lie in the insight and the courage of those men and women responsible for working the system, that they may recognize the barrenness of its impersonal materialism and correct it from within. If mentally disturbed people are to receive residential treatment designed to promote their individuation rather that their 'adjustment to the norm', then the battle of Withymead will have to be fought again, but this time on a national scale, and, one prays, with a happier outcome.

Irene Champernowne had nine years of life ahead of her after her expulsion from Withymead in 1967, and she lived them to the full. Together with Sylvie, she moved to the Cotswolds, where she bought a large stone cottage in the lovely village of Stanton. She was followed there by Molly

Kemp and Euanie Tippett, and by her secretary, Freda Platts, all of whom settled in cottages nearby. Stanton thus became a sort of mini-Withymead, to which people travelled in order to analyse with Irene, make music with Molly and paint with Euanie. In addition to her work at Stanton, Irene spent three days a week in London and one day a week working at the Child Guidance Clinic in Cheltenham. In 1969 she invited me to join her practice in London and our partnership flourished until her death in 1976.

During these years Irene did all she could to keep the Withymead spirit alive. With £5,000 given to her by the parents of a young man who had committed suicide at Withymead during 'the troubles', she founded the Gilbert Champernowne Trust to further the development of psychotherapy through the arts and to help individuals who needed analysis – virtually unobtainable under the National Health Service – to receive it, despite their inability to afford private fees. To date, many people have been helped in this way – far more than could have been envisaged at the time of the original bequest. Under the auspices of the Trust, Irene also began a series of art therapy courses at Amy Buller's old estabishment, Cumberland Lodge, in Windsor Great Park, and these courses have subsequently become a popular annual event. Here the values of Withymead continue to be passed on to growing numbers of men and women con-cerned with the treatment of mental illness by creative means.

What gave Irene most satisfaction as she grew older was the special relationship that developed between her and the young. She felt that a great change had come over young people in England. She found them less conventional, more spontaneous, more genuinely concerned with matters of the spirit than earlier generations had been. Many came to consult her, often travelling long distances at considerable cost to themselves: she loved their earnestness, the easy way in which they called her 'Irene' and treated her as one of themselves, and she was deeply touched by the many signs of appreciation and love that they gave her – and which she returned in abundance.

The last 18 months of her life, however, were a time of protracted suffering. In the late autumn of 1974 she gave a course of lectures at the C.G. Jung Institute in Zurich and returned to England feeling very unwell. She was admitted to Charing Cross Hospital for a check up. There, investigations proved that she had an inoperable cancer. She bore the diagnosis and the painful months that followed with great courage, sharing her ordeal with her patients and friends with extraordinary candour. She lived on from day to day, managing to carry on, she said, 'by steering a course between hope and despair.' She was helped by a memory of climbing in Switzerland many years previously when she had complained to her old mountain guide, 'Alois, I shall never manage those terrible looking peaks.' He replied quite angrily, 'That's not your business. Your business is to look where you put your next foot. And enjoy the view!' She also remembered her mother telling her as a child, 'God never gives us strength for anything but the moment – not for tomorrow, certainly not for next week or ten years hence. He only gives strength for NOW. And the tomorrows will be now when you come to them.' In this manner she was able to keep going, step by step, looking where she put her next foot *and* enjoying the view. She refused all medication until near the end: she was not interested in extending the quantity of life, it was the quality of what remained to her that mattered. Jung once told her, 'We are partly fated and partly free, and the measure of our freedom is our capacity to relate to our fate! She took this to heart and related to her fate in full consciousness and with much dignity. 'I must not settle for death,' she said, 'nor must I struggle for life', and she went on seeing her patients and working for the Trust until the week before she died. She often said she had no wish to retire and hoped to drop dead at her work: it was fitting that she almost managed to do so. She was 75. Those of us who were close to her missed her dreadfully, but were as one in our conviction that the warmth of her love and the example of her life would remain with us, unforgettably, until the day we die.

BIBLIOGRAPHY

Bachofen, J.J. (1967), *Myth, Religion, and Mother Right*, Routledge and Kegan Paul, London.

Bogen, J.E. (1969), 'The other side of the brain: an appositional mind', *Bulletin* of the Los Angeles Neurological Societies, 34, pp. 135–162.

Barton, R. (1959), *Institutional Neurosis*, Wright, Bristol.

Bowlby, J. (1969), *Attachment and Loss: Volume 1: Attachment*, Hogarth Press and the Institute of Psycho-Analysis, London.

Bradley, A.C. (1904), *Shakespearean Tragedy*, Macmillan, London.

Champernowne, Irene, (1980), *A Memoir of Toni Wolff*, C.G. Jung Institute of San Francisco.

Clark, D.H. (1964) *Administrative Therapy*, Tavistock Publications, London.

Clark, D.H. (1974), *Social Therapy in Psychiatry*, Penguin, Harmondsworth.

Crozier, Anne, (1979), 'Attempts at democracy', in *Therapeutic Communities* edited by R.D. Hinshelwood and Nick Manning, pp. 263–271.

Cumming, J. and Cumming, E. (1962), *Ego and Milieu*, Aldine, Chicago.

Goffman, Erving, (1968), *Asylums: Essays on the Social Situation of Mental Patients and Other Inmates*, Penguin, Harmondsworth.

Goldberg, S. (1973), *The Inevitability of Patriarchy*, Maurice Temple Smith, London.

Hillman, James (1975), *Loose Ends*, Spring Publications, Zurich.

Hinshelwood, R.D. and Manning, Nick, (1979), *Therapeutic Communities: Reflections and Progress*, Routledge and Kegan, Paul, London.

Hobson, Robert F. (1879), 'The Messianic community', in *Therapeutic Communities*, edited by R.D. Hinshelwood and Nick Manning, pp. 231–244.

Jansen, Elly, (1980), 'Therapeutic Community Models: IV The Richmond Fellowship', in *The Therapeutic Community*, edited by Elly Jansen, Croom Helm, London.

Jones, Maxwell, (1979), 'The therapeutic community, social

learning and social change', in *Therapeutic Communities*, edited by R.D. Hinshelwood and Nick Manning, pp. 1–9.

Jung, C.G. Most quotations in the text are taken from *the Collected Works of C.G. Jung*, edited by H. Read, M. Fordham, and G. Adler, Routledge and Kegan Paul, London, 1953–1978. Quotation sources are indicated by the volume number followed by the number of the paragraph from which the quotation is taken (e.g., *CW* 16, para. 82). Sources other than *The Collected Works* are here listed chronologically:

Jung, C.G. (1933), *Modern Man in Search of a Soul*, Kegan Paul, London.

Jung, C.G. (1962), *Commentary on The Secret of the Golden Flower*, translated by Cary Baynes, Collins and Routledge and Kegan Paul, London.

Jung, C.G. (1963) *Memories, Dreams, Reflections*, recorded and edited by Aniela Jaffé, Collins and Routledge and Kegan Paul, London.

Kennard, David (1979), 'Thinking about research in a therapeutic community', in *Therapeutic Communities*, edited by R.D. Hinshelwood and Nick Manning, pp. 297–302.

Main, T. (1946), 'The Hospital as a Therapeutic Institution', *Bulletin of the Menninger Clinic*, 10, pp.66.

Main, T. (1980), 'Some Basic Concepts in Therapeutic Community Work', in *The Therapeutic Community*, edited by Elly Jansen, pp. 52–63.

Manning, Nick, (1979), 'Evaluating the therapeutic community', in *Therapeutic Communities*, edited by R.D. Hinshelwood and Nick Manning.

de Mare, P.B. (1972), *Perspectives in Group Psychotherapy – a theoretical background*, Allen and Unwin, London.

Morrice, J.K.W. (1979), 'Basic concepts: a critical review', in *Therapeutic Communities*, edited by R.D. Hinshelwood and Nick Manning, pp. 49–58.

Parks, C.M. (1973), 'Factors determining the persistence of phantom pain in the amputee', *Journal of Psychosomatic Research*, 17, pp. 97–108.

Parsons, T. and Bales, R.F. (1955), *Family, Socialization and Interaction Process*, Freeman, San Francisco.

Pattison, M.E. (1976), *The Experience of Dying*,
Prentice–Hall, Englewood Cliffs.

Rapoport, R.N. (1960), *Community as Doctor*, Tavistock Publications, London.

Riesman, D. (1952), *The Lonely Crowd*, Yale University Press, New Haven.

Rollin, Henry R. (1981), 'Changing face of administration of mental hospitals', Journal of the Royal Society of *Medicine*, 74, pp. 641–644.

Stanton, A. and Schwartz, M. (1954), *The Mental Hospital*, Basic Books, New York.

Stern, Karl, (1966), *The Flight From Woman*, George Allen and Unwin, London.

Stevens, Anthony, (1982), *Archetype: A Natural History of the Self*, Routledge and Kegan Paul, London.

Storr, Anthony, (1972), *The Dynamics of Creation*, Secker and Warburg, London.

Taylor, G.R. (1972), *Rethink*, Secker and Warburg, London.

Weber, M. (1948), 'bureaucracy', in *From Max Weber*, edited by H. Gerth and C. Wright Mills, Routledge and Kegan Paul, London.

Whiteley, Stuart, (1979), 'Progress and reflection', in *Therapeutic Communities*, edited by R.D. Hinshelwood and Nick Manning, Routledge and Kegan Paul, London.

Yates, John (1982). Interview reported in *The Times* of April 6th, under heading 'Computer picks 15 mental hospitals "at risk"'.

Zablocki, Benjamin, (1971), *The Joyful Community*, Penguin Books Inc., Baltimore, Maryland.

Zeigenfuss, J.T. (1976), 'The Therapeutic Community from 1970 to 1975: A review and comment', unpublished thesis, Dauphin County Commission for Treatment and Program Developments, Harrisburg, Pennsylvania.

INDEX

academic psychology, 51
active imagination, 137–139
Adamson, Edward, 125
alcoholism, 51
Allen, Ruth, 71
Allenby, Inge, 59, 85
analogic codification, 134
Analytical Psychology Club, 21, 26
Animus, 111
anxious attachment, 65
Appleby, Miss, 189
archetypes, 141, 146, 148, 155, 171, 233–236
Aristotle, 225
art therapy, 34, 122–147
Ash, Maurice, 69, 160–161, 176
Austen Riggs Medical Center, 116

Bachofen, J.J., 231–232
Bartlet, Dr, 205
Barton, Dr Russell, 43, 78
Barton, The, 70–71, 147, 192, 199, 200
Bates, Hilary, 2
Baynes, Godwin ('Peter'), 14, 22–23, 25, 27
behaviour therapy, 52
Bell, George, 13
Belmont (later Henderson) Hospital, 38, 39, 86
Belton, Ben, 3, 4, 6, 31, 71, 114, 157, 161–162, 169–173, 174, 229
Belton, Jean, 4
Bennet, Dr E.A., 58
Bethlem Royal Hospital, 97
Bettelheim Bruno, 41

Bion, Dr W.R., 38
Birkbeck College, 17
Bogen, Joseph, 116
Bottome, Phyllis, 21
Bowlby, Dr John, 63–65
Bradley, A.C., 234
Buller Amy, 190, 242
Burt, Sir Cyril, 19

Cassel Hospital, 38, 39, 41, 85–86, 159
Castor, 139
catharsis, 225, 227
cerebral hemispheric lateralization, 116–121, 134–135, 138–139
Champernowne, Edward, 13, 27–28
Champernowne, Gilbert, 7; analysis with Godwin Baynes, 15, 33; as consort, 72, 109, 232; biographical details, 9–14; declining years, 170; financial sense, 67–68; meets Irene Broomhall, 14–15; on the size of the community, 157; terminal illness and death, 173–174; works as occupational therapist, 27
Champernowne, Irene (née Broomhall), 1ff; personal analysis with Leonard Brown, 19, with Godwin Baynes, 22, 123, with C.G. Jung, 24–25, 73, 117, 123, with Leonhard Seif, 21, with Toni Wolff, 5–6, 25–26, 73, 112, 117; as mother figure, 72–73, 230–231; as therapist,

Current Coventure Titles

Art as Healing* *by Edward Adamson*   0 904575 24 1
The remedial value of creative self-expression, with over 100 colour illustrations by people in Adamson's care.

The Heart Attack Recovery Book *by Elizabeth Wilde McCormick*
                                                    0 904575 37 3
A look at the emotional and practical problems encountered during rehabilitation, for patients and their families.

The Baby Massage Book* *by Tina Heinl*   0 904575 15 2
"A gentle, helpful and reassuring book." *Illustrated.*

The New Male–Female Relationship* *by Herb Goldberg*
                                                    0 904575 39 X
An immensely encouraging blueprint for a new kind of sexual relationship.

The Challenge of Fate *by Thorwald Dethlefsen*   0 904575 35 7
How life around us reflects our inner nature.

The Unknown Spirit *by Jean Charon*   0 904575 18 7
French physicist Jean Charon explains how "physics has discovered spirit"

The Opening Eye *by Frank McGillion*   0 904575 03 9
The pineal gland and our link with cosmological phenomena.

Relating: An astrological guide to living with others on a small planet* *by Liz Greene*   0 904575 28 4

Looking at Astrology* *by Liz Greene*   0 904576 86 8
A sound introduction to astrology for children. *Illustrated.*

Myth and Today's Consciousness *by Ean Begg*   0 904575 30 6
The mythological expression of forces behind the acceptable face of consciousness.

Germanic Mythology *by Margrit Burri*   0 904575 36 5
The world of myth which belongs to our pre-Roman, pre-Christian, psychic origins.

The Inner World of Childhood* *by Frances G. Wickes*
                                                    0 904576 64 7
The fruits of Frances Wickes' practical experience in child psychology.

The Inner World of Choice* *by Frances G. Wickes*   0 904576 66 3
A reprinting of the classic by Jung's longstanding friend and colleague.

Dynamics of the Self *by Gerhard Adler*   0 904576 92 2
Essays on the themes of the psyche, the self and individuation.

In the Wake of Jung *ed. Molly Tuby*   0 904575 23 3
Articles mostly by working analysts, illustrating the practical application and development of many of Jung's ideas.

In the Wake of Reich *ed. David Boadella*   0 904576 58 2
A collection of important papers by colleagues and students of Reich, including Ola Raknes, Gerda Boyesen and A.S. Neill.

The Symbolic and the Real* *by Ira Progoff*   0 904576 63 9
A programme for personal growth.

Mirror to the Light *by Lewis Thompson, ed. Richard Lannoy*
0 904575 19 5
"Poetic aphorisms of great density and beauty" – Lawrence Durrell.

Prospero's Island: the secret alchemy at the heart of "The Tempest" *by Noel Cobb.*   0 904575 26 8
Illustrated.

A Vision of the Aquarian Age* *by Sir George Trevelyan*
0 904576 52 3
A new spiritual worldview for an age stifled by materialistic values.

A Tent in Which to Pass a Summer Night *by Belle Valerie Gaunt and Sir George Trevelyan*   0 904576 35 3
An anthology of poetry and prose concerning reincarnation and the soul.

Magic Casements *by Sir George Trevelyan*   0 904576 91 4
The use of poetry in the expanding of consciousness.

The Psychology of Nuclear Conflict *ed. Ian Fenton*
0 904575 35 7
Insights and views which become a phenomenology of the subjects for professional and general readers.

The Work of Creation *by Frank Avray Wilson*   0 904575 33 0
The aesthetics of art and science to show a wholistic and human-centred creation.

Withymead *by Anthony Stevens*   0 904575 32 2
A Jungian community for the healing arts.

The Grail Legend *by Emma Jung and M.L. von Franz* 0 904575 31 4

Available from Element Books Ltd., Longmead, Shaftesbury, Dorset SP7 8PL. Telephone Shaftesbury (0747) 51339.

*Coventure edition not available in the United States.